ARE YOU DREAMING?

ARE YOU DREAMING?

Exploring Lucid Dreams: A Comprehensive Guide

DANIEL LOVE

Enchanted Loom Publishing

Published 2013 by Enchanted Loom Publishing
www.enchantedloom.co.uk

First Edition

A CIP catalogue record for this book is available from the British Library.

ISBN 978-0-9574977-0-2

To my parents, whose love has given me the courage
to follow my dreams.

Contents

CONTENTS

1

Are You Dreaming?

Life is the grandest of mysteries. Each and every one of us is the result of an insurmountably vast series of unlikely events; chance moments in time, stretching back to the very dawn of the universe in which we find ourselves. The fact that you are here right now, alive and holding this book, driven by your curious and inquisitive mind is, for want of a better word, a miracle, a true marvel of the most staggering kind. Yet, we all go about our daily lives very much as if it is business as usual; we are here, we exist, this is 'normal'. Sometimes, we all get a little lost in the fog of simply living. There are many mysteries in this universe of ours, we are surrounded by them constantly. This book will tackle only one, but what a mystery it is - the world of dreams.

Sometimes in our lives we have brief moments of exquisite clarity, as if a veil has been lifted from our eyes. Suddenly, we find ourselves acutely aware of ourselves and our surroundings, and the strangeness of it all. The light dancing through the leaves, the feel of the wind against our skin, the curious sensation of simply being. In these moments, it feels as if we have woken up, we have snapped out of our normal routine minds and are seeing the world anew, almost as if for the first time.

In these rare moments, it can seem as if our previous 'normal' way of being was subdued, almost as if we had been sleepwalking through our lives.

But, alas, such moments are rare; some have called them 'peak experiences', for they demonstrate our minds working at their very best, our awareness at its most acute. Putting such peak experiences aside briefly, in our daily lives our minds more often seem to operate on a spectrum of awareness; our mental abilities fluctuate greatly throughout each day, from the groggy, pre-coffee minds of our morning selves, through to the sharp and 'switched on' minds when we feel at our most clear-headed. In whichever of these many states we find ourselves, we have one term to classify them all: 'Awake'.

There is, of course, another state of mind, one in which we spend a considerable amount of our lives. It is, as you have most likely already guessed, the realm of sleep. Sleep, as it is commonly considered, is the antithesis of being awake; it is being without being, a seemingly complete withdrawal from the waking world. But, this is only half the story, the picture as seen by those still awake, observing the state from the outside. It is not until we examine sleep from within that we can understand that it is far from passive. As we will later explore, sleep is a dynamic process, one that is constantly shifting and churning like the ocean tides. Again, like the ocean, it is not until we dive into the realm of sleep that we discover that what lies beneath its apparently benign surface is an entire world, one ripe for exploration and discovery. If we dive deeper still, we will find yet another place, a world within a world. Whilst sleep itself is strange, it is also a stage upon which a more fascinating and peculiar state plays its role: the world of dreams.

On average, most of us spend roughly eight out of twenty-four hours sleeping. If we extrapolate this over the course of a year, we are left with the staggering total of just over one hundred and twenty-one days asleep. Over the period of an average human lifespan, this can account for the mind-boggling duration of approximately twenty-six years spent sleeping, which, for a state of mind that many of us take for granted, is an awfully long time.

Of course, during this vast amount of time spent asleep, we will also spend a great deal of our time dreaming. Whilst we will discuss this in more detail in later chapters, for now it is both important and incredible to note that, for each day of our lives here on planet Earth, eleven per cent of our mental experiences are those spent dreaming. To clarify, this is not eleven per cent of your sleeping activity, but eleven per cent of your entire daily experience of 'reality', each and every day. We humans are many things, but one thing is certain - we are most definitely dreamers.

For the majority of human pursuits, especially those natural urges and needs that require our daily attention, we have often honed our skills in their undertaking, developing elaborate ways in which to incorporate them, in the most pleasant of ways, into our lives. The prime example is that of eating. There could be fewer acts more basic and fundamental to our survival, yet it has spawned schools teaching the elaborate preparation of food, endless books and television shows on the subject, countless professionals in the field and, perhaps most tellingly, restaurants and eateries lining the streets of every town and city on a global scale.

Each and every one of us holds an opinion on the subject; many have taken the time to learn as much as we can and we all, most certainly, have our own particular tastes. Essentially, we have turned a basic human requirement into an art form. The same can be said for almost all of our other basic bodily requirements - with one notable exception. Although the details and social conventions differ for each, sex, exercise and cleanliness have all become areas in which we can study, develop and excel far beyond their simplest forms. Indeed, even the act of the excretion of our waste products has spawned entire industries and inventions. Generally, if there is something we are required to do by the constraints or desires of our biology, we will find ways in which to improve upon them.

So what of dreaming? We spend more time dreaming than we do eating; so where, then, are the expert dreamers or dream artists? How have we, as a species, enhanced this natural biological requirement? The odd truth is that, for most of us, we haven't. Whilst there are experts on sleep and dreams, more often than not their role and knowledge is curative; they are experts, not on the enjoyment or personal exploration of these states, but in resolving problems in their most basic functioning. They are more concerned with curing those who, for one reason or another, do not meet the minimum requirements for healthy living.

There are also those who claim to be able to interpret the meaning of your dreams, or to analyse your personality through their content. Again, this is not so much an expertise on dreaming itself, but rather a review and analysis of events after the fact. Imagine the equivalent for food - if there were 'food interpreters', who would (if they existed) explain what your taste in food says about your personality, or could foretell possible future events from your choice of breakfast. If such a concept strikes you as a little ridiculous, then take time to think about that for a moment. No, we need more than just experts on dreaming from a distance, or reviewers of memories. Instead, we need adventurers and explorers, those who can navigate the dream state whilst it occurs; people who have learnt to consider dreaming as an event, in which you can willingly and actively participate, not simply recall. Fortunately, we live in a time where this is now increasingly possible. There are many, like me (and, should you wish to follow this path, you too can become one of us), who have taken the time to appreciate the absolute wonder and beauty of dreaming with awareness, and who wish to explore and understand this previously overlooked miracle of the human mind. Such people are called Lucid Dreamers, and this book will teach you what you need to know in order to become a fellow traveller on this, the path of lucid dreaming.

Connoisseurs of consciousness

In order to understand how we can participate in our dreams and what is meant by the term 'lucid dreaming', we first need to return to the topic of 'peak experiences', those rare moments where our waking mental clarity is so incredibly clear and engaged that our usual awareness seems dull and somnolent by comparison. We have also seen that the spectrum of consciousness during our waking hours can fluctuate wildly; our mental acuity whilst, say, watching television, can be very different from when we are taking part in a heated intellectual debate, or lost in deep concentration over a complicated task.

Peak experiences seem to transcend all of these aspects; they appear to be the height of our waking awareness. Whilst we all often use words such as 'conscious' or 'awake' rather flippantly, we should always remember that they are umbrella terms and there are dramatic and subtle differences in what they can represent. For example, I may well be awake and conscious at 4am whilst I stumble, bleary-eyed to the kitchen for a glass of water, but how *aware* I am, on the other hand, is open to debate. Compare this to my consciousness during an important meeting, and the two states are barely similar at all.

Dreaming, unlike the other stages of sleep, is characterised by a surprising level of mental activity. When the activity of the dreaming brain is monitored, amazingly there is little observable difference from what we would expect to see if the same brain were engaged in the waking world. From the perspective of the brain, waking and dreaming are very similar experiences indeed.

This can be easily confirmed when we look at the majority of dream reports. For most of us, whilst we are engaged in the process of dreaming, the subjective experience feels essentially identical to that of waking life. We generally believe that what we are experiencing during the dream is really happening to us, and it is not until we awaken that we realise we were mistaken. You may well ask: if the dreaming mind and the waking mind are so similar, why, then, are we not aware that we are dreaming whilst dreaming? This would be a very good question, one for which there are several interesting answers. The first is the matter just discussed, in that consciousness is not a single unwavering state. Whilst our dreaming and waking brains show similar activity, this should not lead us to the conclusion that we will be clear-minded, nor especially aware. Indeed, the mental activity of someone who is heavily under the influence of alcohol would also still register as similar to that of other waking states (and also dreaming), and would very much be considered 'awake' and 'conscious' (well, at least up to a point!), but we would not expect such an individual to be in a position to be making a critical and reasoned assessment of their situation. It would appear that the dreaming brain is in a similar state of inebriation, albeit from our own internally generated chemistry of sleep. Whilst dreaming is a form of consciousness, on the whole it is generally not accompanied by a high level of critical thinking or awareness.

The second reason for our inability to notice our predicament whilst dreaming, is that we are simply not in the habit of questioning the nature of our reality. We rarely, if ever, consider the possibility that we may be dreaming whilst we are awake. Therefore, it is hardly surprising that we are even less likely to ask the question 'Is this a dream?' whilst dreaming, especially considering we are under the influence of the foggy logic that is the result of the chemistry of the dreaming mind.

This is where the concept and training for lucid dreaming steps in. What we are attempting as lucid dreamers is to raise the awareness and critical faculties of our dreaming minds to a level where we can recognise that we are dreaming whilst we are dreaming. In many ways, the experience of lucid dreaming is, to our standard dreams, what the peak experience is to normal waking consciousness. To achieve this state, we will need to become connoisseurs of consciousness; we must learn to navigate and understand the intricacies of our own minds, what it really means to be aware. It is both a fascinating and rewarding undertaking, and our journey is only just beginning.

What is lucid dreaming?

In the simplest possible terms, lucid dreaming is the knowledge that you are dreaming whilst you are dreaming. You remain asleep, you continue to dream; however, your mind becomes imbued with clarity, critical thinking and an awareness of your predicament. It is knowing, without doubt, that the world in which you find yourself is the creation of your own mind, a mental fantasy, or a natural virtual reality; one in which you can, if you wish, exert an almost unlimited control over.

It is, in many ways, an incredibly simple concept; you 'wake up' inside of the dream, and your awareness comes along for the ride. However, as with many simple concepts, there is often room for misunderstanding. So, to clarify the experience of lucid dreaming, let us look at what lucid dreaming is not.

Lucid dreaming is not:

Vivid dreaming: Lucid dreaming is not simply the act of experiencing a particularly vivid or memorable dream. Whilst lucid dreams are more often than not overwhelmingly vivid, memorable and realistic, this is not their defining characteristic. Unless you were absolutely aware at the time of the dream that you were dreaming, then you have not experienced a lucid dream.

Daydreaming or imagination: Lucid dreaming occurs during your regular sleep cycle. It is not an experience of daydreaming, nor that of vivid imagination. In all the most obvious ways, someone who is experiencing a lucid dream is completely and utterly asleep and, just as would be expected during a regular non-lucid dream, will exhibit the rapid eye movements and other traits associated with the state.

A vague feeling: The most commonly mistaken experience for lucidity is the vague and unformed feeling of 'it's only a dream' many of us occasionally experience during our regular dreams. Whilst this could conceivably be considered as an incredibly low level of lucidity, it is far from the experience of true lucid dreaming. The most important aspect for judging the level of lucidity is to consider how appropriate your dreamt behaviour is in regards to the knowledge that you are dreaming. Lucid dreamers know without question that their experience is a dream, therefore they respond accordingly to this understanding. They may, for example, see a hideous dream 'demon' rushing towards them with teeth and claws bared; however, they would feel no fear, knowing that it is only a creation of their mind, which, therefore, frees them from such an inappropriate response. If, on the other hand, they were only harbouring the vaguest of notions that 'it's only a dream', they would very likely still experience abject terror, and run for their lives. Lucidity is about knowledge and informed reasoned responses, not simply an ambiguous belief that is neither fully comprehended nor acted upon.

Unusual sleeping experiences: The world of sleep is full of unusual experiences and events. For example, we can occasionally wake during the night to find our bodies completely paralysed; sometimes, such an experience is also accompanied by startlingly vivid hallucinations. Such a state is called 'Sleep Paralysis' and we shall discuss it further in Chapter 3. It is not, however, a lucid dream, nor does it even particularly resemble one. Neither are the many and varied other peculiar half sleep states that can crop up during a night's sleep.

Lucid dreaming is a distinct state that occurs entirely within the world of dreams; you are neither half awake, nor are you aware of your physical body. The world of sleep is a strange place indeed, but lucid dreaming can only ever occur within the dream state itself.

The experience of lucid dreaming

Unless you have already experienced a lucid dream, it is very difficult to convey the sheer wonder and variety of experiences you may encounter. In the same way that attempting to describe in words the beauty of the ocean or night sky will always pale into comparison to the vibrancy of a first-hand experience. There is a majesty to lucid dreaming that is almost beyond words. To find yourself fully present and aware in another world, a universe within your own mind, is simply so far removed from our daily 'normal' experiences that it can quite literally take your breath away.

For most of us, our non-lucid dreams are something we can only ever recall, not live. Even at their most powerful, we experience their intensity only briefly before waking with a start. Lucidity, on the other hand, places us directly within the experience; we experience our dreams with full awareness as they happen, and no longer are we distant observers straining to recall a fuzzy memory. Your first lucid dream may very well be a life-changing event; it can raise within you all kinds of questions about the nature of our reality and of what it means to be human. It can be profound in ways that transcend language.

To be practical, the best approach is to describe the experience in terms of what we already know, namely the waking world. Take a moment to look around you, let the colours and details of the world flow in through your eyes. Become aware of the sounds of your environment, not only the obvious but also the subtle. Feel the sensations in your body, of temperature, texture, weight. Be aware of your thoughts, your feelings, your mood. Simply take the time to experience what it feels like to exist. Try to really experience this unique moment in time in all its magical and varied details.

Once you feel satisfied that you are somewhat present in the here and now, I would like to ask you a simple question: If I could prove without doubt, that you are dreaming right now, how exactly would you feel? Perhaps you would find it difficult to accept, or maybe you would shrug it off as simply a joke. You may believe that it all feels 'too real' to be a dream. But if it could be proved, would such a realisation surprise you to your very core?

What, then, if I were to tell you that, in this world, you can also experience anything you wish? That your powers are limited only by your imagination? Take time to really think about this for a moment; once again, look around and try to truly understand how it would feel to know for certain that the world you currently inhabit is a dream. If you have a strong imagination and you can genuinely project such a realisation onto your current experience, you are some way towards understanding the enormity of the experience of lucidity.

Just like this present moment, the world of dreams feels entirely convincing, utterly real and immediate. We shall explore this concept further throughout the coming chapters. However, for now, be assured that the experience of lucid dreaming is difficult to be completely prepared for.

As strange as it may sound, one of the difficulties for those new to the subject is being able to truly convince themselves that the overwhelmingly vivid and realistic experience of a lucid dream is only a dream and not reality itself. Even when dreamers have performed all the relevant tests with which to prove that they are indeed dreaming, often the sheer realism is enough for them to hesitate, to doubt. In almost every important respect, a lucid dream feels quite utterly as real as this world. We will go into more detail about how to distinguish between dreams and reality later, giving detailed explanations on the practice of 'reality testing', the method with which we establish the reality we currently inhabit.

For now, look around you once again. Can you really be sure that this moment isn't a dream? Soon you will have the skills required to answer this question with both knowledge and understanding, not relying simply on belief. Soon you will learn that the question 'Are you dreaming?' is relevant not only to every moment of your life, but also - and, more importantly - it is a doorway to another world.

Who am I?

My journey into lucid dreaming started young, and was a trial by fire. At around the age of five years old, I started to suffer terrifying recurrent nightmares. So, as a mechanism to survive my fear of sleeping, I devised a method to overcome them, by attempting to catch the moment where waking turned to dreams. This practice eventually resulted in my own personal discovery of lucid dreaming, one which cured my nightmares and transformed my fear of sleep into a love of dreaming. What had been a world of terror, overnight became a magical world of adventure.

This love of lucid dreaming has lasted my entire life and now, thirty years later, I am as equally enthralled by the subject of lucid dreaming as I was as a young boy, long before I knew there was a name for such a state of mind. The seeds of this early childhood experience were the start of an unbroken thread of study and research into the subject of dreams and lucid dreaming; it was one that, as a young adult, had blossomed into a more serious pursuit. Eventually, with many years of experience and study under my belt, having devoured every available source of information on the topic, I decided I would like to share my experience and knowledge with others. This resulted in what was to become my primary means to disseminate information on the topic for years to come, namely lucid dream workshops.

Over the years of running such workshops, alongside various other avenues of research, I have had the pleasure to meet many wonderful dream enthusiasts, learnt equally as much as I have taught, travelled, researched, experimented and been constantly amazed and enchanted by the endless wonders lucid dreaming has to offer. Lucid dreaming, for me, has been a lifelong friend and a skill which, I believe, has the potential to greatly enhance the lives of its practitioners.

Whilst I may have spent many years researching and teaching lucid dreaming, I would like to make one thing clear: the foremost expert in your dreaming life will always be you. No one else will ever be able to walk this path for you; nor will anyone ever know the workings of your mind, your memories and motivations, with as much insight and understanding as you yourself. There is a real danger in the exploration and study of dreaming for some people to fall into the trap of believing that an expertise of their own dreamworlds makes them an expert in the dreams of others.

Lucid dreaming, and dreams in general, are the very height of subjectivity. Your dreams are formed from the essence of who you are, your life experiences, your hopes and fears; all those very private things that make you unique and individual. We are all travellers on our own personal journey. However, as human beings, we also share much in common, however different our daily lives may be, whatever our upbringing, religion, race or any other factor. We, as a species, all have many more similarities than we have differences.

Knowledge of the subject of dreaming comes in two flavours: an understanding of the processes and science of the dreaming mind, and the experience of having explored and lived your own personal dream journey. This book will address both, the objective facts surrounding the process of dreaming and how they relate to your own experimentation, and the discoveries myself and others have made during our own private adventures, with the hope that they will be relevant and of help in your own explorations.

Consider my writing much as you would consider that of a travel journalist. Should you, for example, read a guide to the city of Paris, you would by no means expect the writer to be the final and only authority on the subject; instead, you would expect a somewhat subjective review and guide to the city which, at the same time, would include relevant and objective facts on the topic. Indeed, writing a book on lucid dreaming is very much like writing a travel guide, for the world of dreams is as much a destination as are any of the great cities of the world. Also, as with any travel guide, simply reading the book can only prepare you for what to expect; you will need to take your own journey to experience the sights and wonders yourself. So, strap yourself in and prepare for lift-off, for your own personal dreamland awaits.

About this book

When I first set out to write this book, my goal was to create a modern, comprehensive and up-to-date guide to lucid dreaming. Essentially, I wanted to write a book I, as an enthusiastic lucid dreamer, would want to read. I believe I have succeeded, and I hope this work will inspire many more to explore their inner universe. Whilst there are already many fantastic books on the topic, the majority of these were published in the late 80s or early 90s and a great deal of development and discovery has occurred in the field since then. I believe that this book contains all the information required to give those new to the subject a well-rounded understanding and knowledge of the topic as it stands today. However, as an experienced lucid dreamer, I am also very aware that there are many other enthusiasts who are looking for more than simply a 'beginner's guide'. So, with this in mind, I have attempted to delve deeper into topics, looking to explore the many subjects involved in depth.

This book is very much a labour of love. It is the culmination of a lifetime spent immersed in the topic and an attempt to share my passion and knowledge of lucid dreaming to a wider audience. By no means should this book be considered either a replacement for, or by any means in competition with, other works in the field. I would prefer it to be considered as simply another source of information among the many wonderful others available. Although, it must be said, there are most certainly fresh ideas and new techniques within.

The best approach towards lucid dreaming, as with many things, is to immerse yourself, looking to read and learn as much as you can from as many varied sources as possible. Whilst I am confident that this work contains all the information that is required to get you started, and more than enough to also sustain many years of personal exploration, I would not want to be so arrogant as to believe that it is the final word, nor the only approach towards the subject. Lucid dreaming is, thankfully, a vast and deep arena, and there is room for many opinions and many paths.

There is an awful lot of information crammed into this work and, whilst a single read will go a long way to help in your understanding, I have designed the book with the intention that it be read several times, or used as an ongoing reference alongside your journey. With this in mind, I have attempted to raise important points when they will be most relevant.

With such things aside, here you will find a comprehensive guide, laid out in a logical step-by-step approach, with the intention of helping you set sail upon the sea of dreams, and to explore how such a journey can enhance both your waking and dreaming lives. The best place to start is, of course, at the beginning, so let us first look at the origins and history of lucid dreaming...

2

A Brief History of Lucid Dreaming

Dreaming is very old indeed. When the first homo sapiens emerged here on planet Earth, some 200,000 years ago, the processes required for REM and dreaming had already been well-established, their evolution having long since taken place in the countless species that had come before us. We humans evolved with dreaming built into our design. We have always been dreamers.

How strange dreams must have been to those early people, for we were then, just as we are now, intelligent beings trying to make sense of the universe we inhabit. We dreamt long before we developed tools, fire or language. But no doubt, once we had made such great leaps forward, dreaming would soon have started to impact upon our waking lives in profound and unusual ways. Now that we had the language with which to communicate our private inner experiences, we would soon discover that we all shared these peculiar nightly events.

I wonder just how much of early human culture was influenced by our dreams? What did our early ancestors make of these mysterious experiences? It is likely they were seen as journeys to another world, maybe a world of spirits; a place where the dead could, once again, be seen, where animals had voices, where men could fly or be transformed, a place in which anything could happen.

Where there is dreaming there is the chance of lucidity, so it is likely that lucid dreaming has equally been part of humanity's long journey through the ages. There is absolutely no reason to believe that just because our distant ancestors were technologically lacking, or simply because they were unaware of the true nature of dreams, that they would be unable to recognise on occasion that they were dreaming. Even today, spontaneous lucidity occurs in young children who have little understanding of the workings of dreams, nor any concept of the existence of lucidity.

Imagine, then, what it was like for those ancient people, living in a culture where dreams were likely to be considered journeys to another world, perhaps the world of the gods. How striking the experience would have been to find yourself lucid and fully conscious, wandering in the realm of the spirits. Such experiences must have felt profoundly significant. Just how much of our ancient past has been guided by such dreams? What impact would they have had, should they have been dreamt by a person of note, such as a tribal or religious leader?

Of course, such ponderings of our distant beginnings can never amount to anything other than speculation. But it seems likely that, for early cultures, when our first primitive explanations of reality were being formed, that dreams, especially those spontaneous lucid dreams, were likely seen as guidance from another realm, as something magical.

As humanity moved forward into the light of recorded history, there is no question that dreams played an influential role in the sculpting of our world. References to dreams that clearly demonstrate their importance abound in religious writings, throughout artistic works and (unsurprisingly) in scientific and philosophical texts. Lucid dreaming, however, has remained up until recently rather more hidden, with only the occasional reference here and there. Entire books could be written about the impact of dreams on human history, but that is not our goal here. So, let us instead look at the role that lucid dreaming has played.

Lucidity in the shadows

In western history, at least up until the past 200 years, interest or musings on what we now call lucid dreaming seems surprisingly scarce. Before this time, there have been only scattered references. Fortunately, there are a few glimpses of insight that demonstrate that, at least for some, lucidity was a subject of interest. But in reality, up until our more recent history, the subject of lucid dreaming has remained mostly hidden in the shadows.

In his treatise on dreams, Aristotle wrote: 'often when one is asleep, there is something in consciousness which declares that what then presents itself is but a dream.' This certainly seems to be a rather unambiguous description of a lucid dream, impressive considering it was written in the fourth century B.C.

Somewhat later (415 A.D.), in a letter written by St Augustine to a priest named Evodius (discussing how the deceased would be able to experience the afterlife without a body), there appears to be an account of what is possibly one of the first recorded lucid dreams. The dreamer in Augustine's account was a physician from Carthage by the name of Gennadius. Gennadius had developed doubts about the possibility of an afterlife. During a series of two dreams, the second in which he became lucid, Gennadius was visited by a beautiful youth of remarkable appearance and commanding presence. In the first of these dreams, Gennadius was asked to follow the youth, to which he dutifully complied, whereupon he was shown a city in which he heard enchanting heavenly music unlike anything he'd ever heard before. He was told by the youth that the singing was the hymn of the blessed and holy. After awakening, Gennadius dismissed the experience as simply a dream. However, on his second night, when, once again, he found himself in the company of his guide, he discovered (through a series of intense philosophical questions and prompting, all initiated by the youth) that he was, in fact, experiencing another dream.

Of course, Gennadius was lucky here, as not many of us are given such a blatant clue to our nightly predicament from our dream characters (indeed, often the opposite is true, as they regularly seem to do anything in their power to convince you that you're experiencing reality and not dreaming at all). Anyhow, this being the case, the information provided by the guide resulted in Gennadius achieving lucidity. The angelic youngster, who it seems had his own axe to grind, continued to explain that, in the same manner to which Gennadius was experiencing the dream, where he was without need for his physical body, so too would he experience the afterlife.

To cut a long story short, by the end of the dream Gennadius was left convinced of the existence of an afterlife. This is perhaps not the most foolproof logic, but considering the thinking of the era and the powerful realism experienced in a lucid dream, his conclusion is not all that surprising. It does, however, seem rather convenient that such a perfect story should fall into the lap of Augustine, especially considering its conclusion so neatly fitted his own arguments for an afterlife. I'll leave the reader to judge if the account sounds plausible, or just an exaggeration or philosophical parable, used in order to support an argument.

Later, still further references are made by the Spanish Sufi master Ibn El-Arabi, who says 'a person must control his thoughts in a dream.' He goes on to explain that 'the development of such a mental alertness is of great value and should be developed by all.' St. Thomas Aquinas also seems to have mentioned lucidity in passing, whilst referring to the work of Aristotle. Tantalising snippets such as these are strewn throughout historical writings; however, generally they never amount to much more than a passing reference or comment in which we can only infer that lucid dreaming was the intended subject.

Meanwhile, and far away from the rather scarce Western interest in lucidity, the monks of Tibetan Buddhism who had long since practised skills in developing alert and focused minds, and were by no means strangers to questioning the nature of reality, had apparently made lucid dreaming an integral part of their religious practices. Such techniques were intimately entwined with their belief system, making them somewhat impenetrable to the uninitiated. Of course, such information was not available to interested western minds at the time, although today there is a good deal written on the subject and, for those of you who are interested in the more esoteric subject of Dream Yoga, I would suggest a good starting point would be the writings of Chogyal Namkhai Norbu.

The dawn of lucidity

It wasn't until 1867 that lucid dreaming first found a foothold in the western world, with the publication of *Les rêves et les moyens de les diriger; observations pratiques* (Dreams and how to guide them, Practical observations) by Marquis d'Hervey de Saint-Denys. It was from these humble beginnings and through the continued work and research of many other enthusiasts that lucid dreaming has become the well-known and much discussed phenomena it is today. Perhaps the easiest way in which to explore this history is to take a brief look at the contributions of these pioneers and where they fit into the history of lucid dreaming. Whilst the history of lucid dreaming is a fascinating subject that could easily fill a book of its own, there simply isn't enough space to explore the subject in too much depth here; as such, the following should be considered as a brief historical overview only. What you'll find is a short synopsis of the contributions to our current knowledge made by each of those whom I believe to be key players. To fully appreciate the work of everyone mentioned, I would thoroughly suggest seeking out a copy of their personal publications, most of which are still readily available.

Marquis d'Hervey de Saint-Denys
(1822-1892)

If asked to name the father of modern lucid dreaming, then Marquis d'Hervey de Saint-Denys is certainly the most eligible candidate. Indeed, contrary to popular belief, it was Hervey de Saint Denys who first coined the term 'lucid dream', albeit in his native French as rêve lucide. Saint-Denys whom, by day, was a distinguished scholar (specialising in studies of the Far East, more specifically China), had been interested in dreaming since his early teenage years, even then keeping a record of his nightly adventures. As an adult, he was a prolific dreamer with both the skills and intelligence required to dutifully record and examine his experiences.

During his exploration of dreams, he managed to record twenty-two highly detailed volumes of observations regarding his dreaming life, covering 1,946 nights spanning a period of over five years. However, it wasn't until his 207th night of dream exploration that he experienced his first lucid dream, which had such a profound impact that he decided to pursue developing techniques to enter the state at will. Six dedicated months later, he records experiencing the state of lucidity on an average of two out of every five nights; after a year, it was three out of four. Eventually, and after fifteen months of nightly practice, Saint-Denys found himself experiencing lucidity virtually every night. Very impressive indeed, considering he was approaching the subject completely alone as a pioneer. There were certainly no how-to books available for him to focus his explorations; it was only his combination of dedication and curiosity that resulted in his discoveries and success.

His major contribution to the field of lucidity was in sharing these experiences in his book *Les rêves et les moyens de les diriger; observations pratiques* (Dreams and how to guide them, Practical observations), published anonymously in 1867 and when he was 45 years of age. It is a fantastic book (and a must read for all lucid dreamers, should you be able to find a copy) and, it would seem, the first publication in which lucid dreaming is demonstrated as a learnable skill. Unfortunately, however, his book failed to be widely distributed or read at the time, resulting in its immediate influence being negligible. Even Freud himself was unable to obtain a copy, resulting in lucid dreaming being conspicuous in its absence from the first edition of his famous work *The interpretation of dreams*. Even in later editions, Freud does little more than very briefly skim over the topic. One can only wonder what directions dream research would have taken should he have been able to obtain a copy.

Saint-Denys, unlike Freud, did not look for hidden meanings in his dream world. Instead, he took a more practical stance. For example, he discovered that, whenever he had a thought within his dreams, it was likely that either that very thought or something closely related would materialise. Based on this, he suggests that anyone looking to increase their enjoyment of dreams should fill their minds with pleasant thoughts from their daily life. Such advice still very much holds true today, and is just one aspect of the role expectation plays in our dreaming lives.

Saint-Denys loved to experiment. During his explorations, he performed countless fascinating tests to push the limits of his dreaming mind. Very much with the scientific mindset, he would constantly test his assumptions with experimentation and keep detailed records of his results. In one such experiment, he wanted to judge the influence that music playing by his bedside would have over the quality of his dreams. However, his motivation for this particular experiment, it seems, may have been driven more by private desires than that of purely scientific curiosity. His goal was to induce a dream involving two women 'about whom it was particularly agreeable for me to dream.' In this experiment, he arranged for an orchestra to play one of a couple of waltzes whenever he had danced with either of these ladies, his plan being to associate a particular waltz with each woman. Alongside this continued waking association during his dances, he also had a custom music box built, designed to play both of these tunes. The music box included a clock mechanism, which allowed him to trigger either tune to play during his sleep. Whilst the journal entries for these musically-induced dreams are somewhat lacking in detail, it would seem the method was successful. Whenever either tune was played during his sleep, he would indeed dream of the relevant woman.

He performed a similar experiment involving scent. During a holiday in the Ardèche region of France, he took with him an unfamiliar bottle of scent, of which he had no previous psychological connections. Throughout his trip he repeatedly exposed himself to this scent, having soaked his handkerchief in it. Again, his plan was to establish an association, this time between a place and a scent. He made certain that, once he had left the region, the bottle would be locked away, so that no new associations could be made. On returning home, he arranged for his servant to sprinkle a few drops of scent upon his pillow whilst he slept. As he had hoped, the experiment was a success and, during these nights, he dreamt once again of visiting the mountains of Ardèche. Of course, there is no reason that modern dreamers cannot perform similar experiments with equal results, although perhaps an obliging partner, rather than a servant, may be more convenient these days.

In recent times, Saint-Denys has earned the respect he so rightly deserves for being the first pioneer of lucid dreaming. An abridged version of his book was republished in English in 1982, which led to a wider understanding of the important role he has played in the field, inspiring and influencing many modern researchers. Indeed, many genuinely consider him the father of lucid dreaming. Unfortunately, at the time of writing, even this version of the book is no longer in print and has become somewhat of a rarity, which is a terrible state of affairs and a sad reflection of earlier times. Hopefully, it will not remain out of print for too long.

His book is full to the brim of fascinating observations and explorations into the role of memory in dreams and even many of his personal techniques for manipulating the dream environment (such as covering his dream eyes should he wish to transform the scene into something more appealing). Perhaps not all of Saint-Denys' conclusions were completely correct; for example, he seemed convinced that a dreamer would be unable to experience anything that he had not previously experienced in waking life, which raises questions, such as: 'why are flying dreams such a common occurrence?'. Whilst it is true that our dreams rely on memory as a basis for their content, our brains are very capable of making approximations of events that we have never directly experienced. It's also worth nothing Saint-Denys didn't fully explore the role that expectation plays in the dreaming experience. However, most of what he writes is surprisingly accurate, even if somewhat limited by the understanding of his time.

Saint-Denys' dedication, experimentation and clarity of thought were traits that all modern lucid dream enthusiasts should at least attempt to emulate, considering that these alone were all he needed to become a nightly lucid dreamer within less than two years. As far as founders go, the lucid dreaming community could not have asked for a finer example.

Frederik Willem van Eeden

(1860-1932)

Frederik van Eeden was a famous Dutch writer and psychiatrist. It is van Eeden to whom the term 'lucid dreaming' is often attributed, due to it becoming the standard term after being published in his paper for the Society of Psychical Research. Whilst it is true that his paper is the first to bring the term into common use, we have already seen that it was originally coined by Saint-Denys. Indeed, the connection to Saint-Denys is clear, as van Eeden himself refers to him in his paper. Regardless of this, van Eeden's paper did a lot to publicise lucid dreaming, bringing knowledge of the state to a wider audience. In the paper, aptly named *A Study of Dreams,* van Eeden lists seven categories of dreams, the seventh being lucid dreaming, of which he had experienced 352 cases between January 1898 and December 1912. This gives him an average of about 25 lucid dreams a year; as a result, it would seem for van Eeden that lucidity was something of a twice-monthly event.

He made several important observations, one being the experience of a dream body. He goes into some detail regarding a dream experiment in which, whilst slipping back towards waking consciousness, he decided to experiment with the concept of two bodies. By being sure that his dream body was in a different position to that of his sleeping body, he was able to witness the transition between the two as he woke. He describes the distinct sensation of having two bodies, creating a 'double recollection', as he puts it. This sensation of transitioning between bodies he refers to as 'most wonderful' and something he enjoyed repeating. Of course, such a simple experiment can be replicated by today's dreamers, with similar results. He also noted that flying or floating in non-lucid dreams was often a sign that lucidity was close at hand, which makes perfect sense as such an experience, being completely out of the normal range of waking human experience, can often cue even those without a knowledge of lucid dreaming to the fact that they are dreaming.

Another of van Eeden's interesting observations was what he called 'the wrong waking-up dream', something he often experienced following a lucid dream. Essentially, these dreams were a convincing copy of the experience of genuinely waking up. In his dream he would believe he had woken up, until the point he would notice an inconsistency, which would indicate the true nature of his predicament. Today, we call these dreams false awakenings, and they are equally as common.

Like Saint-Denys, van Eeden was fond of experimentation. He seemed to especially enjoy exploring the sensory aspect of dreams, constantly pushing to see where its limits lay. Such experiments ranged from tasting wine, which he states had quite the taste of wine, to drawing a cross of spittle on his dream hand, then pushing it against his cheek to feel the wetness, resulting in a convincing reproduction.

In his paper, van Eeden explains that the observations being shared were merely a preliminary sketch of a larger work, which he hoped to complete in later years. Unfortunately, this seems not to have been the case. However, he also mentions that he had previously condensed many of the ideas into a work of art, a book called *The Bride of dreams*. He points out that, by approaching the topic as fiction, it allowed him to deal with delicate matters more freely. This publication is still readily available and is certainly worth a read should you wish to explore his thinking more deeply.

In *A Study of Dreams,* van Eeden covers a broad range of topics, bringing to light many concepts that are still relevant today. However, not all of his thinking stands up to scrutiny and many of his findings contradict those of modern research, although this is hardly surprising considering the limited knowledge of the era. Interestingly, it wasn't until 1969 that van Eeden's real influence on the subject took place when the American psychologist Charles Tart mentioned lucid dreaming in an anthology of papers called *Altered States of Consciousness* (which did a great deal towards raising awareness of the subject). More importantly, he also republished van Eeden's *A Study of Dreams*, thus bringing his work to a much wider audience and influencing the new generation of dream researchers. The paper remains a classic.

Mary Lucy Arnold-Forster
(1861-1951)

Mary Arnold-Forster was an English gentlewoman with a fascination for dreams. She was a woman of high standing, being the daughter of the politician Mervyn Story Maskelyne and becoming wife of the politician and writer Hugh Oakeley Arnold-Forster, the then British secretary of war. In 1921, she published her book *Studies in Dreams*, which outlined her personal experiences and interest in the dreamworld. Whilst lucid dreaming was not the focal point of her book, it does appear that, at least on a few occasions, she managed to achieve the state. What is particularly interesting is how she managed to train herself to recognise her less than pleasant dreams as 'only dreams', an idea that she attempted to teach children, with some success. Her method of choice seemed to be a form of auto-suggestion.

It would seem that flying dreams were a personal favourite of Mary's, something to which I'm sure many modern lucid dreamers can relate. Her knowledge of previous exploration into lucid dreaming appears limited; there are, for example, no references to the work of Saint-Denys. However, her book is a fascinating read and covers a wide range of topics, some particularly unique to her time such as flying dreams in war time. Other topics covered range from dreams of the dead, dream control, dream houses, memory as a dream recorder, and a great deal more. Her book is well-written, modest and fascinating, therefore absolutely worth investing in. She is, perhaps, most famous for saying: 'There are dreams and dreams, and we must get rid of the assumption that they all resemble each other.' It is as relevant today as it was back then and gives a clear insight into her way of thinking.

Hugh George Callaway (Oliver Fox)
(1885-1949)

Hugh George Callaway was an English writer, poet and occultist who wrote under the pen name Oliver Fox. In 1939, he released the work for which he is most well-known, *Astral Projection: A Record of Research* (modern editions have the subtitle A Record of Out-of-the-Body Experiences). From the title alone, one could be forgiven for believing that this book has little to do with lucid dreaming; however, in reality, the content is an ongoing (and very readable) diary of his dreaming experiences, interspersed with musings and discussions on their meaning.

In his book, he mentions that his research began after a lucid dream in 1902, when he was only 16. Lucidity in this early dream was triggered by a rather subtle inconsistency that could easily have slipped unnoticed. The dream itself was rather uneventful; that of a teenage Callaway enjoying the sunrise from the pavement outside his house. It was the pavement, however, that was the key to his awareness. This pavement was not of the usual type but was, instead, made of bluish-grey rectangular stones, with their long sides at right-angles to the curb. In the dream, however, this detail had not been reproduced correctly; instead, the long sides were parallel to the curb. It was only during a casual glance whilst entering his home that the young Callaway noticed this unlikely rearrangement.

For many dreamers, such an inconsistency may go unnoticed, or be justified by some fuzzy-minded logic about night-time roadworks. However, for Callaway, this was not the case. 'The solution flashed upon me,' he says, 'though this glorious summer morning seemed as real as real could be, I was dreaming!' The dream ended briefly after this realisation, but not before Callaway could appreciate the true joy of the situation. He writes: 'Instantly, the vividness of life increased a hundredfold. Never had the sea and sky and trees shone with such glamorous beauty; even the commonplace houses seemed alive and mystically beautiful. Never had I felt so absolutely well, so clear-brained, so inexpressibly free! The sensation was exquisite beyond words.'

It is clear how such a wonderful experience could profoundly move him, and it's unsurprising that this dream started what was to be a lifelong fascination with lucid dreaming - or, to use his own term for the state, dreams of knowledge. In fact, dreams of knowledge is actually a rather good term for lucid dreaming, for it is the knowledge that one is dreaming that sets lucidity apart from the more standard fare of non-lucid dreams.

Callaway was a man with deep esoteric beliefs and this is apparent throughout his work. Unfortunately, it seems that these beliefs somewhat tainted his experience and conclusions regarding lucid dreams. He struggles to fit his experiences of these dreams of knowledge into the framework of his belief system; in doing so, he makes some rather large leaps in logic (more often illogical leaps), often missing the true beauty of the experience in favour of trying to find evidence to support his world view. He seems determined to use the experience of lucidity as evidence for genuinely leaving the body. In some cases, his explanations become so elaborately illogical that you begin to wish you had access to a time machine, so as to visit him and debate the topic in person, if only to save him the mental effort.

In many ways, his book serves as a useful reminder that we should be careful not to let our beliefs influence how we approach new topics, especially topics like lucid dreaming, where expectation plays such a strong role. However, it does seem that the experience of lucid dreaming was something Callaway discovered for himself, isolated from the knowledge of those who went before him. Therefore, it is understandable that such an experience without prior knowledge could lead to some rather elaborate conclusions. His dedication to the subject demands respect, and his skills as a writer make the book an absolute pleasure to read. I find myself returning to it again and again as he paints such a beautiful picture, not only of his dream life, but the era and environment in which he lived. (In fact, he goes as far as to name the streets on which he experienced his dreams; so, should you be British, as am I, it is rather lovely to visit these places to put his experiences into context.)

Many of the techniques he outlines, whilst apparently for astral projection, are still valid lucid dream induction techniques today. Despite my misgivings regarding his conclusions, Callaway, or Mr Fox as he is better known, remains one of my own personal favourite early writers on the topic. More importantly, his experiences have influenced many who have followed in his footsteps.

Filling in the gaps

During the decades following Callaway, a handful of others wrote on the topic of lucid dreaming. Among them was the Russian philosopher Piotr D. Ouspensky, whose main contribution was to highlight the idea of consciously entering a dream directly from waking, rather than developing consciousness during the dream. In 1939, Alward Embury Brown wrote a paper for *The Journal of Abnormal Psychology* entitled 'Dreams in Which the Dreamer Knows He is Asleep' which, it would seem, was directed at countering those sceptics who considered lucid dreaming as nothing more than daydreaming. Brown reported on roughly a hundred of his own lucid dreams, demonstrating in several that he was just as able to use his imagination (or daydream) during a lucid dream as he was whilst awake, helping to distinguish between the two states.

Two years later. Dr Harold von Moers-Messmer published his findings in a German psychology journal, in which he reported on 22 of his lucid dreams. Moers-Messmer was clearly a man in possession of a particularly logical mind, demonstrated by his ability to notice details within dreams that most of us would barely pay attention to in our waking lives. For example, in one dream he is cued into lucidity through his realisation that he is unaware of the time of year; to establish this, he turns his attention to the position of the sun. He writes: 'I check the sun's position. It appears almost straight above me with its usual brightness. This is surprising, as it occurs to me that it is now autumn and the sun was much lower only a short time ago: the sun is now perpendicular to the equator, so here it has to appear at an angle of approximately 45 degrees. So if my shadow does not correspond to my own height, I must be dreaming. I examine it: it is about 30 centimetres long. It takes considerable effort for me to believe this almost blindingly bright landscape and all of its features to be only an illusion.'

Clearly, a man with such an eye for detail and imbued with such a powerful logic is well suited to inducing lucidity. It's probably worth mentioning here, for those that may be worried, that such an extremely honed sense of awareness and logic are not prerequisites for learning to lucid dream. However, logic, observation and discrimination are all powerful tools that are worth developing and will certainly aid you on your journey.

These are just a handful of the many scattered references that bring us to more recent times. Most consist of anecdotal reports of personal experiences. However, it wasn't until the 1960s that the science of lucid dreaming started to truly flourish, with publications like the previously mentioned *Altered States of Consciousness* by Charles Tart and *Lucid Dreams* by Celia Green acting as rocket fuel to propel the topic forward.

Dr Celia Elizabeth Green

One of the more noteworthy events in the recent history of lucid dreaming is the publication of Celia Green's 1968 book *Lucid Dreams*. Green, an English psychophysical and parapsychology researcher and founder of the Institute of Psychophysical Research, took a scholarly approach to the publication, basing much of its content on the work of those we have previously discussed, alongside material from her institute (indeed, for those interested in exploring a more detailed historical overview, her book is certainly a good place to start).

Apart from simply covering the history of the subject, Green took her time to categorise what she viewed as the various types of lucid dream. She also made some pertinent (and also ahead of her time) suggestions about the possibility of a lucid dreamer being able to send signals to the waking world so that it could be recorded on a polygraph. As Stephen LaBerge points out in his book *Lucid Dreaming*, the Institute of Psychophysical Research tends to focus its activities not actually in psychophysical research, but rather parapsychology, which may have limited the appeal of the book among scientists. As LaBerge comments, 'I am afraid that one of the reasons more conventional scientists remained uninclined to study lucid dreams was exactly because parapsychologists were.'

The book itself was the first to give an extensive overview of the history of lucid dreaming whilst, at the same time, assessing the subject as a whole. Pulling all these threads together did a great deal to promote interest in the subject. However, it is far from the easiest of reads, being a little dry for some tastes. In 1994, Green collaborated with Charles McCreery (the research officer of the Psychophysical Research Institute) to release a new publication entitled *Lucid Dreaming: The paradox of consciousness during sleep*, again written in a similar academic style as her earlier work, and offers an updated view and tackles the subject in more depth.

Ann Faraday

A mention should also be made of the psychotherapist Ann Faraday who, in the late 1970s, published two popular books on the subject of dream interpretation and conscious dreaming, namely *Dream Power* and *The Dream Game*. These books went a long way to bringing the idea of lucid dreaming into the wider sphere of public awareness. In addition, Faraday often wrote for the Association for the Study of Dreams newsletter. Her writing was brimming with positivity regarding conscious (lucid) dreaming, which she referred to as one of the most exciting frontiers of human experience.

Her enthusiasm was clearly infectious and she was one of first to place the experience in a language that was accessible to the population at large. It was her belief that the low priority that society placed on dreams contributed to most people's poor recall of them. This is certainly an important point, although not the only factor involved, as the changes in our brain chemistry during the sleeping process have a profound impact on our ability to remember our dreams (and even the regular experience of waking during the night, which most of us also forget). Her books are still available and worth reading, even if only for the optimism and energy towards the subject that they convey.

Dr Patricia Garfield

Another great populariser of lucid dreaming is the internationally renowned expert on dreaming, Patricia Garfield. Perhaps her most famous work is *Creative Dreaming* published in 1974. Garfield has been a prolific writer and, to date, has published ten books ranging across a wide variety of dreaming topics. Garfield is also one of the six co-founders of The International Association for the Study of Dreams (IASD) which was originally called the Association for the Study of Dreams (ASD), an organisation that is the central hub for many of the world's dream experts and enthusiasts. Garfield was the President of the ASD from 1998 to 1999. Her pioneering book *Creative Dreaming* is a fascinating read with many useful tools and techniques for lucid dreaming, as well as covering the place and uses of dreams in many of the world's cultures. Her work has inspired countless others to explore lucid dreaming, including famous lucid dream experts such as Stephen LaBerge. Garfield continues to be a prominent and positive force in the dreaming community and you can discover more about her and her work at her website: www.creativedreaming.org.

Carlos Castaneda

(1925-1998)

The hugely popular books of Carlos Castaneda have almost certainly played a role in raising public interest in the dreaming state, including that of lucid dreaming. Whilst the majority of his work focuses around a form of Shamanism, there are many references to dreaming, the most well-known of which occurs in his third book *Journey to Ixtlan,* where the shaman don Juan teaches the now famous technique of finding one's hands in a dream in order to stabilise it. More recently, his ninth book, *The Art of Dreaming* (published in 1993) apparently covers the complete dream teachings of Don Juan.

To be honest, having read several of these books, including *The Art of Dreaming*, I must say I fall into the camp of those who believe that these are works of fiction rather than fact (there is a good deal of evidence against these books being factual accounts). Very little outlined in the book bears any resemblance to the general consensus of the dreaming or lucid dreaming experience, while a good deal of what is written in the 1993 publication may actually frighten some dreamers away from the experimenting altogether. Personally, I would suggest not taking his work as anything more than an entertaining fiction. However, their popularity alone proves they are, indeed, very entertaining and we owe Castaneda a debt for inspiring so many to explore their minds and inner worlds.

Dr Jayne Gackenbach

Psychologist Jayne Gackenbach is another eminent authority on lucid dreaming. She is both a writer and dream researcher and has produced and collaborated on several publications, including her own *Control your dreams* and as a contributor to the hefty but informative tome *Conscious mind, sleeping brain: Perspectives on lucid dreaming.* She, too, has also held the role as a former president of the International Association for the Study of Dreams.

Before immigrating to Canada, she performed research at the University of Northern Iowa, in areas such as the role personality traits played in influencing one's ability to lucid dream. Her field of research isn't limited purely to that of lucid dreaming and, according to online sources, her latest interest lies in video game players and the development of consciousness.

I would imagine that there is considerable crossover in these areas of research, considering one lies in the internally generated virtual worlds of our dreams, and the other in the externally generated virtual worlds of computer gaming. I would also hazard a guess that the research of those such as Gackenbach will play an increasingly important role as computer technology grows and their generated worlds start to become convincing replicas of reality, as lucid dreams currently are.

Dr Keith Hearne

If lucid dreaming were to be compared to space exploration, then the achievements of English psychologist Keith Hearne could be considered comparable in magnitude to those of NASA during the time of the first moon landing. For it was Hearne who first demonstrated, through a truly ingenious experiment, that a lucid dreamer could consciously signal the waking world from the world of dreams; in other words, a message could be sent from one reality to another. Such a feat was a clear demonstration that lucid dreaming is a genuine and verifiable state, and therefore could now be accepted as a proven phenomenon within the scientific community. Clearly, such ground-breaking research guarantees him a prominent place in the history of lucid dreaming.

During the mid-1970s, Hearne had been working on his PhD at the University of Hull. Hearne wanted to demonstrate that lucid dreaming was a scientifically verifiable mental state. The question was: How? The key, as he discovered, lay in the very area upon which the dreaming stage of sleep is, itself, named, namely REM, or Rapid Eye Movement.

During the REM stage of sleep, the body becomes essentially paralysed; however, the eye and respiratory muscles remain active. Perhaps, if these muscles were behaving in synchronicity with the dreamt actions of the dreamer (i.e. dreamt eye movements affecting physical eye movements, and dreamt breathing patterns occurring in unison with bodily breathing), then a lucid dreamer, having conscious volition, could be asked to send a prearranged signal via one of these routes (specific eye movements or breathing patterns) during the process of dreaming. Such signals could, of course, then be recorded in the waking world alongside the evidence that the subject was indeed experiencing REM. If successful, one would have solid proof that a dreamer can indeed be conscious during REM; lucid dreaming would, then, become a scientifically verified fact.

Hearne opted for the ocular signalling technique, probably because of the ease of recording these movements on an electro-oculogram (EOG) machine, and possibly because it offered a wider set of signalling options. Of course, he also required a proficient lucid dreamer to act as the Oneironaut (dream traveller) who would send these signals. During this period, he met a young man named Alan Worsley, a local shop worker and experienced lucid dreamer. Hearne offered Worsley the chance to become an experimental subject in his research, allowing him the chance to not only prove his abilities as a lucid dreamer, but also earn a little extra money whilst he slept. What Worsley may not have been fully aware of at the time was that he was also to become the lucid dreaming equivalent of Neil Armstrong - the very first dreamer to send a message between worlds.

Prior to the experiment, Hearne arranged with Worsley the specific ocular signals he should send upon realising he was dreaming. These were to be a clear, deliberate set of smooth eye movements from left to right, so as to distinguish them from the more random movements associated with REM and making them clearly visible on the EOG recording. He was also asked to press, if possible, a physical micro-switch, a technique used by previous researchers in the field of sleep and dreams. However, due to the paralysis during dreams, such a method of communication turned out to be unworkable.

Lady Luck was reluctant to play ball initially and, during the first night where Worsley successful entered lucidity and claims to have made the ocular signals, it was later discovered that he had entered the state shortly after the EOG and other devices had been shut down for the night, resulting in no evidence of this event. However, a week later, in the early morning of 12th April, 1975, at approximately 8am, something very special occurred. Hearne, who had spent a sleepless night observing the output of the recording apparatus, noticed something that was not simply the usual random eye movements to be expected. He recalls in his book, *the Dream Machine*:

'Suddenly, out of the jumbled senseless tos and fros of the two eye-movement recording channels, a regular set of large zigzags appeared on the chart. Instantly, I was alert and felt the greatest exhilaration on realising that I was observing the first ever deliberate signals sent from within a dream to the outside. The signals were coming from another world - the world of dreams - and they were as exciting as if they were emanating from some other solar system in space.'

One can only imagine how excited he must have felt. By a strange and fitting coincidence, Hearne noticed that, on the same date in 1961, man's first orbit in space (by Yuri Gagarin) had also taken place.

Meanwhile, in dreamland, Worsley was having an adventure of his own. After approximately half an hour of dreaming, according to the mechanical readouts, his dream was that of wandering the university wearing electrodes. It was this peculiarity that cued him into an awareness that he must be dreaming, thus initiating lucidity. Being well prepared, he immediately performed the prearranged eye signals.

Whilst not the most dramatic lucid dream in terms of content, it is certainly interesting that the dream scenery involved both the university grounds and the electrodes he was wearing whilst sleeping, which demonstrates the power that association and expectation can play in influencing the theme of one's dreams. In fact, Hearne goes on to explain that many of the dream reports of his subjects contained elements that were related to their sleeping circumstances in the lab.

During his continued research into this area, collecting further evidence and examples of ocular signalling from within the dream, Hearne made several other interesting discoveries. One was that lucidity was generally preceded by a burst of especially brisk rapid eye movement, lasting generally around 22 seconds. Another was that, alongside voluntary control of eye movement during lucid dreams, the dreamer was, as predicted, also able to control his rate of breathing; as such, a second form of communication was possible. It was this second form of dream signalling that was the inspiration for the invention of the world's first lucid dream induction device, Hearne's Dream Machine, which we'll discuss shortly.

Following Hearne's achievement, he communicated his data with others in the field, including Professor Allan Rechtschaffen of Chicago University, who had independently been experimenting with ocular signalling during sleep paralysis, and who had responded encouragingly to Hearne's work, and also Prof. William Dement at Stanford University. It was at Stanford University, several years later, in 1978, that the young Stephen LaBerge would produce similar work involving ocular signals during his own research into lucid dreaming.

Hearne delivered his paper during the 1977 postdoctoral Conference in the Behavioural Sciences held at Hull University. The scientific community initially resisted Hearne's work; for example, when the paper was submitted to the British science journal *Nature*, it was rejected on the rather flimsy and peculiar grounds that it would not command wide enough an audience in the scientific community. Other journals also rejected his paper, again on similar grounds. It was, however, published in the journal for The Society for Psychical Research, but such a publication was generally dismissed or avoided by the majority of scientists. However, the media was far more positive in its response and, at the time, news of the discovery generated a good deal of public interest.

Hearne's next big achievement was in the creation of his Dream Machine (U.K. PATENT No 2039741, 20th July, 1983), the world's first device that would help users both overcome nightmares and initiate a lucid dream. For those that are interested, the device is on permanent display (along with his sleep lab records) at the London Science Museum. The device monitored the breathing rate of the user and, when it detected REM (which is also associated with rapid or irregular breathing), it would send a signal to the sleeper in the form of electrical impulses to the wrists (I would imagine this slightly daunting form of signal may have gone some way to reducing its wider public appeal). These signals would be weak enough so as not to wake the dreamer, instead hopefully cueing them into realising they were dreaming. A second, stronger series of alarms would be signalled at the end of REM, allowing the dreamer to awaken and record their dream.

A second use for the machine was to help users avoid having nightmares. The sensitivity of the device could be set to recognise particularly rapid breathing, which is often associated with strong emotional content in a dream. It would then send an alarm to immediately waken the dreamer. The device generated considerable interest in the worldwide media; however, it failed to become a widely distributed device.

In his book *The Dream Machine*, Hearne covers these and many more fascinating discoveries. It should be read by anyone interested in the subject and is still available to purchase as of 2012. Hearne has also, very generously, offered it for free download from his website www.keithhearne.com. (However, I would personally suggest sending a donation should you decide to do this, as clearly both his research and writing have taken a good deal of time and effort and it is only fair to show one's appreciation, especially for such momentous contributions to the field.)

Dr Stephen LaBerge

If you were talk to anyone with an interest in the subject of lucid dreaming, one name that is almost always likely to pop up in conversation is Stephen LaBerge. LaBerge, first and foremost, is perhaps the single most influential modern populariser of lucid dreaming. A psychophysiologist from Stanford University, he started his journey to become one of the most influential lucid dream researchers whilst working on his PhD at the Stanford University Sleep Centre. He had realised that lucid dreaming was a learnable skill and, within seven years, he'd accumulated around 900 personal lucid dreaming reports.

Apparently independently of Hearne, LaBerge also had the idea of ocular signalling from within a lucid dream. On 13th January, 1978, he and Lynn Nagel managed to record their first EOG signals from a lucid dream. However, it took them over a year to repeat this success in September 1979. Finding that the confines of the lab were not conducive to lucidity, LaBerge had the relevant machinery moved to his home, allowing him more freedom to pursue his experiments. By the end of 1979, he had collected considerably more evidence.

Just as Hearne had discovered, LaBerge found publishing this research was not at all easy, with many journals (such as the American scientific journal *Science*) refusing his work. Eventually, and after much pushing, the paper was published in *Perceptual and Motor Skills*, an important but low-key publication.

Whilst it is without question that Hearne was the first to perform and succeed in this line of research, LaBerge claims to have been the first to have had his work peer reviewed. Looking at the history and writings of both Hearne and LaBerge's work, one can deduce that there seems to have been a certain level of rivalry over this issue. One only needs to read between the lines to see that things were getting more than a little heated, with the two scientists both pursuing the same research, and both pushing to be pioneers in the field. However, in hindsight, it's now apparent that, as with many scientific discoveries, a little competition is a good thing (at least, for those of us not involved), pushing both scientists to pursue further research and promote their findings a little more passionately and timely than would perhaps otherwise have been the case. As such, the late 70s and throughout the 80s was an intense time for lucid dreaming research.

LaBerge's influence on the wider community of lucid dreamers is broad, rather than being limited to only this early research. He has written three bestselling books on the topic, *Lucid Dreaming: The power of being aware and awake in your dreams* (1985), *Exploring the World of Lucid Dreaming* (published 1990 and also known by the shorthand ETWOLD) and his third book *Lucid Dreaming: A Concise Guide to Awakening in Your Dreams and in Your Life* (2004), which is a revised and edited compilation of various elements from the previous two works. In general, most enthusiasts agree that his first two books, especially ETWOLD, are his finer works, and are considered essential reading for beginners to the subject (indeed, I recall reading them both when ETWOLD was first published, back in 1990, at the tender age of 14. LaBerge's writing has certainly been a positive influence on this lucid dreamer's journey).

LaBerge founded the Lucidity Institute in 1987. As stated on their website, The Lucidity Institute's primary mission is to 'advance research on the nature and potentials of consciousness and to apply the results of this research to the enhancement of human health and well-being', which is certainly a noble goal. The Institute originally was very active in its research and activities, notably creating some of the world's first widely-distributed lucid dreaming induction devices (similar in concept to Hearne's Dream Machine) available for the public to purchase. The original device was called the Dreamlight, which was shortly replaced with the more compact NovaDreamer. These are no longer available; however, for quite some time their website states that a NovaDreamer 2 is coming soon, although this seems to have been the case for at least the past five years. As such, many independent entrepreneurs and enthusiasts have filled the void left by the NovaDreamer and are currently selling similar devices.

In recent years, things do seem to have become rather quiet at the Institute. In the early days, it produced a regular magazine called *Night Light* in which readers were able to take part in the Institute's experiments. Its website was once the online hub for lucid dream enthusiasts, especially back when it still included a forum. In its heyday, the forum was an absolutely thriving community, full of useful information from others interested in the subject. However, it has long since gone (other, newer websites have taken on the role in its absence) and the site itself is rarely updated, and then only to promote the twice-yearly Hawaiian lucidity workshops which LaBerge runs. Of course, none of this is particularly surprising, as 25 years of promoting lucid dreaming must be rather exhausting. It is, however, a shame to see such a positive influence as the Institute taking somewhat more of a back seat.

LaBerge himself has made endless radio and TV appearances discussing lucid dreaming, held many workshops, influenced a huge number of people to experiment with lucid dreaming through his books and public appearances, and has performed unique and fascinating research into the subject (the latest being the role of the use of cholinesterase inhibitors to promote lucid dreaming). It can easily be said that, without his influence, the knowledge and acceptance of lucid dreaming among both the scientific community and the public at large would be nowhere near the level it is today. We should all be thankful to LaBerge for working so tirelessly in promoting the benefits of lucid dreaming to a wider audience.

Thomas Yuschak

The work of Thomas Yuschak is probably the most notable book regarding lucid dreaming to be released in modern times (post 2005). Yuschak, who holds Master degrees in Mechanical Engineering and Modern Physics, has long been part of the lucid dreaming community. Indeed, I recall many interesting online discussions with him and other enthusiasts during the heyday of the Lucidity Institute's forum, and also shortly after its closure when several members of the community (myself included), still looking for a new home, were using email groups to correspond on our discoveries and experiences.

It was during these email discussions that Yuschak shared his plans to write a book on the use of supplements to induce lucid dreaming. That book was to be called *Advanced Lucid Dreaming: The Power of Supplements*. Soon after, whilst reading an early digital copy that Yushak shared with the group for feedback, it was clear that his work was detailed, scientific and, in many ways, groundbreaking.

Whilst, indeed, it was no doubt inspired by the research of LaBerge (who had yet to have reported widely his own discoveries on the use of supplements, as most of what was known was through hearsay and established through the various patents he has applied for, which even today still seems to be the case), Yuschak's work covered a wide range of supplements beyond just the cholinesterase inhibitors patented by LaBerge; it went into a good deal of detail on their uses, the effect of combinations of supplements and the science behind their effectiveness.

From what I recall, these discussions, and the early circulation of the e-book among our small group, occurred around 2004, and it wasn't until 2006 that his book was eventually made available to the public. Alongside the release of his book, Yuschak also founded a company called AdvancedLD Ltd, which was dedicated to the research, development and teaching of the use of supplements to induce lucidity. However, the website for the company (originally at advancedLD.com) eventually went offline and has not since returned (currently, it would appear the domain has been purchased by others who are using it simply to advertise).

The company, and Yuschak, seem to have vanished from the public eye for the time being. However, the book is still available and is very much the go-to book for any dreamers interested in the use of supplements to induce lucid dreaming. Yuschak, in many ways, reminds me of the early pioneers of lucid dreaming (such as van Eeden) who, through self-experimentation, detailed record-keeping and trial and error, has helped improve the pool of knowledge available to us all. I highly recommend reading his self-published work, even if you do not intend to experiment with supplements, as it offers a unique insight into an alternative method for inducing lucidity.

The present day

In our trek through the history of lucid dreaming, we now find ourselves at the present day. With the advent of the World Wide Web, the ability for lucid dreamers to connect and share information has never been easier. New websites on the subject seem to spring up almost weekly. With so much information available, those who, before, would have perhaps passed over the subject can now casually learn the basics at the click of a button. However, as with much information online, this can be a double-edged sword as, with the appearance of endless information comes an equally high amount of misinformation, and it can sometimes be a bit of a minefield to establish if what you are reading is based on fact, speculation or wishful thinking. The only suggestion I can offer here is to check and double-check your sources and approach everything you learn with a logical and critical mind. Remember, the old saying holds true - don't believe everything you read.

At the time of writing (2012), a small selection of the current big players among the many lucidity resources online include lucidity.com, dreamviews.com, lucidipedia.com, ld4all.com, mortalmist.com, world-of-lucid-dreaming.com, consciousdreaming.com. There are, of course, many more, but please bear in mind that the fickle nature of the Internet means that the quality or nature of these websites may well change over time. Most of these sites also have their own established communities and forums, generally all catering to a slightly different taste or approach. The only way to truly find a place you feel at home is to explore, read and see if the community you are visiting is filled with like-minded dreamers.

These websites are by no means the only online resources, either. Websites such as YouTube have many tutorials created by enthusiasts. One such long-term dream enthusiast is Stephen Berlin, who has made a wonderful selection of videos. Berlin has been involved in the dream community for many, many years, and I'd highly recommend you seek out his videos (currently his YouTube username is stephenberlin).

The modern world of lucid dreaming is a fascinating and constantly evolving place, where new software, devices, mobile phone applications, websites and much more are constantly being produced. As I've already mentioned regarding the Internet, always approach any available products with a critical mind, remembering that lucid dreaming is one of nature's free gifts. If, what is on offer, seems too good to be true (look out for phrases like 'learn to lucid dream in two weeks' or 'guaranteed lucid dreams') and is also being charged for, then be cautious, as it is unlikely to live up to its claims.

Of course, there are also many fantastic useful products and resources available, just be careful to read the reviews so that you can make an informed decision. Also, keep in mind that lucid dreaming is a skill that takes time and practice, and there are no easy shortcuts. As with any skill, your dedication and time will be required to master it. By using your common sense, you will find that the modern world of lucid dreaming is a thriving and diverse community that is ever-evolving and growing. Your waking adventures as a dream enthusiast will likely be just as fun as your nightly wanderings in dreamland.

3
The Landscape of Sleep

Sleep is perhaps one of the strangest facets of the human experience. It is so very ordinary, yet oh so peculiar; a nightly oddity that all but a few of us take for granted. Yet, there is no human behaviour more common. We all spend a third of our lives asleep, roughly 26 years should we be fortunate and live to reach our expectancy. We will spend more of our lives sleeping than we will spend building our families, eating, enjoying music and the arts, engaging in sex, exploring our creative endeavours, or any number of those many experiences that make us human. Sleep, as much as any of the more acclaimed human pursuits, defines us as a species. Yet, for many of us the landscape of sleep remains a mystery, a mystery which we rarely, if ever, stop to question. For lucid dreamers, this cannot be the case, for to master the world of dreams we must first learn to navigate the ocean of sleep; to do that, we need to become familiar with it, to understand it.

Sleep is somewhat of a misleading word, as it implies a single unchanging state. But sleeping is anything but a simple, passive withdrawal from the world; rather, it is a dynamic and varied process. In this chapter we shall take a look at the nature of sleep, we shall learn its landscape and familiarise ourselves with its features and landmarks. Whilst our final destination may well be the land of dreams, our journey there will be far from uneventful.

The topics we'll cover are intimately entwined with the experience of dreaming. Understanding these unique phenomena and the nature of sleep is vital, if only to prepare you for the sometimes shocking and bizarre events you are likely to encounter. The dynamic and shifting sleeping mind is an exotic and unusual place, far from our usual waking experience. Whilst for many the secret lives of our sleeping minds lay hidden somewhere between apathy and the natural amnesia that accompanies sleep, as lucid dreamers wandering consciously into the twilight realms of slumber, we must be prepared to face these unique experiences head on.

As any good explorer will tell you, the best way to plan an expedition is to first acquire a map of the territory. Fortunately for us, we have such a map, an overview of the environment of sleep. Our map is called the Sleep Cycle.

The sleep cycle

We humans are creatures that operate in cycles. Having evolved here on planet Earth with its 24-hour rhythm of day and night and its monthly cycle of the moon and the tides, it is unsurprising that the internal processes that govern us also closely mimic these natural cycles. Any biological cycle that repeats on a daily basis is called a circadian rhythm, the sleep cycle being perhaps the most familiar of the circadian rhythms. The circadian 'clock' that governs our internal daily cycles is located in the suprachiasmatic nucleus (SCN), a pair of distinct grouping of cells located in the part of the brain known as the hypothalamus. Should the SCN be destroyed, either accidentally or experimentally, it results in a complete lack of a regular sleep and waking rhythm.

The seasonal ebb and flow of the length of the day and night is established by the SCN, by gathering information on the duration of daylight from the retina. This information is then passed on to the pineal gland which, in turn, regulates the release of the hormone Melatonin. Levels of Melatonin peak during the night and are low during daylight hours. Of course, many other important chemical changes are also taking place during this process and throughout our entire night's sleep. Levels of the stress hormone Cortisol and the neurotransmitters Serotonin and Acetylcholine (among others) all play vital roles in the regulation and nature of our sleep cycle. Whilst, for our purposes, the specific details of this intricate chemical interplay are not vital (although I do recommend researching them further) it is important to be aware that our sleeping mind is in a continual state of flux; it is constantly changing, which, from our subjective viewpoint, exhibits itself in the varied stages and experiences of sleep.

Our daily cycle between sleep and waking is just the stage upon which the more detailed sleep cycle plays its part. The sleep cycle itself is further broken into distinct stages, all with their own unique characteristics. Up until relatively recently, these were categorised as five distinct stages, the first four falling under the banner of NREM (non rapid eye movement) and the final being REM (rapid eye movement). This system was standardised in 1968 by Allan Rechtschaffen and Anthony Kales in the 'R&K sleep scoring manual'. The stages were simply referred to as stage 1, stage 2, stage 3, stage 4 and REM. In 2004, the American Academy of Sleep Medicine (AASM) commissioned the AASM Visual Scoring Task Force to review the R&K scoring system. As a result, in 2007 the AASM published their new scoring system, of which the most dramatic change was to combine stages 3 and 4 into a single stage called N3 (the N here again stands for Non-REM). The resultant changes now mean that the stages of sleep are referred to as N1, N2, N3 and REM (N3 is also referred to as delta sleep or slow-wave sleep (SWS)). Whilst a small change, it is important to note and helps avoid confusion when reading older texts on the subject of the sleep cycle. For the sake of remaining current, I shall be using the AASM system throughout the book.

To understand the sleep cycle, let us first take a look at the differences between these four stages of sleep, after which we'll examine how our brains move through these stages throughout the night.

Stage N1 (occasionally referred to as somnolence or drowsy sleep) is the first port of call as we drift into sleep. It refers to the transition of the brain from the alpha waves of waking experience (at a frequency of 8-13 Hz) to theta waves (of a frequency of 4-7 Hz). During N1, you will lose a degree of muscle tone and most of your awareness of the external world. The delightfully named phenomenon, the Hypnic Jerk (also less amusingly known as a myoclonic twitch), is common in N1. You have almost certainly experienced a Hypnic Jerk; it is a sudden twitch or movement in your body whilst falling asleep that can potentially briefly awaken you. The experience is often preceded by a sensation of falling. Another unusual experience often reported in N1 is that of Hypnagogic Hallucination, also known as hypnagogia; these are essentially mini dreamlets, short visual and auditory hallucinations you experience as you drift into sleep. We shall discuss hypnagogia in more detail shortly. Many people, when woken from N1, will often claim not to have been asleep at all, instead reporting being lost in deep thought. However, N1 is most certainly a form of sleep.

Stage N2 is a prolific stage of sleep, generally accounting for 44-55% of sleep in adults. During N2, muscular activity decreases further, heart rate lowers and body temperature starts to decrease. N2 is characterised by the observation of sleep spindles ranging from 11 to 16 Hz (commonly 12-14 Hz) and K-complexes. Sleep spindles and K-complexes are bursts of brain activity that are visible by the recording of electrical activity along the scalp using an electroencephalograph (EEG). Sleep spindles are seen as a burst of brain activity that immediately follows muscle twitching. It is believed by some researchers that, during sleep spindles, the brain (especially in the young) is learning which nerves control specific muscles.

Spindles are generated in the thalamus and have been shown to aid restful sleep when external sounds create a disturbance to the sleeper's environment. Sleep spindles are also associated with the learning and integration of new information, as well as directed remembering and forgetting. The K-complex is the largest observable EEG event in a healthy human brain. K-complexes have two likely functions. Firstly, suppressing cortical arousal to events which the sleeping brain evaluates not to signal danger and, secondly, aiding memory consolidation. The subjective experience of N2 is a complete lack of conscious awareness of the external environment.

Stage N3 (also referred to as slow wave or deep sleep) is the deepest level of sleep. It is characterised by the presence of a minimum of 20% delta waves ranging from 0.5-2 Hz and having a peak-to-peak amplitude >75 μV. In older texts using the R&K standard, N3 is divided into two distinct stages - stage 3, which was defined by 20-50% of delta waves, and stage 4 with greater than 50% delta waves. These are now combined and considered a single stage. It is during N3 that many of the more unusual sleeping behaviours (known as parasomnias) occur. Sleepwalking (somnambulism), bed wetting (nocturnal enuresis), night terrors (not to be confused with nightmares) and sleep talking (somniloquy) all occur during N3. It is very difficult to wake those in N3;

however, should you succeed, they are likely to experience a good deal of disorientation and may take some time to regain full alert consciousness (the common myth that waking a sleepwalker is fatal is just that, a myth). Subjectively, the experience of N3 can be summed up with common phrases like 'dead to the world' or 'fast asleep'. Being the deepest stage of sleep, it is the point during sleep in which we are at our most distant from the familiar experience of waking consciousness.

Rapid Eye Movement (REM) in adult humans typically occupies 20-25% of total sleep, being about 90-120 minutes of an average night's sleep. Also known as Paradoxical sleep, it is distinct in many ways from the three stages of NREM, most notably by being the stage of sleep in which the vast majority of dreaming occurs. Perhaps surprisingly, it wasn't until the 1950s that REM was first identified and defined, by researchers Nathaniel Kleitman, Eugene Aserinsky, and Jon Birtwell. Criteria for REM sleep include rapid eye movement, but also low muscle tone and rapid low-voltage EEG. Breathing and heart rate are irregular during REM, resembling that of waking. Body temperature is also poorly regulated. Both males and females experience genital engorgement during REM, with both genders displaying the characteristics associated with sexual arousal.

Specific neurons located in the brain stem (in the pontine tegmentum) and known as REM sleep-on-cells are especially active during REM and are possibly the causes of its occurrence. During REM, we experience an almost complete bodily paralysis (not quite complete, one of the obvious exceptions being the continued movement of the eyes) known as REM atonia, a state in which the motor neurons are not stimulated, resulting in a lack of muscle movements. This is a fortunate state of affairs for, should we lack this paralysis, we would be prone to physically act out our dreams. Such a condition does indeed exist, called REM behaviour disorder, wherein sufferers truly act out their dreams, often risking damaging themselves or their bed partners (fortunately, this condition can be treated).

Whilst it may seem logical that the rapid eye movements that are the namesake of this state would be due to the eyes acting out their dreamt gaze, this behaviour occurs for both those born blind and in foetuses, raising the question as to whether this is the only reason for its occurrence. To confound matters further, the movements of each eye are not necessarily unified, resulting in a lack of a fixation point. However, lucid dreamers who have been asked to perform a specific ocular signal from within a dream are able to do so and the corresponding physical eye movements can be discerned unambiguously via Electrooculography (or EOG, a technique for measuring the resting potential of the retina).

Whilst the rapid eye movement of the REM state may not be purely the result of dreamt eye movements, there is certainly a meaningful and usable correlation between the two. Of course, for lucid dreamers REM is the state that elicits the most interest, being the home of dreams. It is perhaps unnecessary to describe the subjective experience of REM, for we are all familiar with how it feels to dream. However, for those dreams which are not lucid, the REM state is a strange state of sleep indeed, for it is the one state in which we mistake our sleeping experience for waking reality. Unless lucid dreaming, we all believe our dreams are reality - that is, until we awaken.

We transition between these four stages of sleep throughout the night, generally in the sequence **N1 > N2 > N3 > N2 > N1 > REM** then repeating. We complete an entire cycle of all four stages roughly every 90 minutes (although nature is never quite this exact - in reality, it's somewhere between 70-120 minutes). On an average night, we will repeat subtle variations of this cycle four to six times. The first half of the night is the dominion of N3, or Deep Sleep. During these first four hours or so of sleep, the restorative N3 appears to be the primary focus, with only short periods spent in REM. As the night progresses, the focus slowly shifts towards REM and, with each complete cycle, the length of REM gradually increases. Approximately half-way through an average night's sleep our brains will normally cease entering N3 altogether and, instead, cycle through stages **N1 > N2 > N1 > REM** then repeating, with progressively more time spent in the REM phase as each cycle passes. By the end of a night's sleep, REM is at its peak with a great deal of the cycle spent largely in this stage. It is also normal throughout the night to occasionally briefly awaken following REM, although most occurrences of this are usually immediately forgotten. It's assumed this happens to allow the sleeper an opportunity to shift their sleeping position.

The cycle as outlined is only a generic sketch of the average sleep cycle. In reality, each night's sleep will rarely be quite such a perfectly choreographed event, as outside disturbances, diet, the activities you've experienced the day before can all play their part in either breaking the cycle or shifting the body's requirements for each stage (and thus the duration spent in them). However, the body will always attempt to stick as closely to this cycle as is possible, making the basic premise of the night being split into two phases still valid. In general, the first half of a night will revolve around NREM, the latter REM. Such information is, of course, incredibly important when attempting to induce lucidity. Whilst lucid dreaming can and does occur in the early stages of the night, it is far more common in the latter half and, as we near waking, not only this but the dreams themselves will be of a much longer duration.

With an outline of the landscape of sleep in place, let's take a look at some of the oddities you are likely to experience on your journey throughout sleep and on the path to becoming a proficient lucid dreamer.

Hypnagogia and hypnagogic hallucinations

The rather beautifully named Hypnagogia comes from the Greek *hypnos* 'sleep' and *agōgos* 'leading' or 'inducing', so can be considered to mean 'leading into sleep'. The term was coined by Dr Andreas Mavromatis in his 1983 thesis and further published in his book *'Hypnagogia' the Unique State of Consciousness Between Wakefulness and Sleep*. Hypnagogia is a transitional period between wakefulness and sleep and is often associated with the N1 stage of sleep, though lucid dreamers report the experience of hypnagogic hallucinations whilst entering REM directly from waking. Generally, the term hypnagogia is used in the lucid dreaming community as a shorthand to refer to the hypnagogic hallucinations that accompany this state, rather than the state itself.

Hypnagogic hallucinations are a common occurrence and are likely to have been experienced by most sleepers at some point during their lives, especially during periods in which they are particularly tired or having experienced mild sleep deprivation. As such, references to the experience are littered throughout literary history with famous names such as Aristotle, Iamblichus, Cardano, and Simon Forman among many others, all having made references to the phenomena. In more recent times, accounts abound, an example of which is Edgar Allan Poe's description of his 'fancies' that he experienced on the brink of sleep.

The experience of hypnagogic hallucinations can be startlingly vivid, often with an intensity that rivals dreams themselves (though far less dynamic and very much shorter-lived). In general, they are primarily visual in nature, although auditory hallucinations are almost as common, either occurring with a visual element or alone (tactile and olfactory hallucinations are also possible).

Visual hallucinations generally start simply, either as simple geometric patterns of moving light and colour (called phosphenes), often building in complexity and vividity until a more comprehensive and realistic scene emerges. For example, a hypnagogic hallucination may originate as a series of faint lights moving towards and around you; as their intensity and complexity builds, a convincing scene of travelling by car through an underground tunnel may suddenly emerge, built, it would seem, upon the simpler visual elements that preceded it.

Equally, however, fully-formed scenes can emerge immediately and without the requirement of prior, less complicated visuals. The topic and scenes of these more concrete images can be seemingly limitlessly varied, although in general they are reported to often be either static, or rapidly shift from one unrelated scene to another. The simpler patterns of light tend to be a little more consistent, at least initially, appearing not altogether dissimilar (in hue and texture) to the optical effect of a residual image (or after image) that you can experience shortly after being exposed to a bright scene. As these simpler images build in complexity, so too does the variety of how they may be expressed. Often, when the observer suddenly becomes consciously aware of the formation of hypnagogic hallucinations, especially the more vivid scenes, the effect can be shattered, returning the observer to the more mundane experience of the darkness behind closed eyes. However, a prolonged reverie in these visual hypnagogia is certainly by no means impossible.

Some of the auditory hypnagogic hallucinations that are regularly reported are loud noises (such as smashing glass, banging doors etc.), familiar noises (ringing doorbells, the sound of the phone), or voices (commonly the subject's name being called, or snippets of conversation). Generally, these are all brief in duration and indistinguishable from the actual experience of such an event. In deeper levels of hypnagogia, music can sometimes be heard, once again with a level of clarity and realism that makes it entirely convincing.

Hypnagogic hallucinations may, on occasion, result in a sudden waking, often accompanied by a hypnic jerk (a genuine physical movement, often related to the hypnagogic event experienced). Such awakenings when they do occur are often caused by either auditory hallucinations being a little too convincing (did the doorbell really ring?), the hallucinated experience being of a frightening or shocking nature, or an overly convincing tactile hallucination of, say, falling.

Hypnagogic hallucinations can often be influenced by activities prior to sleep, especially those that are prolonged and repetitive. This has been dubbed the 'tetris effect', after the popular video game Tetris (presumably, whoever chose this term had the experience after intensively playing the game before sleep, maybe in an attempt to avoid writing a paper on sleep psychology). Those who work in repetitive jobs are likely to experience this effect, especially in the early days of such work (I myself can recall endless rows of hypnagogic strawberries after a brief childhood summer job as a strawberry picker). It would seem that a combination of novelty and the repetition of an experience are important factors here. Interestingly, the tetris effect can also generate experiences of the less commonly reported tactile hypnagogic hallucinations. Spending time out at sea, walking through snow or wet sand, sky diving, or any number of novel physical sensations can all be replayed (following a day of such experiences) during that night's hypnagogia.

Many lucid dreamers, during early morning naps, can 'surf' the waves of hypnagogia until fully-formed dreams emerge. In such cases, tactile hallucinations are normally also apparent, either occurring naturally or by attempts to consciously induce them (various techniques for this are available. See the 'Impossible Movement Practice' in the chapter on Techniques.) Bear in mind, however, that the hypnagogia at the start of a night's sleep will almost certainly be followed by a long period of NREM and not dreaming sleep, so such 'surfing' is only valid in morning attempts to return to sleep.

Yet more hallucinations can be experienced as we exit sleep; whilst similar (but not identical) phenomena as hypnagogia, they are referred to as hypnopompic (as you may have guessed, 'pompic' comes from the greek *pompē* which means 'to send away'). These are most likely experienced shortly following a fully-fledged dream and when the dreamer has not completely returned to full waking consciousness.

Hypnagogia is a subject with which most experienced lucid dreamers are intimately aware and fond of, and can become a tell-tale sign (during a morning nap) that dreaming is not far off. As you become more accustomed to your nightly sleeping experiences, you too will likely notice your hypnagogic experiences far more often. Whilst not all experiences are pleasant, nor are they as involved and immersive as the dreaming experience itself, hypnagogia is a fascinating phenomenon and well worth taking the time to document and experiment with.

Sleep paralysis

Of all the many unusual experiences during the night, sleep paralysis, when it occurs, can be one of the most potentially confusing and disturbing. Sleep paralysis is essentially a mistiming of REM atonia, the process in which bodily movements are shut down during REM to avoid our living out the actions of our dreams. This atonia is a perfectly natural safety mechanism and we all unknowingly experience it several times a night during each REM period. Normally, REM atonia should start and end along with REM itself; however, in the case of sleep paralysis, this atonia can occur either prior to REM (known as hypnagogic or predormital sleep paralysis) or immediately following it (hypnopompic or postdormital sleep paralysis).

In both cases, where this atonia persists outside of REM state, the experiencer is by all accounts otherwise awake. The paralysis itself can last anything from a few seconds to up to several minutes (in incredibly rare cases, there are reports of it having persisted for several hours). During the experience, the subject is physically unable to move or speak, with the exception being (as with REM) the continued ability to move the eyes. Whilst unusual, sleep paralysis is harmless and perfectly safe.

The experience of sleep paralysis is often accompanied by vivid open-eyed hypnagogic or hypnopompic hallucinations, which has led some researchers to believe that some accounts of ghostly apparitions and alien abductions are as a result of the state. Indeed, it's believed that the medieval legend of the incubus and succubus (spirits that attack sleepers in the night, either sexually or through suffocation, or both) are early attempts to explain the experience of sleep paralysis and its accompanying hallucinations. For the record, the incubus was a male spirit that preyed on females, while the succubus was its female counterpart who attacked males.

Similar accounts of spirits and demons performing nightly attacks abound throughout the folklore of different cultures (in Turkey, the demon is called a *djinn*, in Finland a *mare*; Fijians refer to the experience as *kana tevoro*, for

Americans it's the *old hag*, to name but a few), lending credence to the idea that these experiences are the result of a naturally occurring and common human experience, and not a genuine supernatural attack. Of course, such an experience can be absolutely terrifying for those who experience it, especially those who lack a prior knowledge or understanding of the cause of sleep paralysis. As a result, panic often sets in, which can be rather counterproductive, often prolonging the experience and intensifying the ghoulishness of the hallucinations. As a rule, a calm witnessing acceptance of the event is the best approach, although admittedly this is much easier to say than do; writing it is one thing, but staying calm whilst an utterly convincing and drooling demon is gnashing only inches from your face… well, that may take more courage. One hint that seems to work well for ending especially terrifying experiences is to simply hold your breath (we retain control over our breathing rate, both whilst dreaming and during sleep paralysis); it seems that the sudden lack of air shocks the body to respond, often returning the subject to complete and mobile wakefulness, if perhaps somewhat breathless and shaken up.

Not all sleep paralysis experiences are quite this dramatic or terrifying. Many are simply the experience of the atonia itself, with no accompanying hallucinations. However, for those who are unaware of the possibility of paralysis, this in itself can be a frightening event. The hallucinations themselves also are not limited to the demons of folklore as, whilst these are common, other hallucinations also occur.

It would seem that your expectations play a large role here; what, for some, may be a demon, while for others it may be an alien encounter, a less fantastical alternative may simply be the hallucination of a human intruder. It is the combined expectation between the paralysis itself (which implies helplessness, and vulnerability to attack) and your own worldview and beliefs of who or what may perform such an attack that generates the scenario you'll experience.

For those who are prepared and are aware of the possibility of paralysis, these expectations are no longer as relevant, opening the hallucinatory experience to much wider possibilities. Sensations of floating, bodily vibrations and distortions, hallucinations of insects or animals moving around the room, flashes of light and colour, strange sounds, etc., are all equally possible and only a small selection from the wide variety of unusual experiences your mind may generate.

The causes of sleep paralysis are many and varied, although generally its occurrence is the result of anything that dramatically throws the sleep cycle out of its normal pattern. For example, sleep deprivation, insomnia, an irregular sleeping pattern, stress, the use of stimulants, certain ADHD medications, physical exhaustion, and sleeping in the supine position (lying on your back) are all factors that can play a role in instigating paralysis. Whilst none of these factors alone guarantee the experience, they all greatly increase the chances of its manifestation.

For lucid dreamers, to whom sleep paralysis is a known and expected phenomenon, such an event is warmly greeted rather than feared. Knowing that the paralysis and the hallucinations are the result of REM atonia and hypnagogia respectively, this makes them absolutely sure signs that REM is very close indeed. In fact, the experience of sleep paralysis is almost certainly the single most favourable time to attempt to induce a lucid dream, as your mind and body have already made virtually all the preparations required for REM to occur; it is simply a matter of enjoying the unusual experience whilst remaining consciously aware and waiting for the dream to begin. With psychological preparation and an understanding that the advent of sleep paralysis is natural and perfectly harmless, we can turn an otherwise frightening experience into something exhilarating, enjoyable and, ultimately, the doorway to another world.

Nightmares

Of the many features of the landscape of sleep, one of the most infamous is the nightmare. Despite the modern use of the word 'mare' to mean a female horse, the 'mare' in nightmare actually refers to the old English word for demon, a demon that torments sleepers. As is common knowledge, a nightmare is not a separate sleeping phenomenon in its own right, but simply a type of dream, albeit an especially unpleasant and memorable dream. Being a form of dream, nightmares happen during the REM phase of the night so their occurrence (based on the varying length and regularity of REM throughout the night) are more likely in the later stages of sleep as we near awakening.

Interestingly, studies of dreams have established that approximately 75% of dreams contain negative emotions or content. It would seem if it is the case that nightmares are simply a matter of degree, if the majority of dreams contain seeds of negative experience, then nightmares are those dreams in which the seeds take root. If it is indeed true and such a large proportion of dreams are at least mildly unpleasant in nature, it is compelling reason to develop the skills required for lucid dreaming, considering just how much of our time is spent in this state (ignoring NREM, 11% of our daily mental activity is spent dreaming). The existence of nightmares only solidifies this argument.

If we define a nightmare as a dream in which the negative content is strong enough to wake us from our sleep cycle, then reports show that such dreams occur approximately once a month. However, it is likely that, due to the amnesia that surrounds sleep, many more experiences of nightmares are forgotten than remembered; as such, their occurrence is likely to be very much higher than this. Children and teenagers are more prone to nightmares than adults, and the rates of such experiences seem to gradually decrease in adults as we age. However, waking levels of fearfulness do seem to show a correlation with the occurrence of nightmares, while those of us who are more timid or fearful in daily life are more prone to frightening and disturbing dreams.

The causes of nightmares are varied; stresses and anxieties in our daily lives are a common trigger, as is sickness or injury. Sleeping in an uncomfortable or awkward position is likely to increase their likelihood also. The common folk wisdom of eating cheese before bed resulting in a nightmare may have a grain of truth to it; eating late can increase the metabolism and brain activity, which will interfere with restful sleep. Add to this that certain difficult to digest foods, made even harder to digest by our lying rather than upright position, could result in indigestion, which will further disrupt our sleep. As for cheese itself, it certainly falls into the difficult to digest category. It is also worth noting that cheese is a reasonably good source of choline, a nutrient which can help aid in the recall of dreams, so perhaps there is a little truth to the old wives' tale yet.

For most of us, nightmares are little more than an unpleasant and somewhat rare inconvenience. However, in certain cases, the regularity and intensity of nightmares can become so strong that it verges on debilitating. Often in these cases the cause of the nightmare is a genuine traumatic event that occurred in waking life, the post-traumatic stress of such an event triggering nightmares in which the dreamer re-lives the scenario again and again.

Fortunately, such nightmares are treatable and respond well to a procedure called imagery rehearsal developed by Harvard psychologist Deirdre Barrett.

The process simply is to regularly imagine the nightmare (during waking hours) with an alternative and positive outcome - essentially, rewriting the plot with a happy ending. Such a process is akin to dream incubation, which we shall discuss later. However, should you give this a little thought, you will realise that the lucid dreaming allows you to perform this practice during the dream itself, allowing a direct interaction with the nightmare and a rewriting of the outcome and your response to events as the dream itself plays out. We shall look at the process of overcoming nightmares via lucidity in more depth in Chapter 7.

False awakenings

It's well known that our minds can play tricks on us. In the realm of slumber, those tricks can take on a whole new level of cunning. Perhaps the most devious of all the nightly illusions is the false awakening. A false awakening is, as the name suggests, a vivid dream in which the dreamer believes they have woken. The level of realism (not in the sense of how real it feels, but in the duplication of realistic events) can vary greatly in such a dream. Some false awakenings can be near carbon copies of the actual experience of waking. In such hyper realistic dreams, the dreamer often simply goes about their usual daily routine, until either the dream diverges into the more standard dreaming fare, or they simply awaken genuinely. They can create a very bizarre sense of deja vu, leading the subject to question, once they genuinely awaken, if they truly have.

Such a feeling can be increased even further should the less common occurrence of multiple false awakenings raise its head. In such cases, the dreamer experiences a false awakening, apparently wakes from it, only to discover they are within yet another false awakening. This process can repeat several times, leading the dreamer to feel somewhat like a Russian matryoshka doll, with each illusion of reality nested within another.

Multiple false awakenings are a relatively uncommon experience, although most people will experience something along these lines at least once in their lifetime. Indeed, the philosopher Bertrand Russell claims to have experienced roughly a hundred consecutive false awakenings whilst awakening from general anaesthetic. Such a claim is, of course, impossible to substantiate, but who knows? The human mind is full of surprises. The strangeness of such events has led to false awakenings being a popular theme in many works of fiction, with films such as the (rather entertaining) 1945 film '*Dead of Night*' wherein the entire plot was based around the concept. More recently, '*Vanilla Sky*' starts with a great example of a realistic false awakening (and also includes various hidden, and not so hidden, references to lucid dreaming).

Not all false awakenings are such convincing replicas of your daily morning routine. In many experiences, the only plausible aspect of the dream is the awakening itself, with the environment you find yourself in being anything from a very distorted representation of your own bedroom, a bedroom from your past, or simply some utterly fictional or unlikely environment. This type of false awakening seems somewhat more common. Dream researcher Celia Green classifies these less realistic false awakenings as a Type 1 false awakening, being the more common of the two experiences. The less common, but more convincing replicas, she refers to as a Type 2.

In reality, there is probably not nearly such a clear distinction, as it would seem that the realism of such events can fall anywhere on a subtle spectrum ranging from hyper real to the absurd. For example, in a recent false awakening I experienced a near perfect copy of my own bedroom; the lighting for the time of day was perfect, and items I had left on my desk before sleeping were in the place I'd expect them to be. However, as I went to open the curtains, upon doing so I was greeted with a view that was absolutely unexpected, certainly not the usual scenery viewable from my window. In its place was a convincing scene of a futuristic city. Luckily, this resulted in a fantastic lucid dream. However, should I be asked to classify this as a Type 1 or Type 2 false awakening, I'd simply not be able to do so, as it fell somewhere between the two categories. The lesson here is not to get too hung up on classifications, as the dreaming mind isn't nearly as neat and predictable as we'd like it to be.

A common theme for many false awakenings is of running late, regardless of the environment in which one seems to awaken. The commonality here is generally that of being rushed. More often than not, such dreams occur when a genuine and important waking event is expected, or if a similar real life event has occurred recently. Job interviews, important meetings, exams, etc., are all triggers for such dreams. Strangely, many people will dream of running late for their school exams way into their adult life, long after such concerns continue to be relevant. It would seem the level of importance we place on our waking life experiences plays a large part in the role they take in our dreams, which is of value to note when developing the skills required for lucid dreaming. If nothing else, false awakenings teach us the powerful role that expectation plays in influencing the content and direction of our dream lives. More often than not, false awakenings occur in the period of REM directly prior to waking. It would seem that at least a part of our mind is preparing itself to awaken and, as such, this expectation influences the content of our dream, and voila, we dream of waking up. This explains the increased occurrence of false awakenings on the night prior to important events - our mind is more intensely focused on the importance of waking on time, increasing the power of expectation and therefore the likelihood of influence over the dream.

False awakenings are also especially common following lucid dreams, often when a dreamer realises the dream is coming to an end and thoroughly expects to shortly awaken (and whilst, hopefully, remembering to attempt one of the methods to prolong the dream - we'll cover those later). What occurs instead (as you'll have guessed) is a very convincing dream of waking. Again, it is this strong expectation that influences the theme and direction of the dream. It is likely, as you become more experienced in your lucidity practices, that false awakening will become a common occurrence in your own dream life. Be prepared for them, and always remember to question if you are still dreaming upon awakening.

4

The Bare Essentials

So now, with a deeper understanding of the background of lucid dreaming, and a familiarity with the terrain within which we shall be traversing, it is time to turn our attention to the processes required to become a lucid dreamer. We shall soon find ourselves in a world of techniques, a diverse range of devious methods that will allow you to access and master the software of your mind. There are many paths and methods you can choose; however, before you choose a technique, you must first learn the bare essentials.

Regardless of which technique or combination of techniques you eventually choose to experiment with, there are certain prerequisites that are the essential foundations upon which all other lucidity practices rely. It's easy for both novice and experienced lucid dreamers, excited by the prospect of grand adventures, to overlook or skip the basics in favour of the more exotic and complicated techniques. But beware, as there are no shortcuts in dream training; attempting to scrimp on the basics is a recipe for frustration, and will almost certainly lead to more work in the long run.

For experienced lucid dreamers who are going through a 'dry spell', simply returning to the basics and making sure your foundations are solid can be the fastest way to return to form. Consider the following practices to be the dreamer's equivalent to a musician learning the scales; they are simple, but they are also effective and the foundation that shall hold everything else you do firmly in place. If you put the effort into mastering the basics, you shall be much more effective when you move into deeper waters.

To be clear, it is impossible to stress strongly enough the importance of strong foundations. Don't be fooled by the simplicity of the following concepts; they are your dreamer's toolbelt and, without them, you will never truly master lucidity.

Many of the concepts outlined here will be returned or referred to later, to clarify how they fit into the broader picture of an effective technique, and their place in the three-tier system for a balanced dream practice. For the sake of simplicity, I shall attempt where possible to list only the crucial elements of these bare essentials. However, the fundamental nature of these basics does require their subtle nuances and details to be explored and understood in detail.

Dream recall

Unquestionably, the very first place any aspiring lucid dreamer or dream enthusiast should start is in developing good dream recall, or the ability to be able to remember one's dreams. It may seem almost too obvious to mention, but clearly without dream recall any other dream practices become exercises in futility. Strangely, the degree of natural talent for dream recall seems to be rather randomly spread out over the population. You will have most likely noticed this yourself when discussing dreams with your peers - some people recall long, vivid dreams almost nightly, whilst others' recall is so poor they will swear they don't even dream at all (of course, this is impossible, as we all dream far more than we believe; it is the recall of these dreams that is the issue here).

Most of us fall somewhere in the middle of this spectrum, often fluctuating wildly from one end to the other, depending on our health and current lifestyle. Aside from any inherent psychological or biological predispositions in this department, the most plausible explanation for this seemingly random spread of abilities across the population is likely due to the varied habits and lifestyles of individuals. Should this be the case, as it almost certainly seems to be, it means that virtually anyone can develop high-quality dream recall with a combination of practice, understanding of the processes involved and a few lifestyle changes.

Before we even start discussing the finer details, it's important to accept that what we are trying to achieve when recalling our dreams is an act in defiance of our own biological design. For whatever reasons, evolution has imbued sleep with its own form of amnesia. During our nightly sleep cycle, we all pass through roughly five periods of REM sleep every night (that's five dreaming periods a night), yet most of us recall only those dreams from which we awaken directly. Therefore, it's clear that what we are attempting is something that will require more than just willpower alone.

One reason behind this nightly amnesia appears to be the complicated fluctuations in our brain chemistry as it moves through the various stages of sleep. Without wishing to go into too much detail at this point (we shall return to the importance of brain chemistry in Chapter 5), it would appear that the constantly changing levels of a neurotransmitter called Acetylcholine throughout our sleep can be considered the 'smoking gun' for tracing the source of our forgetfulness.

Acetylcholine (ACh) is vital in the formation of memories and also plays a major role in the regulation of sleep. ACh levels fluctuate dramatically during our sleep cycle, reaching their lowest levels during the deep non-REM stages of sleep and returning to near waking levels during REM. This may well help explain why our dream recall (especially for the dreams earlier in the night) can be so poor. Considering that our dreams are sandwiched between periods of incredibly low ACh levels, and thus times of very poor memory formation and retrieval, is it at all surprising that they are so prone to being forgotten?

Indeed, there are already many lucid dream enthusiasts who are attempting to turn the chemical balance in their own favour and are experimenting with chemicals such as Galantamine (a fascinating chemical which we shall discuss in Chapter 5), an anticholinergic agent or cholinesterase inhibitor, which essentially blocks the effects of an enzyme called Acetylcholinesterase (AChE), the function of which is to break down ACh. Blocking AChE allows for increased levels of ACh and thus improved recall and memory formation during sleep.

I'd also speculate that AChE levels may be elevated during sleep, which would further compound functional memory. However, due my limited knowledge of neurochemistry and difficulty finding reliable sources to confirm or deny this, I cannot state this as fact. Still, whatever the specific chemical cocktail that inebriates our sleep, the most important point to remember here is that our sleeping minds are operating on a very different level from that of waking.

I mention all this in advance to put our available options for improving dream recall into perspective. Given that our brains are neurochemically prone to poor memory whilst sleeping, we must be especially vigilant in holding onto and recording what memories do pass through the veil of amnesia. What we are attempting is indeed rather difficult, but it is far from impossible. It is simply important to understand the processes involved so as to set our expectations to reasonable levels and avoid chastising ourselves too harshly when we come up against difficulties.

Warnings aside, the first port of call for developing dream recall starts (perhaps slightly counter intuitively) not upon awakening, but upon retiring for bed. As with a great deal of lucidity training, motivation is your most potent tool, and it is before sleep that you must (with the sufficient motivation) prime your mind to be prepared to recall your dreams upon awakening. This brings into play a certain mindset or mental trick that most of us are already familiar with and which will continue to be of use in more advanced dream practices later.

The process is similar to those times when you (in lieu of a real alarm) need to set your mental alarm clock to awaken you at a certain time. Most of us are familiar with this phenomenon; indeed, even when we do set our real-world alarm clocks, we often find ourselves awakening briefly before the alarm itself goes off. This is an example of 'prospective memory', remembering to perform a task in the future.

The mindset involved here I call 'Priming' and its uses extend beyond dream recall alone. The principle is simple. Upon retiring for sleep, you set the intention clearly in your mind to recall your dreams upon awakening. Say to yourself as you lie in bed 'The very first thing I'll do upon waking will be to lie still and recall my dreams'. It sounds simple, and really it is; however, it may take a little practice to engage the exact mental mechanisms required before you find it effective. Whilst priming is simple in practice, being a purely mental process it's very tricky to give specific instructions on how it is achieved. The trick is to really try and implement the thought using the very same part of your mind involved in setting your internal alarm clock. Once you've succeeded in achieving this mental trick, you'll find it becomes second nature rather quickly. Please do try to remember the inner steps you take to achieve this mental process, as 'priming' is a multi-purpose tool and you shall be using it elsewhere in your dream practices.

Whilst on the subject of pre-sleep activities, it may be useful to mention that many people report that, upon retiring for bed, they experience a sudden recall of the previous night's dreams, dreams that they had assumed had been completely forgotten. Whilst this doesn't occur for everyone (I myself cannot claim to have experienced this), reports of this phenomenon are rather widespread, so be prepared for this experience and be ready to record whatever comes to mind.

An often overlooked area for improving dream recall is perhaps the most obvious of all, namely the environment in which you sleep. When embarking on your journey into dream exploration, it is important to make sure your bedroom is as conducive to restful and undisturbed sleep as is possible. Whilst realistically we all may have to live with certain limitations and compromises in this respect, there is almost always room for improvement. Be sure to the best of your abilities to minimise disturbances. Unwanted noise, light pollution, etc., can generally be easily dealt with by the use of a sleep mask and ear plugs (I'll cover these in more detail shortly).

If you share a bedroom, discuss your sleeping requirements with your partner and attempt to find a diplomatic solution that suits you both. The quality of your bed, your nightclothes, bedroom decor, even the freshness of your bed linen can all play their part in improving the quality of your sleep and, by proxy, your recall. Aim to keep any tools you shall be using in your practices easily accessible and in a familiar order.

Your sleep environment also extends beyond these merely physical matters. Aim to have a short period of calm both prior to and after sleep. Take time to unwind before sleep and upon awakening; give yourself ample time to review your night's activities before being forced into dealing with the more practical matters of the day. If this means a slight adjustment in your sleeping patterns, so be it; being awoken by an alarm clock and thrown into an immediate rush for the day will not only kill your dream recall, but will also impact the quality of your sleep. As a pleasant side effect, you shall likely notice your improved sleeping environment and the calm start and finish to your day will improve your mood and energy levels throughout the day.

As mentioned earlier, a sleep mask is an invaluable tool for improving your dream life and recall. Again, it is a subject that often remains absent from discussions on dreaming. I would go as far as to say that a sleep mask is an essential item for any serious dream enthusiast. Apart from its obvious use to minimise any visual disturbance of your sleep, it also seems to vastly improve dream recall upon awakening.

I am of the belief that light plays an important role in inducing the shift from the internalised world of dreams to the external world of waking. It is likely that stimulation of the optic nerve upon awakening sets in motion a process of chemical changes within the brain, some of which, it would seem plausible, result in the sudden loss of dreaming memories. To the best of my knowledge, there have been as yet no studies to confirm this theory, but my own experience and multiple accounts of other dream enthusiasts seem to add weight to the possibility. Even if this were not to be the case, it is undeniable that a sleep mask greatly reduces the immediate distractions of awakening and allows you to focus on the task of recall.

Another fantastic boon of using a sleep mask is that it can greatly aid lucidity induction itself. Once you make a habit of wearing a sleep mask each time you sleep, you will soon start to experience dreams in which you appear to awaken normally (false awakenings). However, more often than not these false awakenings also, rather conveniently, forget to include a dream version of your sleep mask. This is the perfect sign that you are still dreaming - knowing that you fell asleep wearing a mask and awakening with vision is the perfect clue that things are not all they seem to be, and a great gateway into a lucid dream. Indeed, I often prime myself before sleep that 'the next time I can see I shall be dreaming', which can be a very effective tactic, but we are getting ahead of ourselves here!

Experiment with various sleep masks, as almost certainly the cheap items you find in travel shops will not be up to the task. There are plenty of quality masks available but, with the endless variation in the shapes and sizes of the human head, it's impossible to suggest one that will be perfect for all. I would, however, recommend those that allow you to open your eyes whilst still wearing them and retain complete darkness (generally, they have a foam body with an indent cut in the position of the eyes); they not only feel far less claustrophobic, but they are far more comfortable and effective. Earplugs have many of the same benefits as a sleep mask and I'd also recommend them for improved dream recall. However, if you do wish to use earplugs, a word of caution is advised. Whilst they can be great at blocking out unwanted distractions, safety is an issue. They are best used only if you share a bed with a partner who does not use them, or if you can be certain that they are not so effective as to block out warnings of danger, such as your smoke alarm. Apply your common sense to their use and, if in doubt, err on the side of caution.

This brings us to another device that is intimately connected to sleep and plays a role of both the friend and foe of the aspiring dreamer - the alarm clock. As a rule, an alarm clock can be the single most potent way to instantly erase dream recall. Being so abruptly woken is a very effective way to shatter whatever memories you would have otherwise retained. However, as a result of living in the real world of deadlines and work schedules, only very few of us have the luxury of waking up the old-fashioned natural way.

So, how do we fit our dream practices around the stresses and demands of everyday life? The trick is to attempt to find ways to awaken smoothly, using an alarm clock only as the final reminder should other methods fail. As we discussed earlier, we all have a natural ability to prime our own internal body clocks to wake us at a desired time; this is certainly the preferable approach, so try combining your dream recall priming with the intention to awaken 15 minutes before your alarm clock is due to sound.

If you find this method too unreliable, or it just simply doesn't work for your personal schedule, another option is to purchase a secondary alarm clock, one that can be set to play an MP3 or CD of your choice. Set this alarm 15 minutes prior to your original alarm, have the volume low and choose a piece of music that starts softly and gradually builds in volume and intensity, ideally a piece without lyrics. This is a much smoother way to return to the waking world and will greatly enhance your ability to recall your dreams. In fact, it can also work as a lucidity induction method in itself, as often the music will incorporate itself into your dreams long before it awakens you, cueing you to become aware you are still asleep and dreaming. Of course, should the music fail to wake you, your original alarm will still sound at its designated time.

A dreamer's relationship to his or her alarm clock is not all bad. Many lucidity techniques require waking during the night which, without an alarm, can be very difficult indeed. Again, should you find yourself experimenting with these methods at a later date, using a softer musical alarm is certainly the more pleasant approach.

The alarm clock could also benefit those who find developing dream recall especially difficult. Often, the reason for these problems is that, due to a rigid sleeping pattern, they have fallen into the unfortunate situation of waking from sleep during the deep non-REM phases of sleep when dream recall is near impossible. If you find yourself in this situation, then using an alarm to adjust your waking time so that it falls within REM will increase your dream recall immensely (again, I'd advise the musical alarm approach). It will also vastly improve your mood and alertness for the day (as waking from REM generally results in a much clearer mind than waking drowsily from NREM).

When attempting a wake time adjustment, experiment with increments of 15 or 20 minutes until you find the sweet spot. The sleep cycle is essentially a recurring 90-minute pattern in which we phase between the various sleep stages, with REM occurring at the latter end. As such, you should never need to adjust your wake time any further than 90 minutes in either direction to awaken directly from REM. Bear in mind, this will only be effective if your sleeping pattern is very rigid to the point that you are falling asleep and waking up at the same time each day. Also, should adjusting your waking time prove difficult or impossible, you can equally adjust the time you go to bed to achieve the same result. Indeed, the best solution for anyone suffering from poor dream recall due to a strict waking schedule is to simply to go to bed earlier. We all try to push our limits and, whilst we may appear to be able to function on very little sleep, the quality of both our dreaming and waking lives will suffer as a result.

With these fundamentals covered, it's time to turn our attention to the actual process of dream recall upon awakening. As discussed, the ideal scenario is to wake up as naturally as possible, preferably without an alarm, but follow the previous advice should this be unavoidable. At this point, you should find yourself returning smoothly to the waking world, undisturbed and with plenty of time available for the task at hand.

The most important advice now is to minimise all distractions, lie still, allow your eyes to remain closed, and put aside any thoughts or worries about the day ahead. Should your priming have been effective, these thoughts should be your very first upon waking and shall come naturally. Under ideal circumstances, you will find yourself having woken directly from a dream, with a vivid clear memory of the events. If this be the case, remain still and mentally rehearse the previous dream, taking the time to go over the events and details, making sure they are firmly committed to memory. Once you feel comfortable that you've successfully memorised the dream, you should quickly get up, making sure your first activity is to physically record your notes.

It's important to mention at this point that dream memories can be as slippery as a fish. You can easily believe, whilst you are lying in this calm state, that you have a firm grasp on your memories, only to find your recall rapidly slipping away upon interacting with the waking world. I believe this may be due to the relative difference in the intensity between dreaming and waking stimuli. It may be the reason our dreams appear so realistic and vivid at the time of experiencing them; as we retreat into sleep, our mental threshold for what is considered 'notable activity' increases in sensitivity, essentially amplifying the normally subdued nature of thoughts, allowing them to become the fully-fledged world of dreams.

However, upon awakening, the cacophony of waking experience flooding into our senses at the full intensity of a genuine sensory experience throws into stark contrast the comparably feeble nature of mental activity that has been the focus of our attention up until that point. Or, to use a metaphor, in a quiet room even a whisper can seem loud, but the very same whisper can quickly be lost in the noise of a bustling street. So, perhaps upon awakening our brain is reminded of what constitutes the 'intensity of a real experience' and then, comparing this against the previous dream experiences (which, in its heightened state of sensitivity, it mistook as real), quickly corrects its mistake and promptly disregards.

Should your morning dream recall be less than perfect, the key principle is the same - focus on the task and avoid distractions. Work with whatever memories you have, focus on them and extrapolate likely scenarios and connections. The trick here is to be persistent - keep going until you feel you've managed to retrieve as many of your memories as possible. Focus on emotions, places, people, sensations - the whole range of possible experiences.

If you've woken with absolutely no recall, turn your attention to how you feel. Are your emotions positive or negative? Have you woken in a good mood? Try and work backwards and discover why you feel the way you do. You could also try a little word association (pick the first word that pops into your head) to see if this jogs any memories. It's likely that the thoughts and experiences of your dreams are still unconsciously partially active, so also try randomly picking a few names and places out of your mind to see if these kick-start the relevant memories.

More often than not, simply putting the effort into attempting to recall will (given a little time) bring rewards. If you reach the conclusion that there is absolutely nothing happening, allow yourself a mental distraction; let your mind wander to any pleasant subject you wish. We've all experienced having a 'word on the tip of our tongue' and discover it is often the case that it pops back into memory just as you start to think about something else; the same can be true of dream memories. So, should your persistence seem futile, do allow yourself a break. If, after all your efforts, you still come out empty-handed, still take time to record the details of your sleep and your mood upon getting up.

A common experience that many have is that often seemingly forgotten dreams can suddenly come flooding back later in the day. More often than not, these flashes of recall are triggered by an event closely related to the content of your dream, although this is not always the case. As such, it is good practice to always carry a notepad and pen for such occasions; needless to say, it's a handy habit to develop regardless of dream training!

If nothing else, one thing that is certain when it comes to improving dream recall is that practice makes perfect. Initially, it may seem a struggle to garner even slithers of recollection, but with time and perseverance your efforts will pay off. As you learn how your own mind and memory functions, you will develop your own tricks to enhance your recall.

These newfound skills are not only limited to your dreaming life; as you master your memory and develop a greater understanding of its workings, soon you shall see a marked improvement in your daily mental abilities also. Of course, this works both ways, as working on improving your waking memory will also feed back into improvements in dream recall. As with much of the skills developed in dream practice, nothing is standalone; the skills you learn are easily transferable to other areas of your life. A little effort in the early days can go a long way to improving many aspects of your life.

The dream journal

You shall never own a more important book on dreams than your dream journal. It is the first port of call for anyone interested in exploring the dreamworld and should be your constant companion throughout your journey. Don't be fooled (as are many) into thinking it is optional. On the face of things, it may appear that a simple record of your nightly adventures couldn't possibly be of such great importance, but your dream journal will serve multiple purposes, all equally vital to your growth and in developing understanding of your dreaming life.

Many explorers like to choose a beautiful journal, something that inspires them and demonstrates the value they place in their relationship with their dreams; others, on the other hand, may find an expensive journal daunting and will avoid 'messing it up' with the inevitable scribblings and notes that will need recording. Establish early on your own personal tendencies when it comes to this kind of behaviour, as a blank, beautiful journal is of absolutely no use to anyone. If you fall into the latter camp, simply use a basic notebook. Choose as your journal whatever will inspire you to make full use of it. Whatever you choose, be prepared to record not only beautiful, well-written dreams, but also fragments, notes, doodles, pictures or anything else that may be of relevance. This is not a place to be coy or selective; consider it as a repository of all and anything that relates to your dreaming life.

The absolute primary purpose of a dream journal is data collection. Record everything, however seemingly insignificant. Remember also, a dream journal is not simply for recording dreams alone; it is a place to store any information regarding the circumstances and details of anything that may have influenced your sleeping experience. These details can range from (and are not limited to) the time you retired, the time you awoke, any disturbances in your sleep, your mental and emotional states on both retiring and awakening, dietary details, hormonal cycles, medication, techniques used, unusual sleep phenomena (such as sleep paralysis or hypnagogia), dream goals, activities before sleep (or anything during the day that you may feel could influence your dreams), worries or any other absorbing thoughts. Literally anything that may be of relevance to your sleep and dreaming experiences.

The goal of this information gathering is to build an ongoing powerhouse of data. The details you collect here will give you a goldmine you can return to again and again, full of insight into the workings of your mind, your personal idiosyncrasies and the nature of your dreaming life. Over time you shall develop, with the aid of your journal, a familiarity second to none, of how the cogs behind the workings of both yourself and your dreaming mind turn.

Don't be fooled into believing that an entry into your journal, once written, is simply a record completed and forgotten, as it will become an interactive part of your dreaming practices. You shall return to your previously recorded dreams (and the additional information surrounding them) again and again, sieving through the data like a prospector searching for gold, hunting down dreamsigns (a subject we shall cover shortly) and discovering nuggets of insight and connections that shall aid your continuing journey into self-discovery. With this in mind, always leave sufficient space beside each journal entry for future notes.

On a painfully practical note, there are certain troublesome details to keeping a dream journal that are often overlooked, or simply left out of the discussion by some of those teaching the subject (possibly for fear of frightening people off). However, it would be both misleading and pointless for me to avoid this topic, as preparation for difficulties is half the battle won.

First and foremost, do not expect keeping a regular journal to be easy, as it most certainly isn't. Waking up in the middle of the night to make notes, or simply recording as much detail as you can first thing upon awakening, can take an almost herculean act of motivation. Be prepared to find that, on occasion, writing your journal will instil in you the very same negative feelings to which you are almost certainly already familiar, and have associated with a common bedroom device, namely the alarm clock. Indeed, journaling can bring with it an almost identical unpleasantness to that of the well-known experience of being awoken to the jarring sound of your bedroom alarm on those days you've been forced to set it all too early.

Just as with your alarm clock, the very times when you will be required to interact with your journal will also coincide with your mental and physical energy levels being at their absolute lowest. More importantly, unlike an alarm, there is no 'snooze button' for your journal; if you miss an opportunity to record the details of your dreams, either from laziness or distraction, they will almost certainly be lost forever to the fog of amnesia, which is the dream journalist's worst enemy.

There are, however, a couple of helpful solutions to counter these problems - or, at least, lessen the effort required for dream journaling. Firstly, build into your morning and evening schedule a fixed time for journaling (evenings for recording details proceeding sleep, mornings for the dreams themselves). Ideally, this should be the very first and last activity of your day. The best way to do this is to combine your writing with another morning activity so as to build a regular habit, such as over a cup of tea or breakfast. If you do choose to follow this route, though, be sure not to leave a large gap between waking and writing, as dream memories fade fast. Indeed, if there is to be any gap at all between waking and writing your journal in full, then you must also make brief notes immediately upon waking, such as keywords that will trigger the relevant memories for when you sit down to write out the complete account.

The only real way to establish the best system for yourself is to experiment, as you'll soon discover what does or does not work for you. This leads us neatly into the second tip for reducing the effort of dream journaling - the electronic voice recorder. Of all the gadgets in the dreamer's arsenal, the voice recorder has to be one of the most handy and stress-reducing of all inventions. I'd go as far as to say that, if you are serious about dream journaling, a voice recorder is an absolute must have. The advantages are obvious - there is no fumbling for a pen and paper in the middle of the night, nor disturbing yourself (or your partner) with the glare of a bedside lamp. Instead, you can keep your recorder easily accessible under your pillow, ready to record whenever it is needed.

When purchasing a voice recorder, the best advice is to look for something simple. Avoid the models with complicated menus and with too many buttons; what you are looking for is a simple device, with a large tactile record button (something you can feel for in the dark), and ideally one that also acts as the power switch. You'll be using this device often, in conditions where your drowsy mind will appreciate the forethought of purchasing a device that is simple to operate. Again, there is a warning to be made here - do not fall into the trap of merely recording your dreams on the device and then deciding to write them into your journal at some later date. As the saying goes, 'tomorrow never comes', so be prompt with transferring your recordings to paper.

Follow the previous advice on writing your dream journal at a daily set time, but instead of making physical notes first thing upon awakening you'll simply be making a voice recording. One of the real benefits of a recorder is that you can record your notes whilst your eyes are still closed. This can be incredibly beneficial when you intend to return to sleep to practise further lucidity techniques, or simply to help aid dream recall.

These tips can greatly reduce the stresses involved in keeping a regular journal, and I wholeheartedly recommend them. So, with a little preparation and motivation, whilst at times you may still find journaling a little daunting, the rewards will greatly outweigh the costs.

To recap, a dream journal is a dreamer's best friend and, without it, you will soon find yourself struggling to develop a familiarity with your dream life. Keep to a strict daily schedule for making entries into your journal, in which you will record as much detail from your dreams, sleep-related activities and daytime influences as possible. Should you awaken with no dream recall, you should absolutely still write whatever information is relevant.

Remember to keep some space next to each entry in preparation for those times you shall be reviewing your data, in order to make future notes. Most importantly, however, have fun and enjoy the process. Remind yourself regularly that you are compiling a record of your most personal and private adventures, adventures that, without your journal, would have been lost forever. Remember also that, with every page written, you are a step closer to developing an intimate relationship with your dream life, one which will, in time, bring you unimaginable experiences and self-knowledge, truly the key to unlocking your wildest dreams!

Dreamsigns

If your dream life were a detective story, then dreamsigns would play the role of the trail of clues leading you to the conclusion of 'whodunit'. In this intriguing case, the perpetrator our inner detective is tracking is the dreaming mind and the reward for successfully cracking the case is lucidity. We're all very aware that dreams are different from waking life; however, if pushed for an answer, most people struggle to define exactly what this difference is. Often, the general response is something along the lines of 'strange', 'weird', 'bizarre' or other vague words of that ilk. These answers are, for most people (to whom dreams are simply a nightly curiosity), sufficient.

But why would we aspiring lucid dreamers attempt to define the peculiar nature of dreams? The simple answer is that knowledge is power. Developing an intimate understanding of how our dreams differ from waking experiences prepares us to respond appropriately when we spot these soon to be familiar signs that we are dreaming. In essence, dreamsigns are the fingerprints of dreaming; the unique events, nature and elements of our personal dream worlds, that distinguish them from our everyday world of waking.

Before we delve into the process of establishing your personal dreamsigns, it is useful to distinguish the more fundamental differences between dreaming and waking. So, let's sidetrack from the immediate task at hand, for a moment, and consider these.

Interestingly, if you were to be shown a brain scan of your dreaming mind, its activity would appear almost indistinguishable from that of an equivalent scan taken whilst you were awake. On the most basic level, the dreaming and waking mind are very similar places to inhabit. There is perhaps good reason for this. In a very real sense, it could be said that every experience you'll ever have could be considered a form of dream.

Now, before I'm accused of rushing off on a metaphysical tangent, I'll try to explain what I mean by this. Firstly, let's ask the question, what exactly is a dream? If we simplify the concept to its absolute basics, a dream could be defined as a mental model of an experience. This may seem rather obvious, but what is perhaps less obvious (probably because we've lived our whole life in this way) is that our waking experience of the world can be defined in exactly the same way.

The words you are reading on this page right now are not the words themselves - those 'real' words exist outside of your brain and always will. What is actually happening is that the evidence of their existence originating on the physical page is transmitted via light into your optic nerves, where they are converted into data impulses and fired off towards the relevant areas of your brain to be interpreted. The words you are experiencing at this moment are the result of that process and are a model of those external words, a model that exists inside your skull. Your brain is constantly modelling the outside world, inferring details of that world via the information supplied by your five senses. In a very real sense, you experience the world around you by proxy - you experience the model.

It is undoubtedly a difficult concept to fully accept, mostly because our brains are so good at their job, but it's not difficult to confirm through experience. There are endless optical illusions (and plenty of auditory and other sensory illusions) that demonstrate how our minds are modelling the world. Indeed, a funnier and possibly more accurate term for these kinds of illusions would be 'brain failures', for a great deal of them are effective only because they take advantage of inherent weaknesses in our brain's abilities and exploit processing errors. Various mind-altering substances, hallucinogens being one of the most demonstrative in this respect, also clearly show us that our seemingly solid grasp of waking reality is indeed a mental model which is easily distorted.

The point I am making here is that, regardless of whether you are dreaming or awake, your experience of either world is a kind of mental model. This is important for two reasons. Firstly, knowing this can help you understand that the transition between waking and dreaming isn't as dramatic as it may have otherwise seemed, this knowledge can greatly help dissolve any mental blocks for achieving lucidity. Secondly, and more relevant for the topic of dreamsigns, it brings us closer to understanding the differences and similarities between dreaming and waking.

I understand that the point of mental models can be a little difficult to grasp, so I'll use a simple thought experiment to clarify. Imagine if you will a video camera, a DVD player and a screen. Both the camera and player are attached wirelessly to the screen. Whatever the camera points at appears on the screen. When the camera is turned off, the DVD player seamlessly switches on and plays previous random recordings based on what has been seen by the camera. Imagine that you are in a locked room and your only knowledge of the outside world was via this screen. You could never see what the camera is seeing directly (it is outside of your room), only what it reports to you via the screen. In such a scenario, it would be correct to call the images on the screen a 'model' of reality.

The question is, would you be able to establish if what you are viewing is the result of the live video feed, or a previous recording from the DVD player based purely on the quality of the picture alone? Both would appear equally as vivid and 'real' (by your standards). However, should you be lucky and realise there are certain quirks to how the DVD player operates, with that information you may be able to learn to notice these details and establish if the feed is either live or a recording.

In this example, as you will have guessed, the camera represents your senses, the screen your mental model of the world and the DVD player the processes which generate your dreams (memory etc.). Whilst this is an oversimplification, the point remains the same. It is almost impossible to distinguish between dreams and our experience of reality based on how 'real' they appear or feel to us, as both are always models or representations of reality. Dreamsigns, on the other hand, could be considered the 'quirks in the player' and we can learn to notice these.

If we are to accept that all our experiences are mental models, then the next logical question is, what differentiates them? The answer, which may well be apparent to you already, is the source of the information upon which the model is based. Whilst awake, our model of the world is being constantly updated and refined based on the information available to our senses. This is obviously not the case when dreaming. The model of the world we experience whilst dreaming is (with a few exceptions) built not from the stable consistent information afforded to us by our senses, but instead is formed from a combination of our memories, expectations and other attributes of our own minds. This is a crucial point and the foundation upon which much of the concept of dreamsigns is based.

Armed with this knowledge, hopefully it is apparent that, when attempting to spot clues to establish if one is dreaming, we are not looking for a qualitative difference in how realistic the experience feels or appears, but instead we are (among other things) on the lookout for issues with stability and a plausibility of the events unfolding. In other words, 'it seems so real' is never a relevant, nor effective, line of thinking, and is certainly not a conclusion that will establish which world you are experiencing.

Both the dreaming and waking states are confined within their own set of rules. The rules of the world of waking are governed by the strict and stable laws of physics, laws that by their nature remain independent from our opinions or thoughts of them (ignoring certain recent discoveries in quantum physics, but for our purposes we don't need to think about that). Gravity, for example, will remain, no matter how hard we attempt to wish it away. On the flip side, the rules of the dreaming world are completely dependent upon our minds. Our thoughts, beliefs, memories and the limitations of our brain's processing abilities are the roots from which the tree of dreams grows. These properties, on which the rules of dreamland are built, are flexible and not anchored in the laws of a stable external world. Gravity, in the case of dreaming, is an assumption based upon memory and experience. When in dreamland, we can indeed wish gravity away.

Again, a vastly over-simplistic but useful way to think about the difference between the waking and dreaming worlds is this: Whilst awake, our thoughts and moods are largely the result of the events occurring around us. Dreaming is the reverse. In dreams, the environment and events we find ourselves in are the result of our thoughts, expectations and mood.

Of course, whilst dreaming, the apparent events around us still impact our moods, only those moods then feed back to further fuel and create those events we experience. This can go some way to explain the intense emotions so often reported in dreams. Because our thoughts directly create our environments and, in turn, those environments influence our thoughts, a feedback loop is established and can quickly escalate the seed of a thought or emotion into a full-blown tsunami of intensity. In extreme cases when this process spirals out of control, we call those dreams 'nightmares'.

Getting started

Now we've looked into the primary differences between dreams and waking experience, it's time to move onto the more practical side of things, to discover the individual landscape and landmarks of your personal dreamlife. By this point, you should have developed your dream recall and have a rapidly growing collection of dreams recorded in your journal. You may well have already noticed certain recurring themes or quirks to your dreamlife; these are your first most glaringly apparent clues, the more obvious of your dreamsigns. Now it is time to pull out our detective's magnifying glass and take an even closer look at the evidence we have acquired in our dream journals.

It's important to note that what we are about to discuss is by no means a one-off exercise; it should become a regular event in your dream practices. I would suggest performing the following cataloguing and evaluation of your dreamsigns on roughly a weekly basis. Perhaps, like me, you could make it an activity for a lazy Sunday afternoon, when there is little else to distract you. Initially, however, you may find it useful to perform this exercise daily immediately after writing the account of your dream in your journal.

It would be useful to invest in a quality set of highlighter pens as this will make the whole task of marking your dreamsigns much easier. What we are about to do is to go through your dream records with a fine-tooth comb and establish the themes and occurrences that make your dreams unique to you. Prepare yourself with some notepaper (in addition to the blank space after each entry you've already reserved in your journal) and your highlighter pens.

The best place to start is at the beginning, so simply read through your dreams and highlight anything that stands out as unusual, improbable or simply impossible. We are not simply looking for just scenery, imagery or events, but also emotions, your own reactions to events, thoughts, sensations and the behaviour of dream characters. Absolutely anything (from the entire range of human experience) that, in waking life, you would consider out of the ordinary. Pay particular attention to coincidences; due to the self-generated nature of dreams and the role of expectation, coincidental occurrences happen far more often when dreaming than in waking life. Really do keep an open mind and a keen eye; even time can distort in dreams and, if it does, that too would count as a dreamsign.

I'd like to quickly mention here that, while writing on the subject of dreamsigns, I've been surprised at just how tricky it's been to choose the best approach towards describing them. Whilst it's a simple concept in essence, the sheer range of dream experiences that it covers can make it very tricky to pin down. I'm sharing this with you to further clarify the scope of potential candidates for dreamsigns, and partly to avoid writing a long list of possibilities, a list that could never be truly comprehensive. Instead, I will rely on your intelligence as a reader and reiterate that, in a nutshell, anything you experience in a dream could potentially be a dreamsign, depending on how striking you find its implausibility, and how out of place its occurrence would be in your waking life.

Here's a short example of a randomly selected dream from my own journal. It's a typical short, non-lucid dream and, whilst nothing of any real significance occurs, it still has many dreamsigns. Examples of what I would consider to be obvious dreamsigns are in bold.

I'm standing in the ***living room of my childhood home****. The house is empty and it's late afternoon.* ***I feel a strange sense of urgency*** *to get out of the house and into the back garden, although on attempting to open the door I find* ***the lock is jammed and won't budge****. My mother enters the house and asks how my day has been; she mentions she has just read an article on the new Aquarium that has opened in a nearby town.* ***The scene shifts*** *and I now find myself standing in the garden. It's a bright sunny day and I take time to soak up the sunshine. As I look up, I notice various shadows in the sky, they move closer and I notice that rather than birds* ***a shoal of fish is swimming through the sky****. I think to myself* ***this is a strange coincidence,*** *considering the previous conversation, but quickly* ***justify what I am seeing by assuming a rare breed of flying fish must have escaped the Aquarium****.*

As you'll notice in this dream example, there are multiple types of dreamsigns ranging from distorted time (finding myself in my childhood home), unusual emotions (sense of urgency), malfunctioning devices (jammed lock), a sudden shift in scenery, an impossible event (flying fish), an unlikely coincidence (discussion of aquarium followed by sighting of the fish) and, finally, poor reasoning skills (justification for the flying fish). All of these dreamsigns range across the scale from improbable to impossible should they have occurred during my daily life.

This dream should, by all accounts, have resulted in lucidity. However, additional notes in my journal also recorded that this dream occurred early in the night and after retiring for bed in an especially drowsy state. Be prepared for many similar 'missed opportunities' in your own dreams, and don't beat yourself up too harshly for not always noticing the signs as they occur in the dream. Missed dreamsigns whilst dreaming are far more common than those you'll notice, and should be considered lessons in where you need to improve your vigilance and awareness.

As you work through each dream, highlight the individual dreamsigns. Use the space in your journal at the end of each dream to classify the types of dreamsigns that have occurred within that dream. The best way to do this is to give each dreamsign both a broad and specific classification. The terms you use to classify each dreamsign are best left up to you. You'll find it much easier to remember and work with any terminology you have decided upon yourself. As a rule, you want to use a broad term to describe the basis of what occurred, such as 'time distortion' or 'unusually strong emotion', and a more specific phrase to sum up the details, for example 'travelled back in time' or 'feeling of urgency'. I'll use the previous dream as an example of my own system. The following dreamsign classifications are the result of following the above process (and listed as they appear in my own journal).

Time Travel - Travelled back in time
Unusually strong emotion - Feeling of urgency
Malfunctioning device - Stuck lock
Scene shift - Change of environment
Impossible event - Shoal of flying fish
Coincidence - Conversation influences reality
Uncritical assumption - Poor reasoning skills

If you reference these against the example dream, it should help clarify the kind of verbal distillation you're aiming to achieve. The broad classification is designed to help you establish the frequency of similar dreamsign themes throughout your journal, whilst the more detailed descriptive phrase will allow you to hunt down any dreamsigns in which the specific details occur regularly. For example, my above dreamsign broad-classification of 'impossible event' is apparent throughout many of my dreams, but the details of each actual event can vary a great deal (it is not flying fish that occur often, but the unlikely or impossible events themselves). However, in the example of 'Unusually strong emotion', both the broad-classification (theme) and the specifics the 'sense of urgency' happen often.

As you work through your own journal classifying your dreamsigns, you too shall start to notice similar recurring themes. As a rule, the broader classifications, due to their wider scope, shall be all the more frequent. You will, however, start to notice that more specific dreamsigns will also crop up again and again; this becomes especially noticeable as your dream journal grows over time. For the sake of convenience, I'll refer to the broader classifications as 'dreamsign themes' and the specific dreamsigns as simply 'Dreamsigns', regardless of the words we use to describe them. Both are still technically dreamsigns and equally as important in the ongoing process that we'll soon be covering - it's just linguistically tidier.

Apart from the personal dreamsigns that you will be uncovering yourself, I feel it is important to mention that there are three events that I believe every lucid dreamer should always consider as potential dreamsigns. I've touched briefly on them earlier, but their importance is such that it's useful to reiterate them here. They are as follows: any coincidental occurrence, strong emotions, and any time you justify or explain away unusual occurrences without taking into account the possibility that the explanation for them could be that you're dreaming (this is often overlooked as a dreamsign itself). These three dreamsign themes appear to be both prevalent and universal amongst dreamers, so it's important to be prepared for when they occur.

Now that you've taken the time to classify the dreamsigns for each dream recorded in your journal, phase two of the process begins. Work through the listed dreamsigns in your journal, making a copy of these onto your notepaper. The goal now is to collect similar dreamsigns and dreamsign themes into groups, with the intention of establishing your more prevalent dreamsigns. This is to help you develop a familiarity with the more common occurrences in your dreamlife. You'll most likely notice that many dreamsigns are simply one-offs, and just the inevitable unusual happenings of dreamland. Others, especially dreamsign themes, will happen with more regularity.

Using your own powers of deduction, forge a list of your most commonly occurring dreamsigns. This list will help you focus your attention for the next stage in your dream practices (which we shall discuss shortly). A great way to do this is to categorise your dreamsign list by regularity, a dream equivalent to the musical charts 'top ten' (please don't misunderstand this to mean you will only need to list ten dreamsigns - it's just an analogy!). Include as many dreamsigns as possible and try to commit as many (especially the more common) to memory as possible. It's good practice to print out an attractive copy of your list and keep it near your bedside so you can review it before retiring to bed. It's also useful to keep a copy with you throughout the day and review it when you have a quiet moment to yourself.

Remember once again that this is a fluid list, one that will grow and become more refined over time as your dreamsign dataset grows, and as you continue to regularly perform the above task.

This practice of becoming familiar with your dreamsigns will most likely in itself result in several spontaneous lucid dreams. Simply learning the landscape of your mind and how your dreamlife operates will increase the chances of you noticing your dreamsigns whilst dreaming, and will cue you into recognising them as dreams. However, this is just the tip of the iceberg.

Next, we shall be discussing how to amplify this process a thousandfold, using what is, in my opinion, the central premise of lucid dreaming.

Reality testing

There is some truth in the stories and fairy tales of old. Sometimes, when the time is right and the conditions are just so, a person who has undergone certain rituals and taken their time with mysterious preparations, can look out at the universe and utter a single, seemingly magical phrase, a question. If their intentions are genuine, their preparations in earnest, and they possess the correct mental fortitude, all the wishes of their heart will be granted. The world around them, will be forever magically transformed. In this new and enchanted land, they shall become ruler of all they see.

Whilst this may read as a passage from some fictional tale, putting artistic licence aside, what you've just read could well be considered an interpretation of the journey of a lucid dreamer. Truth really can be stranger than fiction. It's probably clear that the 'enchanting land' refers to the world of lucid dreaming, and the 'mysterious preparations' the training we are undertaking. So, what then is this magical phrase, the question, the key to this world? We'll come to that shortly.

With our feet firmly back on terra firma, let's take a more practical look at the next essential step towards mastering lucidity. So far, you've been working on developing your dream recall, forming a bridge of memory between the two worlds. With the information you've gathered, you've developed a record of your nightly adventures in your dream journal. You've distilled those records into dreamsigns, the fingerprints of your dreams. Further still, you've categorised and listed these in such a way that you're becoming increasingly familiar with the nature of your dreams and are prepared for the kinds of experiences you are most likely to encounter.

Now, without wishing by any means to belittle the hard work and importance of what we've done so far, as it truly is vital for our success, it can be said that our practises up until this point have been of a passive nature. By passive, what I am trying to say is that we have been processing and working with only that information our dreams have given us. We may well have taken active steps to improve our access to this information, but the general theme has been that of a receptive nature; we've been scouting the territory, getting to know it. Now it is time to become active, to make our own mark by adding something genuinely new to our dreaming life.

To do so, it's time to learn what I truly believe is the fundamental centrepiece of all lucid dreaming practice: the 'reality test'. This practice is so ingrained in our journey, in the subject itself, that it could perhaps be considered the defining behaviour (and mindset) that distinguishes a lucid dreamer from the population at large. Indeed, as it becomes part of your lifestyle, you'll be entering into a small group of individuals to whom this practice has become second nature. On rare occasions, you may well spot or be spotted by fellow lucid dreamers performing a reality test, and recognise your kinship.

The reality test, being such a vital element of lucid dreaming, has (as is often the way with such things) been called by various different names. The most commonly used terms are: reality test, reality check, state test, state check and critical state test. Whenever you come across these terms, just be aware that they are all referring to the same process. The choice of 'fashionable' terminology changes over the years and depends equally as much on whom you're talking with. I feel that 'critical state test' is probably the most accurate term, but it's failed to become popular, probably because it's just not all that catchy. Whilst all of the names have their own descriptive pros and cons, in order to avoid jumping between terminologies I'll just be using 'reality test' throughout this book. It's far more important to fully understand the process involved than the name we give it, but feel free to use whatever you feel most comfortable with.

So, what does a reality test involve? Before we look at this in detail, let me ask you a question. Are you dreaming? I'm asking this in all seriousness - and yes, I absolutely mean, are you dreaming right now? I would suggest taking a moment or two to really ponder this question. Sincerely ask yourself 'Am I dreaming?' and be ready to justify whichever conclusion you reach. Once you've given it a little thought, continue reading.

Now that you have your answer (and don't worry if it's just 'I don't think so'), I'd like to hazard a guess at a few assumptions you may have made. Firstly, I would expect that, like most, you will have found it difficult to ask this question in complete seriousness. This is perfectly normal considering it is at odds with a lifetime of social programming regarding the nature of reality. Secondly, perhaps you reached your conclusion based on how vivid and real your current experience feels. Again, a perfectly normal response. However, as you have already learnt in the previous section on dreamsigns, this is not a valid set of criteria on which to base your judgment.

Finally, did you ask yourself this question with the presumption that the most likely answer would be 'no', that this couldn't be a dream? If so, remind yourself that a question asked with a prior assumption can be a huge barrier to discovering the truth. Of course, all of the above are completely normal responses for those who've yet to be trained in how to perform a reality test (and, of course, congratulations for those of you to whom these assumptions do not apply). We shall be covering how best to resolve these issues and others shortly.

Now, how often have you asked yourself this question, 'Am I dreaming?' in your daily life? Chances are you have rarely, if ever (ignoring those of you with an interest in philosophical thinking or are already seasoned lucid dreamers). This is an important point. Considering that a good deal of your life is spent in the dreaming state, where the correct answer to the question would be a resounding 'Yes!' (resulting in a lucid dream), to never ask the question is an issue that needs to be resolved. This is where the reality test fits in.

It should be apparent by this point that the 'magical phrase' from the opening of this section is referring to the question upon which reality testing is based. The question 'Am I dreaming?', 'Is this a dream?', or whichever way you wish to word it, is the keystone upon which the reality test is built. I feel it is such a fundamental and important question, that the title of this book is itself designed to cue you into performing a reality test whenever you see it.

You may well at this point be asking 'Yes, but how do I successfully answer this question?' This is a very good point, as a question raised without the ability to discern the correct answer is of no use to us at all. A reality test is a two-stage process, the first of which, being the question itself, we shall be covering in detail next. The second stage is learning the tools required to correctly reach a conclusion. So, before we learn how to correctly answer the question, let's first learn to ask the question properly.

It may seem a little unusual to take time learning how to ask a question properly. However, as we've already seen, this is no ordinary question and there are certain pitfalls that we need to avoid. The best starting point is to establish when and where we shall be performing our reality tests. The answer to this is really rather simple: anywhere and everywhere! But let's be a little more specific.

The goal of developing the habit of reality testing during our waking hours is for eventually, once the habit becomes second nature, to find this behaviour being transferred to our dreamlife. If we never ask the question whilst we are awake, how can we possibly expect to be asking it whilst dreaming? Dreams as a rule are based upon the events, behaviours and preoccupations of our waking lives. If a behaviour becomes a regular fixture in our waking psychology, it will only be a matter of time before it transfers to our dreams. With this in mind, you must be prepared, if you are serious about developing the skills required for lucid dreaming, to make reality testing an integral part of your daily life. Realistically, you should expect to be performing these tests a bare minimum of between 5-10 times daily, and often much more.

Whilst simply performing reality tests regularly and randomly throughout the day can in itself be a successful practice, if we wish to really increase their effectiveness, then the best approach is to focus our efforts into performing them at key events, events that closely resemble our dream lives. On the most basic level, be prepared to perform a reality test at any point during your day where unexpected, unusual or dreamlike occurrences take place.

Fortunately for us, we can take this a step further. We've already invested the time and effort in developing a familiarity with our dreams when we established our list of our commonly occurring dreamsigns. This list will act as our road map, showing us when and where our reality tests will be most effectively implemented during our waking hours.

Throughout your day, keep a keen lookout for waking events that resemble your dreamsigns. Even events with vague similarities should be a cue to perform a reality test. For example, should one of your common dreamsigns be the theme of running late or rushing, whenever you find yourself in a similar position whilst awake this should be your sign to perform a reality test. Remember, too, that dreamsigns can equally be internal states (emotions, thoughts, etc.) as much as external events. The key here is to develop an ongoing state of mind in which you are regularly assessing your situation and prepared for dreamlike events to cue you into performing a test. However, don't limit your reality tests only to your personal dreamsigns. Whilst they are indeed the most potent cues, any unusual or dreamlike event should be sufficient justification.

On a related note, a frustratingly common dreamsign and cue to reality test, which often slips under the radar for many a new lucid dreamer, is the theme of discussing lucid dreaming itself. There are few dreams that can leave you kicking yourself quite as much as those where you've been discussing lucid dreaming, whilst dreaming, yet failed to notice. As such, if you wish to avoid this embarrassing state of affairs, make a concerted effort to reality test whenever discussing the subject of dreams in your waking life.

Put simply, reality testing will become a new fixture, a regular habit in your daily routine. You will find yourself becoming increasingly tuned-in to noticing dreamlike events happening in your daily life.

Now that we've established when and where you will be performing reality tests, we need to focus on asking the question with the required conviction. As we covered earlier, it's very difficult when starting out in dream practices to truly be open to the idea that we really could be dreaming at any moment. The side effect of this is that, when we ask ourselves 'Am I dreaming?' we do so in a way that lacks seriousness. The only real way to counter this mindset is to understand what percentage of our lives is actually spent dreaming. The average adult spends roughly eight hours a night sleeping. Of those eight hours, approximately two hours are spent in REM (dreaming) sleep. So, for two of our already limited twenty-four hours a day, we are dreaming. That's seven hundred and thirty hours a year, or thirty days. **For every year of our life, we spend one month dreaming!** That's a huge amount of time in which the question 'Am I dreaming?' is absolutely the most important question to be asking.

Yet, almost universally among humans, during that month we spend dreaming, we all simply assume (for no reason other than it being out of habit) that we are experiencing the waking world. Most people are only aware a dream was a dream once they awaken. Learning to seriously ask 'Am I dreaming?' can set you apart from the masses, potentially stopping you from being completely and utterly wrong in your assumptions about which world you inhabit. Completely wrong, every single second, for an entire month, each and every year!

At the risk of appearing to be belabouring my point, I'm going to repeat this concept because it's so very important. Each day you spend two hours dreaming. Out of a total of twenty-four hours, six are spent in unconscious sleep, sixteen waking and two dreaming. That's eighteen hours of brain activity a day. What this means is that, for eleven per cent of the daily time that your brain is active (REM and waking brain activity are virtually identical), you are dreaming. I'll repeat, eleven per cent of your daily experience is a dream. To put this in perspective, your lunch break (assuming it's half an hour) is less than three per cent of your daily experience, and I very much doubt you consider your lunch break an insignificant part of your day! Make it clear in your mind that it is not foolish to question your reality, considering the human condition, it is foolish not to.

An additional mental trick that greatly increases the hit rate for a successful reality test is to enter it with the assumption that the most likely outcome will be to discover you are dreaming. As we covered earlier, this is a reversal of the mindset for which most people perform their tests. The reason for doing so is twofold.

Firstly, it is to help counter the fuzzy-minded logic that you will experience whilst dreaming. By assuming that the outcome of our test will be proof that we are indeed dreaming, we lessen the chances that our poor dreaming logic will fail us. Because the onus is now switched to proving we are *not* dreaming, should we fail to perform our test with the required vigour then the result will be to believe we are dreaming and, as such, favour lucidity.

Secondly, we need to proactively reprogramme a lifetime's worth of assumptions that all experiences are waking experiences. One of the biggest hurdles to successful lucid dreaming is coming to terms with just how convincingly real the experience feels. In my own experience, I've performed reality tests that clearly demonstrated that what I was currently experiencing was a dream, yet the sheer vibrant realism of the dream, combined with an ingrained social programming that 'dreams feel unreal' and 'if I feel like I'm awake then I must be', can really shake your conviction.

By approaching a reality test with the genuine belief that the more probable outcome is proof you are dreaming, this will help us improve our ability to accept our experience as a dream when, indeed, the test proves it to be so. In short, approach your reality tests with the following mindset: 'Should I question my reality, then the chances are that I am, in fact, dreaming.'

So, we've examined how and when we will approach this all-important question. Now it's time to learn how to correctly discern reality from dreaming.

In the previous section on dreamsigns, we covered the essential differences between dreaming and waking experiences. We established that the defining factor was not the realism of the experience, but the source of the information from which our current mental model was built. In the simplest possible terms, waking experiences are stable, while dreams are unstable. This fact is the crux upon which most versions of the reality test are based. To successfully answer the question 'Am I dreaming?' we must examine the stability of the world we currently find ourselves in. This can be achieved in a number of ways.

The most primitive (but by no means ineffective) approach is to simply observe the situation in which you find yourself. Scrutinise everything - where you are, who you're with, how you got to be where you are, your memories preceding this experience, the plausibility of your feelings and environment. Look for absolutely anything that is unusual or would not make sense in your waking life. You're essentially performing the same task you performed whilst looking for dreamsigns in your journal, only this time you'll be applying that mindset to the world around you. Be wary for possible poor judgement on your own behalf; be ready to justify your conclusions and explanation for events to a high standard. This approach is the basis for every reality test you will perform.

Next, I shall be outlining some rather more focused and specific tests. However, regardless of which tests you use, they should always be accompanied by this scrutiny of your current circumstances. The key here is to look for instability, rifts in cause and effect and simply impossible or improbable events (such as unlikely coincidences).

To be really precise in our testing, we need to look for certain aspects of dreamland that are consistently unstable. In my personal experience (and as backed up by the reports of many, many dreamers), the basis for one of the most effective reality tests seems to be the dreaming mind's inability to generate stable, written text. The following two reality tests are my own personal favourites, and I've found them to be the most consistently reliable tests I've used.

Morphing text test

This test really is simplicity in itself. When you feel compelled to test your reality, look for any kind of text available in your immediate environment. This can be anything at all from the number plate of a car, a shop or road sign, the text in a book or magazine, or the writing on a coin. The only important factor here is to choose something where the text will remain the same and the item remain stationary long enough for you to read it, look away, then reread it. An advert on the side of a moving bus, for example, is a poor choice.

The test itself is incredibly basic: read the text, look away, whilst looking away 'will' the text to change, then look back and scrutinise the text for any differences. That's it. When dreaming, the text will almost always change. Changes in the text can range from incredibly blatant (I've seen street signs upon a second look read 'you're dreaming!') to subtle (such as a change in font or colour). Remember, any change whatsoever is solid proof that you are dreaming.

Being such a simple test, it's easy to quickly repeat should you feel it necessary. Be warned, though, that doubt can be the enemy here. If the text changed on the first test, yet you doubt yourself and recheck, you're risking falling into the mindset of creating a false justification and missing out on a chance at lucidity. Be careful.

Of course, the easiest way to guarantee this test will always be available under all circumstances is to always carry with you something with suitable text. Perhaps wear a pendant or bracelet with lettering, or carry a business card in your wallet. I myself have gone to what may be considered slightly extreme lengths in this regards and have had the word 'Dream?' tattooed on my inner right wrist. This acts not only as guaranteed text for performing this reality test, but also as a constant reminder to question my reality. Perhaps too extreme for most, but the principle is sound and I suggest improvising a less permanent alternative that achieves the same result.

As an aside for those of you who may be interested, or already have text-based tattoos, I have found another interesting quirk is that, in dreams, if I rub the tattoo, it behaves as if it is written with non-permanent ink and can be smeared, or distorted, which itself acts as another form of reality test and proof of dreaming. Whilst I've not experimented with the following myself, perhaps the same effect could be achieved with a mole or birthmark. So, for the curious non-tattooed dreamers out there, perhaps you could experiment and discover your own new reality test based on this concept.

Digital watch test

This could be considered the 'big brother' of the previous reality test. Whilst it's essentially the same principle, the enhancements do justify it being considered a test in its own right. We've covered how the dreaming mind struggles with keeping written text stable, but another area in which stability is also reliably inconsistent is the display of digital clocks. Initially, you may think that this is just a repeat of the previous test, with only the source of the text being different. However, it would seem that it is not simply the mind's issue with generating stable text that comes into play here, but rather a second stability issue also compounds the effect.

It appears that the dreaming brain also has problems generating the flow of numerical sequencing that a digital clock displays. Of course, being an internally-generated model of a digital clock, there is no external mechanism systematically counting upwards in the correct sequence of time. For our brain to successfully model a digital clock, it would also need to expend the resources towards dedicating a part of itself as a precise timekeeper - which, it would appear, is not the case. As such, a digital display of time in dreamland can be even more reliably unstable than simply text itself.

Practically, the test is a repeat of the morphing text test, in that you read the time, look away (willing it to change), then look back. Any change is evidence that you are dreaming. Unlike the text test in a great number of cases, the display on your digital watch (or clock) will be jumbled or bizarre in appearance on the very first reading. Upon looking away and back, the effect is often increased with the display becoming even more nonsensical, or sometimes morphed into a more convincing temporarily stable version of itself. Whatever the case, should you ever encounter a digital display of time behaving incorrectly, assume it's a sign you're dreaming.

Of course, unlike printed text, there is the added issue of the possibility of a genuine mechanical malfunction of a waking world digital clock to consider. Firstly, your brain is absolutely going to attempt to justify a wacky digital display by jumping to the conclusion that it is a faulty real world display - don't fall for this. Make it your default assumption that any digital display that is malfunctioning is almost certainly a dreamsign happening before your eyes and proof that you are dreaming. The probability of it being a real world malfunction is very low. However, with safety firmly in mind, and because in the real world digital displays can indeed malfunction, it is wise to back up your conclusion with a second reality test (checking another digital display, or using the morphing text test, for example), as well as always performing the basic reality test of critically observing your current state and environment as outlined earlier.

In practice, you'll soon grow accustomed to performing several different reality tests in tandem. This helps avoid the rare cases when a dream is unusually stable and a single test fails to demonstrate you're dreaming. Also, the increased evidence of several tests also instils a greater confidence in your knowledge that you are dreaming. These are such important points I'll risk repeating myself for absolute clarity here: **whilst faults can occur in digital displays in waking life, it is rare and, as such, an unlikely explanation. Always assume a malfunctioning device is evidence of dreaming; only ever dismiss this conclusion once you've discovered it cannot be backed up with further reality tests. Equally, do not engage in dangerous or embarrassing behaviours until you've fully established your state with further testing**.

We shall return to safe dreaming practices later. For now, let's take a closer look at the benefits of the digital watch test. As mentioned, this is a very reliable test, and the combined instability factors genuinely make this one of the least likely tests to give incorrect results.

Digital watches are incredibly convenient and can be worn at all times, giving you a guaranteed reality test on your wrist whenever you need one. Choose your watch wisely; you'll want to use one with a clear easy-to-read display, and one that is visible under all lighting conditions. In my experience, the high power LED display watches offer the best viewing under the widest conditions. The last thing you want is to be unable to perform a test because of glare from the sun, or because it's too dark and you can't read your display. It would be only a matter of time before you dreamt of these poor viewing conditions and lost the chance at lucidity due to them. So, make absolutely sure your watch has either a backlight, or the display itself is generated by light (as is the case with an LED watch).

It's also useful if your display also shows the passage of seconds. Because these so rapidly change, they are often one of the trickiest things for the brain to duplicate and, as such, are almost always displayed incorrectly in dreams. I'd also suggest purchasing a watch with physical printed (or engraved) text somewhere on its display, as this will allow you to also perform the morphing text test using your watch.

Another nice (but by no means necessary) feature that many lucid dreamers look for when choosing their watch is a customisable scrolling message. There are various models that allow for this function, and often the message scrolls past shortly after displaying the time. You can set this to anything you like, a firm favourite of mine being something along the lines of 'Are you dreaming?' or simply 'Dream?' The added complexity of this kind of display allows for more errors in duplication by the dreaming mind and, as such, increased chances for spotting mistakes. It also increases the duration you spend observing your watch, giving you more time to really focus on your reality test.

A perhaps obvious point to mention here is that analogue watches or clocks are not suitable for reality tests. For some reason, the dreaming mind has much less trouble reproducing them. I believe this is because of the smooth visual way in which time is represented on the analogue display. It would seem our minds are much better at reproducing the consistent flow and logical movement of the hands of a clock rather than the more abstract switching numbers of a digital display.

This would seem to make sense, if you consider how our brains have evolved in an analogue world, one where the sun sweeps smoothly across the sky, where the stars turn in the heavens, and where a leaf thrown into a river will move gently in the direction of its flow. An analogue clock duplicates this kind of predictable flowing behaviour. This may also explain why, generally, many of us prefer the aesthetic of an analogue clock to that of a digital display. Unfortunately, pleasant aesthetics or not, for the purposes of lucid dreaming, it is the digital watch that we'll be using.

One last thing to note that is relevant to both previous tests is a devious little trick the dreaming mind likes to play that can throw you completely off guard. Should you be wearing a digital watch or carrying text with a view to performing a reality test, be prepared for the possibility that, whilst in a dream, your dreaming mind will concoct a scenario in which it removes these items from your dream. This can leave you in a position where you are unable to reality test. There are two solutions to this problem. The first is to make it a very firm habit to always have your reality test tools to hand, no matter what. This way, at any time you find yourself without them, it will itself become a glaring dreamsign. The second option is to be prepared with the following reality test, namely the nose pinch test.

The nose pinch test

The nose pinch test is somewhat unique among reality tests. Rather than focusing on the inherent instability within dreams as its premise, instead it takes a wholly different approach, using the nonphysical nature of the dream body (the model of your body you inhabit whilst dreaming) as its basis. Essentially, what we'll be doing is exploiting a glitch in this model, a glitch that, once spotted, is proof positive of our dreaming state.

Like the previous tests, the actual process involved is the height of simplicity: to perform the test, you tightly pinch your nose, blocking the air supply to your nostrils. Once firmly blocked, you simply attempt to breathe through your (now sealed) nose. Of course, whilst awake this is all rather futile, as you'll obviously be unable to breathe. However, whilst dreaming, your dream fingers are pinching a dream nose, neither of which have any impact at all on your real source of air - which, of course, is the physical nose attached to your physical body that lies undisturbed sleeping in your bed.

As is no doubt apparent, pinching an imaginary dreaming nose will not stop your ability to breathe. Instead, what you'll experience in the dream is the slightly unnerving sensation of breathing through a sealed nose. The test results are straightforward: if you can breathe through a pinched nose, you're dreaming, if not you're awake. This is a fascinating and also incredibly useful reality test.

The benefit of this method over the previous two tests is that it requires no additional props or environmental conditions to perform. You should, under virtually all dreaming circumstances, have a nose and fingers with which to pinch it. A further benefit is it can be performed in complete darkness. Also, it's rather subtle - while, under some circumstances, glancing at your watch may appear as socially inappropriate or rude, a quick and simple pinch of the nose can (especially with a handkerchief) be performed under a slightly more socially acceptable guise.

You may well be asking, if this test offers so many advantages over the previous two, then why do I not consider it a personal favourite? Well, in many ways, I do. Almost always when performing a reality test, I'll combine either of the previous two text-based tests followed up with the nose pinch. I am a strong believer in combining tests as it acts as a backup. Should, for whatever reason, the conditions of the dream lessen the effectiveness of a particular test (a particularly stable dream, for example), then having the habit of following up with a secondary test (especially, as in this case, one that is based on an alternative premise) is a great advantage. I would very much suggest you develop the same habit.

The reason the nose pinch test itself is not my primary testing method is because I feel it to be slightly less reliable. That is by no means to say that it's unreliable, simply that reports of it failing to deliver the correct results are slightly higher than that of the previous tests. This may be a simple matter of biology, as breathing whilst sleeping can be slightly erratic and, on occasions, disturbed by issues with health (the common cold, for example), or even something as simple as snoring. Such breathing issues may well be the cause of the rare false-negative results with the nose pinch test.

Whilst these issues are uncommon, the elusive nature of lucidity being as it is means that we should always be aiming for the most effective, consistent tactics available. As such, I wholeheartedly recommend the above three tests as the best reality testing techniques, but with the caveat that the nose pinch test should be used as the secondary follow-up test to either of the text-stability tests. This minimises failure rates to the best of your abilities and will avoid the frustrations that can arise when relying utterly on one single test.

Other reality tests

Should you spend any time searching online, or have read other works on lucid dreaming, you will have almost certainly stumbled across a whole host of different reality test techniques. In general, I would advise approaching these with careful consideration. Always question the logical basis upon which a test is based. Ask yourself 'Why would the outcome of this test be different in a dream from waking?' and 'How reliable is this test likely to be?'

There are, of course, other great tests out there, such as the 'light switch test', where you simply switch a light on and off. In dreams, it can often be difficult to suddenly change lighting in this way, and instead of the desired result you'll experience a convincing blown light bulb. This test has been confirmed as effective by a great deal of dreamers. It has been suggested that the reason behind this may be that the brain has difficulty in generating sudden dramatic lighting changes. Although possible, I do question this logic somewhat, as I've had dreams involving sunrises and lightning, both examples of impressive light changes. I've also lit candles in dreams without issue, creating the same results you'd see in waking experience (I accept, of course, that candle light is a much more subtle shift in light).

It may well be that there are several factors at play causing this phenomenon. Electrical devices on the whole do tend to behave in strange ways during dreams. Also, conscious attempts at sudden changes in lighting may be difficult for the brain to deal with (rather than those that play a part in the general theme of the dream). I can't give a conclusive answer to this question, but I can say that I've even heard reports from people with no knowledge of lucid dreaming or the 'light switch test' itself mentioning issues with light switches in their dreams. It does indeed seem to be a genuine phenomenon of the dreaming mind.

Such a test is worth experimenting with, but I'd caution against using it as a primary reality test, simply due to the limitations of needing a light switch with which to perform it. Also, lacking a general understanding of how and why this phenomenon exists means we open ourselves up to becoming victims of variables that we are unaware of. The general rule of thumb for a good reality test is consistent results and a sound logic for why those results occur. If nothing else, malfunctioning light switches are a great dreamsign.

Another popular test is to simply examine your hands to look for anything unusual or inconsistent, such as longer fingers, moles you don't have, or even someone else's hands. Many beginners use this as their default test because of its simplicity. I personally would seriously advise against using it as a test. Whilst it can be effective on some occasions (there are, indeed, rare occasions in dreams when your hands will appear different), there is no sound reasoning for why this should be a consistent occurrence. Yes, dreams are unstable, but they are also based upon the information stored within our memories.

Our hands are perhaps the single most familiar part of our body. They are regularly within our visual field. It stands to reason, then, that we should have some pretty clear memories of how our hands should appear and, as such, it would seem unlikely our brains would have issues with creating a model of them. I'd go as far as to say that our hands would be one of the easiest body parts for our brains to recreate. I believe this particular reality test works only for those who believe and expect it to work, being a kind of dream placebo. Expectation is unreliable and not a good basis for a reality test. Experiment with this test by all means, if you're curious, but using it as a regular reality test is almost a guarantee for future failure and frustration. I'd suggest saving yourself the headaches it will cause.

Once again, the occurrence of distorted hands, whilst not a reliable test, is a useful dreamsign to look out for (due to the impossible nature of this occurrence in reality). Also, rather than using your hands to perform a reality test, instead use occasions in which you consciously notice your hands as a trigger to do a reality test. As such an event is a common occurrence in your daily life, this will be a great way to make regular reality testing part of your daily routine, as you are also very likely to see your hands during a dream. Of course, once you see your hands and are reminded to reality test, choose one of the stable tests available (such as the nose pinch).

There are many reality tests similar to the 'hand test' that are either based upon rather flimsy logic, or are impractical for regular use. So, please approach research into less well-known reality tests with a critical and logical mind. In many cases, what is being observed are dreamsigns rather than suitable reality tests.

One last example is an often cited reality test where you are required to jump in the air and attempt to defy gravity. The theory is that, if you perform this in a dream and 'will' yourself to fall slower (as gravity is optional) and you indeed descend at a slower rate, it's proof you're dreaming. Whilst by no means wrong (as this is entirely possible in a dream), I believe this test is once again based upon expectation which, as we've already discussed, is too fickle a beast to trust for these purposes. There will simply be times in dreams where you'll have a perfectly convincing experience of gravity and completely miss your chance for lucidity. Also, as you will be reality testing many times throughout your waking hours, it is simply impractical to jump in the air every time something unusual occurs (unless, of course, you are looking to win Eccentric of the Year Award).

With the above warnings aside, I genuinely believe that the morphing text, the digital watch and the nose pinch tests are the three most effective reality tests. They prepare you for virtually all available scenarios and are based upon sound reasoning and genuine dream phenomena. Not only this, but they have been proven to be effective by many lucid dreamers. You really shouldn't need to experiment with other tests if effectiveness is all you're looking for (curiosity and experimentation are other matters entirely).

Another point of interest on the topic of reality testing is the use of electrical reminder devices to help cue you to perform a reality test throughout the day. There are several products available, often originally designed to help those who are required to take medication regularly through the day. These can be used for our own purposes. They range from watches that vibrate at specific intervals, or devices you can attach to your key ring.

The basic idea behind these devices is that they can be set to give regular reminders (normally in the form of a vibration) to perform a task at preset intervals or specific times during your day. For those of you who may struggle with remembering to perform regular daily reality tests, these devices can be a great way to kick-start the habit. There is, of course, no substitute for developing a good prospective memory, as this will be vital for successful lucidity, but it is better to use a tool to aid this development if you truly are struggling, rather than to simply give up altogether. But, as a general rule, it's best to avoid the use of such devices unless you absolutely do require them.

A final and interesting aspect to reality testing is a side effect of the practice that can be greatly beneficial to our daily lives. I actually believe this to be one of the true benefits and hidden gems of lucid dreaming practice. A great deal of the times we'll be performing our tests will be those very same times our emotions are running high, or we are 'lost in the moment' due to the strangeness or intensity of an event. Reality testing acts as a buffer during these times, a moment to step back and reflect on the events and emotions in which we find ourselves.

As such, continued lucid dream practice can help develop a calmer and more even-handed approach to our lives. Rather than fall victim to simply unconsciously reacting to events, we have developed the skill to temporarily step back, and be a little more objective to our world. Over time, you may find your reality testing helps lower your stress levels and cause you to be less prone to impulsive reactionary behaviour. Your life, as well as your dreams, may become a little more lucid.

Reality testing in a nutshell

The reality test is the core of lucid dreaming practice. It will, in most cases, be the last thing you do before embarking on a lucid dream. Perform reality tests a minimum of 5-10 times daily and at any point in your waking life that resembles a dream. Always perform your tests with clarity of thought, absolute seriousness and thoroughly. If you find yourself falling into the trap of mindlessly going through the motions, be aware that you are doing nothing more than developing a bad habit, one that will lessen rather than strengthen your chances of lucidity. Be consistent by performing your choice of tests in the same order each time; this will help build the habit faster and shorten the time it will take to transfer into your dream life. The following is a typical reality test:

1) Notice a dreamlike event.
2) Genuinely and seriously ask yourself 'Am I dreaming?' Assume that the most likely answer is that you are.
3) Pay close attention to your environment and feelings - are there any other signs you may be dreaming?
4) Perform either the morphing test or digital watch test. Whatever the result, be sure to be logical in your conclusions.
5) Perform the nose pinch test. Again, assess the result logically.
6) If, after both tests, you are still unsure of your state, perform your tests again. Continue to assume you are most likely dreaming.

7) Should your combined results prove negative (that you're not dreaming), take the time to consider what you would have done if the results had been otherwise. Daydream about how your lucid dream would have panned out.
8) Should the results prove positive (you are dreaming), then take a moment to consider if there is anything you had previously planned to do, then enjoy your lucid dream!

Now that you understand the intricacies of reality testing, you are well on your way to becoming a proficient lucid dreamer. Try to really integrate what you've learnt into your daily life, I cannot stress enough just how pivotal reality testing is to the whole subject. Make reality testing part of who you are, and your dreams really will be transformed. Next, we'll discuss the final bare essential in your dream practices: dream incubation.

Dream Incubation/Preparing what to dream

Since at least the time of the Egyptians, people have been attempting to influence the contents of their nightly adventures through dream incubation. Healing temples were used in ancient Greece, known as an 'Asclepieion'. These temples were named in honour of their god of medicine, Asclepios. In these temples, seekers would use focused prayer in an attempt to influence the content of their dreams. Their goal was to dream of a cure or answer to their issue. After spending the night sleeping in the temple, they would report the resultant dream to the priest, who would then analyse it and prescribe a cure. Similar practices and temples have been used in the Middle East and the Roman Empire.

Dream incubation (influencing the content of your dreams through pre-sleep activities) has no doubt played its part in countless other human cultures throughout history. Our use of dream incubation will be somewhat less elaborate than that of the Asclepieion temples. However, we do have one big advantage in that, whereas the dreamers of the sleep temples were simply attempting to influence the vague theme of their dream, we as lucid dreamers (knowing that, once lucid, we can dream virtually what we wish) can be far more specific in our goals. At the most basic level, we simply need to decide in advance the tasks we wish to accomplish in our lucid dreams.

Technically, what we are discussing are two slightly different concepts:

dream incubation and goal setting. Dream incubation has traditionally been the term used to define the process of attempting, before sleep, to influence the general theme of the dream. Goal setting is, as the name suggests, choosing in advance what you will do once you find yourself in a lucid dream. For our purposes, the boundaries between these two concepts overlap and can easily be blurred into a more general hybrid of the two ideas. Goal setting is our primary concern, preparing ourselves to make the most out of our lucid dreams once they occur. Influencing the theme of the dream is of less immediate importance, as lucidity itself negates to some extent the need to do so. The techniques for both of these activities are, however, essentially identical.

During conversations with lucid dreamers, one common issue that seems to arise is that, although hours might have been spent in preparation and training to achieve their lucid dream, when they suddenly find themselves awake and aware in the dream, they have forgotten one important element: what they are going to do next! As a result, many lucid dreamers ad lib their dreams, exploring the environment or impulsively doing the first thing that springs to mind.

This is by all means a perfectly valid approach to lucid dreaming, as you are of course free to do whatever you wish. However, often upon awakening and pondering the true potential of the situation you have just experienced, you may find that you kick yourself for not doing something a little more grand or spectacular. The best way to make the most of your lucid dreams is to plan in advance what it is you wish to use them for, what adventures and experiments you want to try out.

The solution should be apparent: prepare and decide before you sleep the various goals you wish to achieve. In practical terms, this is as simple as writing a list of 'things to do', or your wish list of dream adventures. Before bed, review your list, decide which goal you would like to achieve should you become lucid that night. These goals really can be anything you like. We'll discuss a few ideas for uses of lucid dreaming later in the book, but really the sky's the limit and you can be as creative and daring as you wish. It's a good idea, also, to write your night's dream goal in your journal before retiring to bed, as this helps crystallise your intention and also allows you to review how successful you have been upon awakening. It's best to choose only one goal per night; this helps to keep your mind focused and lessens the chances of confusion or forgetfulness.

The very act of choosing a dream goal and writing it prior to sleep in your journal is itself a form of dream incubation. You can take this a step further, into the true old-fashioned form of incubation, and meditate and reflect upon your goal as you fall asleep. Try to imagine how the dream would pan out, visualise the events as they unfold. This process uses much the same mindset of 'priming' we discussed earlier. Of course, when incubating your dream in this way, be sure to also include the thought that you will be lucid and aware in the dream. A benefit of this form of incubation is that it may well influence your eventual dream scenery to closely resemble that of your incubation visualisation. This improves your chances of lucidity and also has the added bonus of placing you in exactly the right environment in which you can perform your dream goal.

Should you find yourself lucid in an environment that seems unsuitable for your dream goal (for example, in a desert when your dream goal was to experience breathing under water) you have several options. The first is to continue to pursue your goal regardless, you can attempt dream scenery changes, rapid travel to other dream locales, etc., until you achieve your desired outcome. You could also simply choose another of your previously chosen goals that are more suitable for the environment you find yourself in. Whilst this seemingly contradicts the idea of choosing one goal per night, for experienced lucid dreamers who review their dream goals regularly, this becomes less problematic.

On occasions, you may find that, for one reason or another, your dream stubbornly refuses to play ball, and your attempts to pursue your goal keep coming up against obstacles. In these situations, it's useful to know when to admit defeat and instead explore the dream on its own terms, which can often be equally as rewarding. As for why this occurs, negative expectation is usually the culprit - dream control is almost entirely an act of learning to focus your expectations for the desired result. Those new to lucid dreaming can, on occasion, unwittingly project negative expectations, such as a lack of belief that something is possible; as such, the dream complies with your expectations and gives you exactly the outcome you subconsciously expect. We'll discuss the finer details of dream control in Chapter 6.

There is little more to mention on the subject of goal setting and dream incubation. The key points here are that the process keeps us focused, motivated and prepared. The experience of becoming lucid can be quite overwhelming and disorienting at times, so preparation in advance can greatly improve your initial orientation within the dream world and increases your chances of really getting the most out of your lucid dreaming experience. As is the motto of the Boy Scouts, so it is the motto of dreamers: 'Be prepared!'

So, now we have come to the end of the bare essentials of lucid dream practice. These tools alone are enough for those with a casual interest to experience regular, if somewhat sporadic, lucid dreams. They should become second nature, a part of who you are and integral to your daily life. Please don't take them for granted, as they are the backbone to every other lucidity technique.

The techniques that follow will help us hone our efforts and focus these preparations to allow us to choose on exactly which nights we wish to become lucid. Without the bare essentials, however, none of the following techniques will be particularly effective. Lucid dreaming practice is holistic; it requires all the pieces of the puzzle to be in their correct place. Your overall effectiveness as a dreamer is only as strong as the weakest link in your entire system. Master these foundations; only then will the techniques that follow become the sharpened and accurate tools they are designed to be.

5

Lucidity Techniques

With our foundations in place, it's now time to turn our attention to the various techniques available for directly inducing lucid dreams. It is important to remember that there is no 'one size fits all' method, so experimentation with what works for you is very important here. With this in mind, I'll be sharing several tried and tested techniques, some already firmly established in the dream community, while others will be inventions and adaptations of my own that I feel would be beneficial to share with a wider audience. All techniques outlined will be based on and backed up with sound principles and logic, and all have been tested by fellow dreamers (including myself) to be of a high degree of effectiveness (once again with the caveat that no single technique is effective for all dreamers). I'll also be focusing on the strengths and weaknesses of each technique with suggestions for how to combine or adapt methods to improve the odds of success.

Before delving into the techniques themselves, I'll shortly be sharing a general theory outlining what I believe constitutes the vital elements of an effective lucidity induction technique, and the reasoning behind this line of thinking. The techniques that follow will continue to refer back to this principle and be classified in such a way as to allow you to understand where they fit into the wider picture, thus enabling you the freedom to explore the concept further. This may all sound rather complicated, but don't worry - it really isn't that difficult. We'll just be looking at lucidity induction techniques in detail, with the aim to understand how to best achieve our goals.

Importantly, we first need to cover the two varieties of lucid dreams you will be aiming to achieve, as the techniques you choose will depend greatly on which type of lucid dream you intend to attempt.

Types of lucid dream initiation

A lucid dream is, in essence, the meeting of two seemingly contradictory states of mind: dreaming and consciousness. When combining any two factors, there are two approaches - you can either add A to B, or add B to A. In our case, we can either add dreams to consciousness or consciousness to dreams. Both approaches require different tactics and each have their own unique personalities. In his 1990 book *Exploring the world of lucid dreaming*, Dr Stephen LaBerge coined two terms to define each of these approaches: Wake Initiated Lucid Dream (commonly referred to as WILD) as the term for adding dreaming to consciousness, and Dream Initiated Lucid Dream (DILD) for the reverse, adding consciousness to dreaming. These have become the standard terminology across the board and, as such, they are what I shall use throughout this book.

Once combined, dreaming and conscious awareness will always result in a lucid dream, but the wider community of lucid dreamers regularly refers to WILDs and DILDs as unique entities, two different types of lucid dreams. There is good reason behind this as, whilst a lucid dream may well always be a lucid dream, how you enter into it can have a profound impact on the nature of the experience. These two definitions themselves are also very handy for distinguishing between the aims of the various techniques. Some techniques are aimed purely at achieving DILDs, others towards WILDs, with the rare few attempting to cover both approaches. When we cover the techniques later in this chapter, I shall be clearly marking which form of dream initiation each technique is aiming to produce. Let's look at how these two forms of lucid dream differ.

Dream initiated lucid dreams

Dream Initiated Lucid Dreams (DILDs) are, by far, the most common form of lucid dream. The experience is of discovering that you are dreaming whilst dreaming. They are also the most likely type of lucid dream to be experienced spontaneously, even by those with no prior knowledge of the existence of lucid dreaming itself. Generally, they are triggered by the dreamer noticing an inconsistency (a dreamsign) during the dream, which brings them to the realisation that they are dreaming.

The majority of DILDs occur from a sudden realisation, an 'Aha!' moment where one becomes clued into what is really going on (you're dreaming). This realisation is usually caused by a dreamsign but can occur spontaneously. There are exceptions to this rule, where dreamers find lucidity creeps up on them or is simply just present. In such DILDs, you will either simply just know you are dreaming (this is common with experienced lucid dreamers, who have become familiar with how it feels to be dreaming), or conscious awareness slowly fades in throughout the dream with the realisation happening in a much less dramatic fashion. In the latter case (the pre-lucid stage), which is a kind of half awareness of the fact that you are dreaming, this can be as far as your consciousness progresses in the dream, never quite achieving lucidity (these are not true lucid dreams, but more a kind of grey area between standard and lucid dreaming).

A lucid dream can only be defined as a DILD if there has been a lapse in conscious awareness between falling asleep and the moment of lucidity itself. It will occur during any REM phase throughout a night's sleep, either with or without waking during the sleeping process.

Due to the spontaneous nature of a DILD, the dream scene in which you find yourself can be limitlessly varied. Your level of lucid alertness and consciousness can fluctuate greatly also. Generally speaking, whichever state is being added to the other (in the case of a DILD, its consciousness) will be the state you need to focus on stabilising. As the primary state of a DILD is dreaming, it will initially be the dominant of the two states, so once consciousness is added you will need to spend a little time grounding yourself and attempting to increase your awareness. In other words, at the start of a DILD the dream will most likely be very vivid and stable, but your consciousness may well not.

A DILD can begin at any point of an already established non-lucid dream. For beginners, many of their first DILDs occur at the latter end of a dream, generally due to their brain chemistry gearing up towards the waking state, resulting in their critical faculties becoming more astute. This partly explains the frustrating experience for many new lucid dreamers achieving lucidity, only to awaken shortly after (it can be further explained by the excitement of this realisation shocking them into awakening). As experience in lucid dreaming grows and as our dream practices progress, we can move the initiation of a DILD further towards the start rather than end of the dream, allowing for a longer, more satisfying, lucid dream. There are also techniques for prolonging the dreaming experience, and we shall discuss those in detail in Chapter 6.

DILDs are somewhat easier to induce than WILDs, most likely due to the fact that a dream already contains elements of conscious activity. As such, we are simply looking to increase the conscious element to the critical level where it becomes fully activated and useful. In contrast, a WILD starts with consciousness, where (unless exhausted to the point of hallucination) there are no elements of dreaming already present, so we are attempting a more dramatic shift in mental states.

Out of the two initiation options, DILDs most closely resemble the 'normal' experience of our regular, non-lucid dreams. Indeed, they require the standard process of dreaming to be underway before they can even occur. As such, when discussing lucid dreams, most practitioners are more often than not referring to the experience of a DILD.

In the simplest possible terms, a DILD is a lucid dream that starts during a non-lucid dream. Your consciousness 'switches on' at some point during a dream, transforming it into a lucid dream.

Wake initiated lucid dreams

Wake initiated lucid dreams (WILDs) are a far more elusive and peculiar phenomena than that of the DILD. The experience, stripped down to its bare bones, is that of falling asleep consciously, directly into a dream. One minute you will be lying in your bed fully awake, the next (and generally after some rather bizarre experiences) you'll have slipped with full awareness into the dream world. It is less likely for those without experience of lucid dreaming to spontaneously experience a WILD; on the rare occurrence they do, they often erroneously classify it as something else entirely, such as an 'out of body experience' or 'astral projection'. Whilst I do not wish to enter the debate into the existence or not of such esoteric phenomena, I will mention that many accounts of astral travel share a striking and, unlikely to be coincidental, resemblance to the experience of a WILD.

WILDs require a certain balancing act between alert consciousness and 'letting go', allowing yourself to relax just enough to fall asleep. The experience is hard to describe, but it's not unlike lying on a sandy beach, just close enough so that you can feel the sea lapping your feet, waiting for the tide to come in and draw you out into the sea (in our case, the sea of dreams).

WILDs by definition require a period of wakefulness from which to initiate them. As such, the most common time to attempt them is in the early morning, just after waking when you can easily slip back into sleep. Of course, they can also be attempted at any other point during a night's sleep should you awaken.

The more calculated nature of a WILD, combined with the smooth transition from waking experience into the dream, means that often the dream scene in which you find yourself will closely resemble the environment in which you are sleeping. For example, if you've attempted to induce a WILD during an early morning nap in your bedroom, there is a high probability that the dream itself will start with a reproduction of your bedroom, and with you getting out of bed (or perhaps floating out of it). This makes a good deal of sense, as expectation is a powerful creative tool in dreamland. As your consciousness has remained unbroken, your brain is likely to expect to be in the same environment in which your WILD attempt was initiated.

However, this is not always the case. Sometimes, during the process of falling asleep, you will find a vivid thought thoroughly materialises into a full-blown dream, in which you are suddenly a part. In such cases, the initial scenery of the dream can be as varied as your imagination will allow.

Common experiences during the early stages of WILD attempts are unusual bodily experiences, such as the feeling of electrical vibrations running through your body, extra limbs, or bizarre distortions of bodily parts. The feelings of dropping or floating are also commonly reported. You may experience temperature changes, the feeling of something or someone touching your body, strange noises, voices or people calling your name (all of which seem utterly convincing). Be prepared for all kinds of strange and possibly disturbing experiences.

WILDs are not for the faint-hearted. Bodily paralysis is also a common experience (sleep paralysis is a natural phenomenon, one designed to stop us physically acting out our dreams and injuring ourselves). Whilst normal, this can be frightening if not expected. All these and much more can happen whilst falling into a dream. The key here is to remain calm, conscious and aware that everything that is happening is part of the natural process of falling asleep. Whilst bizarre, these experiences are fantastic signs that you are close to entering the dreamworld and on track for a successful WILD attempt.

As mentioned during our discussion on DILDs, whichever element is secondary in our mixing of dreams and waking, it will likely be the weaker and less stable of the two. In the case of WILDs, it is the dream itself that is the secondary element. As such, WILDs can begin with a strong and aware consciousness but with an unstable or incomplete dreaming environment. Indeed, in my own experiences of WILDs I have regularly found that the dream itself forms around me, often building in strength and vividness as the dream continues. Oddly, for me I find this 'dream building' seems to occur in distinct stages, often the auditory and tactile aspects of the dream being the first to form.

I'll give a generic example of one of my common WILD experiences:

I find myself in a dark space without any visual element. However, initially I feel the position of my dream body and the environment in which it is placed (the feeling of the floor against feet or body). If I feel around, I can make out - through the sense of touch - the different aspects to the environment. Generally, by this stage I can clap my hands, speak, etc., as sounds have also joined the proceedings. Eventually, after a short period of this, the visual element of the dream will finally form, although not always completely. My mind likes to use the trick of giving my vision a blur, as if I've something in my eyes and they can't focus correctly. Sooner or later, this will clear and I'll find myself in a fully-formed dream environment. Another trick my mind plays, whilst the visual element forms, is that of low lighting. Perhaps I can make out the dim light of a candle in the distance, the light of which grows as the dream scenery coalesces.

Should you find yourself in an incomplete dream environment, the trick is to continue interacting with the dream until it is fully formed. Please don't worry and think that you're stuck in a dream without vision, as this is so incredibly unlikely it's barely worth considering. Instead, just patiently wait for the visual element to form and help it along by interacting with the dream using your other senses. You have to let your mind know that you take the experience seriously, that you are accepting the dream as the genuine world around you. The more you engage, the more rapidly the dream will form.

The other reason to engage (especially using your sense of touch), in the early stages of dream formation, is to avoid your mind switching its focus back to your real physical body, as it lies motionless in your bed. Keep the dream sensations strong for your dream body, and they will hopefully take priority over your physical body long enough for the dream to fully build.

A real benefit of a WILD is that you will always be entering a dream at its very beginning. This gives you the reassurance that you are likely to experience a relatively long period of dreaming. Also, with WILD attempts being best made after awakening in the morning, the REM phase that you will enter into will also potentially be the longest of the night. WILDs are a great way to experience long, lucid dreams with a high degree of clarity in your conscious thought. Whilst they may be slightly harder to initiate, they are certainly worth the effort.

Now that we have an understanding of the types of dreams we are aiming for, it's time to get to the meat of the subject and look at the techniques we'll be using to achieve them.

The three pillars of lucidity

To put our efforts to best effect and to get the most out of the techniques we use, it's useful to put them into a framework that helps us understand why and how they work. Over my years of studying and practising lucid dreaming, I often found myself both frustrated and confused by one seemingly inexplicable occurrence, when I would use the same induction technique on different nights, but with wildly fluctuating success rates. Some nights, lucidity would be a breeze - using the technique of my choice, I would effortlessly achieve my goal. Bolstered by the success, I would use the same technique on a following attempt, only to fail. Why was this? It seemed I was following the same procedures yet getting different results.

Over the years this same experience would continue to raise its head. There were, of course, certain techniques that would prove generally more successful than others, yet even those still failed to be consistently reliable. Discussing lucidity among fellow researchers and enthusiasts, it soon became apparent that I was not alone in this experience. The general consensus of opinion was that lucidity was, by its nature, elusive, and that we all must find our own personal key to success, that no technique is guaranteed. Whilst, on most levels, I agreed with this conclusion, and still do, it felt somewhat lacking, almost coming across as a convenient excuse to just accept the situation.

I would also notice over the years that my success at inducing lucidity would fluctuate over time. There would be phases in my life when lucidity seemed to come almost without effort; at other times, there were 'dry spells', where it became so difficult I almost started to believe it was impossible, and that my memories of previous lucid dreamers were some kind of delusion. Any experienced lucid dreamer will probably relate to this. Frustratingly, there seemed to be no correlation between the effort and preparation I would put in and my success rate. Indeed, during many of my dry spells, I would be investing more effort. This seemed completely illogical. There must have been variables that were not being taken into account.

Having spent the vast majority of my life as a committed lucid dreamer, this was a problem that I'd wrestled with for a long time. Luckily, a relatively recent discovery and advancement of lucid dream induction helped put the first pieces of the puzzle into place, confirming what I had already believed to be the case, and pointed me in what I believe is the right direction for at least partly solving this conundrum.

It was the sudden emergence of the supplement galantamine into the lucid dreaming community (around 2004 - shortly after Stephen LaBerge applied for a patent for the use of cholinesterase inhibitors, such as galantamine, to promote lucid dreaming) that really helped clarify where the gaps in previous lucid dream induction techniques were to be found.

Galantamine is classified as an Acetylcholinesterase (AChE) inhibitor. AChE is the substance that breaks down Acetylcholine (ACh) within the brain. When used, galantamine will inhibit AChE allowing for increased ACh levels. Elevated levels of ACh are associated with improved memory, clarity of thought, improved learning abilities and also prolonged REM. Bear in mind that usually ACh levels are highest during waking and REM, but also at their lowest during non-REM sleep. With the specifics aside, what we had here was a supplement you could take during your sleep cycle that would greatly improve your chances of attaining lucidity.

So, what did this mean? It meant that the state of your brain chemistry was an absolutely vital factor when accomplishing effective lucidity induction. Whilst this may seem obvious, here we had solid proof that galantamine could change your brain chemistry, making lucidity easier.

Up until this point, and even still today, the majority of well-established lucidity induction techniques focused almost entirely upon the psychological preparation and mental training for lucid dreaming. By psychological, I'm referring to the learnt skills and mental preparations required for inducing lucidity (for example, reality testing, recognising dream signs, critical thinking, etc. - anything that is an activity in which you prepare or use your mental faculties.)

An analogy I often use when explaining the above is as follows. Imagine you have been told that, in two weeks' time, you will be taking part in a chess tournament. You spend the fortnight leading up to the tournament studying everything there is to know about chess, learning the techniques of a good player, memorising the rules, learning about the other players. By the day of the tournament, you feel confident that you have completed all the psychological preparation required to play a good game. Unfortunately, you'd not been told one very important factor about the tournament, namely you will be required to drink an entire bottle of whisky before playing! Now, no matter how mentally prepared you are for the match, the chemical effect of the whisky on your brain will seriously affect your ability to play. There is no way to 'think your way out' of being drunk, so you'll be stuck with your inebriated brain chemistry during the match.

Whilst not a perfect analogy, the situation we face as lucid dreamers is similar. The majority of techniques and training available focus on mental training and psychological skills. We are, however, faced with our own form of inebriation, being our altered dreaming brain chemistry. During our waking hours, we are training a mind that is in a very different state to the mind we will eventually be working with.

In our above analogy, in order to perform well, the fictional player would need prior knowledge of his predicament, allowing him the chance to perhaps practise his skills whilst under the influence (or maybe spending time developing a tolerance to alcohol). Alternatively, he would need a 'magic sobering pill' that would counter the effects of the alcohol. In the case of lucid dreaming, that pill would be something like galantamine.

I'll sidetrack briefly here to put some readers' minds at rest. I am by no means about to base the rest of this book around simply promoting the benefits of galantamine (or any other substances for lucidity induction, for that matter). Whilst they are certainly a useful option to have available, I am a strong believer that the true beauty of lucid dreaming is that it is one of nature's free gifts. To become reliant on an external chemical would, in my opinion, effectively destroy one of the best things about lucid dreaming, which is that it is natural, free and available for all. Galantamine is being discussed because its effectiveness at improving lucidity induction sheds light on the lucid dreaming communities' previous overdependence on mostly psychological techniques. There are natural ways to achieve brain chemistry changes that will increase our success. We'll discuss those shortly.

To get back on track, how does altered brain chemistry fit into the problem of unreliable induction techniques? Certainly, fluctuations in our brain chemistry could possibly explain why a technique would be effective one night and not another. However, this alone didn't seem to be the case.

When galantamine first became available, I was both sceptical and slightly worried. Firstly, I assumed that this may be another lucid dreaming snake-oil product, just a way to take people's money, a sham. Secondly, should this be the real deal, a perfect 'lucidity pill', it could create a generation of mindless lucid dreamers who needed do nothing more than pop a pill.

It seemed to me that, whilst the psychological skills developed for lucid dreaming may not be all there is to induction, those skills did have a great deal of positive influence in the daily lives and minds of lucidity practitioners. Would critical thinking and mindfulness be thrown aside and replaced with pill-popping hedonists? Luckily, this wasn't the case.

Being curious, I decided to purchase some galantamine and give it a try. The experience was impressive - my dream recall was greatly improved and the length of my dreams extended by an impressive degree. But was lucidity guaranteed? Well, no, although it is a great aid (on nights when it was effective, it was very effective indeed). Still, the original problem of unreliable techniques reared its head again. Whilst galantamine certainly seemed to greatly increase my chances of lucidity and lengthen my REM by an impressive margin, it was still no absolute guarantee. Clearly, brain chemistry was only one variable out of several that needed to be in place.

With my worries about galantamine undermining lucid dreaming practices aside, I decided to continue my dream practices mostly chemical-free and follow a path generally independent from external requirements (I do still occasionally use galantamine, perhaps a couple of times a year, when I feel the need for a night of intense long periods of dreaming, or to help break a persistent dry spell). However, a valuable lesson had been learnt: psychological preparation was only part of the puzzle and brain chemistry another. However, even with both in place, there was still something unaccounted for, still something that was influencing reliability.

The third element, the missing part of the puzzle, is timing. Timing is something experienced lucid dreamers are already very aware of. Without the proper timing of a lucidity attempt, no amount of psychological preparedness, nor finely-tuned brain chemistry, will result in a lucid dream. It's really rather obvious, but clearly you need to be initiating your attempt when REM sleep is likely to occur. As an extreme example, you decide one afternoon to attempt lucidity; you've taken galantamine, so your brain chemistry is favourable, you've spent months undertaking all the relevant psychological preparations, but you're making your attempt at a time of day when REM sleep is highly improbable. Of course, the chances are you will fail.

Whilst an exaggerated example, this highlights the problem. Indeed, should any of the three elements of psychology, brain chemistry or timing - be missing, then your lucidity attempt will be prone to fail. I believe my previous occasional failures with the galantamine experiments were due to either poorly-timed attempts, which missed the critical point where REM dreaming and the Galantamine peak should have occurred simultaneously, or, more likely, in not putting enough focus on the required psychological methods and preparation, probably due to an overconfidence in the effectiveness of galantamine.

In my mind, this accounts for the unreliability factor that has been, up until now, our problem. Whilst many lucid dreaming techniques may well be more effective than others, I believe this is because they account for two of these vital factors (whilst the less effective techniques focus on only one). The unreliability is due to leaving to chance the third element. To reliably and effectively induce a lucid dream, you need a technique, or combination of techniques, that cover all three bases. Like a tripod that needs all three legs to be stable, a lucid dream requires all three factors to be in place. I call these the three pillars of lucidity.

To clarify here, you can become a regular and proficient lucid dreamer using the techniques already widely available. I and many others have reached a level where, to all intents and purposes, we can claim we dream lucidly at will. However, even when you reach this state you can still be plagued by the unreliability factor. This is why, when browsing lucidity forums, there is so much discussion on (and invention of) induction techniques.

Lucid dreamers are struggling to find the 'holy grail', the constantly reliable 100% induction technique. It is the unreliability factor that drives this obsession. Even seasoned lucid dreamers can feel their confidence undermined when they will inevitably make the occasional failed attempt using a technique that is normally effective for them. It is not the technique that is the problem, it is having not fully accounted for the correct balance of all three variables. As for the 'holy grail' technique, I do still believe that each lucid dreamer must find their own adaptation or combination of techniques that works for them personally. However, with an understanding of the three pillars of lucidity, we are in a much better position to focus our efforts and find our own 'grail'.

Let's look at these 'three pillars' in a little more depth so that we can be sure they are all properly in place when attempting our inductions.

Pillar One: Psychology

Any lucidity induction attempt requires a solid psychological preparation. This is the basis for almost all lucidity training. A great deal of the techniques and methods available concentrate upon developing a strong psychological preparedness, as well as entering an induction attempt with the proper mental focus and motivation. This covers the general day-to-day training of our minds such as the methods outlined in the bare essentials. Reality tests are a perfect example - we train ourselves to perform them when we notice a dreamsign or dreamlike events. This is psychological training in action.

Psychological induction techniques are those techniques that require mental focus, memory techniques, the ability to remain alert and aware, counting yourself to sleep, etc. In other words, anything that requires the development of mental skills or habits. As previously mentioned, I'd say that as much as 80% to 90% of material written on lucid dreaming tends to focus on mental preparation. It's the core of our training and the majority of the preparations you make will be psychological. When choosing your method for lucidity induction, you must be sure to have put in the sufficient psychological training and preparation. Equally important is that you remain motivated and focused during your attempt. It is easy to fall into the trap of taking a somewhat lazy approach, half-heartedly making a lucidity attempt. Doing so will seriously weaken the psychological pillar of your induction and greatly increase your chances of failure.

Pillar Two: Timing

Here we are looking to attempt our lucidity induction at the optimal time. It really is quite a tricky topic to discuss as, the further we delve, the more complicated it becomes. There are just so many variables involved. Either way, for an induction technique to succeed, it requires good timing.

As mentioned earlier, most lucid dreaming techniques focus on psychological preparations, with only a few that include the stipulation of precise timing. When timing is mentioned in many techniques, it is often a little vague, normally along the lines of suggesting performing the technique in the morning hours, when REM is more prevalent. This is good advice, and is the most basic principle for improved timing of induction attempts. However, it is imprecise and, therefore, leaves a lot up to chance. Certainly, should you take no other advice from this section other than this, you will improve your success rate. You will find the majority of your induction attempts should be best made after five hours of sleep, when REM increases in both length and regularity.

To really increase the reliability of our induction attempts, we need to hone our timing skills and look towards ways of trying to ensure that our attempts will always occur when REM is imminent. This is where things become a little more complicated.

By tracking and becoming accustomed to the intricacies and characteristics of our own sleep cycle, we can learn to focus our efforts to always occur just prior to an REM period, ideally skipping any of the non-REM phases of sleep. DILD inductions, unless attempted after a period of waking, will remain difficult (but not completely impossible) to influence in this regards.

Precise skill with timing can be difficult to master, because we simply have no obvious indication upon waking which stage of sleep we will enter should we return to bed. Will we be lucky and enter directly into REM or less fortunate and enter non-REM (NREM)?

Given time and good observation skills, you can start to develop a familiarity with how it feels to be on the brink of REM, or recognise the stage of sleep from which you have just awoken.

One of the more reliable ways to virtually guarantee entering REM directly is to have just awoken from a very brief dream. So, always pay attention to the stage of sleep from which you have woken. If you do find you've woken from a particularly short dream, it is highly likely that you could easily and rapidly re-enter REM, so it's best not to delay and to make your attempt immediately (although you may wish to spend a little time improving your brain chemistry beforehand, which we'll cover in the brain chemistry section).

This is the ideal timing scenario, as there really is no better clue that you're ready for REM than that of waking from a short dream. Under such circumstances, you can further test the probability that you're returning to REM by being observant of how you drift back into sleep. If you notice hypnagogia, then this is a great sign that REM is on its way. On the other hand, you may notice your mind becoming dulled, or simply going blank; this could be a sign that you're entering NREM sleep, so it may be worth aborting or delaying your attempt.

Each person's processes will be different in this respect, so pay attention to your own personal experiences of falling back to sleep and learn from them. Look for your own reliable signs. This will take experimentation, but over time (and with several failed and successful attempts) you will learn to judge if your mind is heading towards REM or NREM. The key here is to document your experiments so you can become familiar with how your own mind works.

If the dream you have woken from has been longer, especially if you feel particularly alert by the end, this is often a sign that you've completed an REM phase. It may still be worth attempting an immediate return to sleep, as it's possible you still have more dreaming to do. However, in this scenario, pay particular attention to how you feel as you're falling back into sleep and be ready to abort or delay your attempt if the signs do not look favourable. If you have completed an REM phase, you will be entering a fresh sleep cycle, meaning a long period of NREM, and your likelihood of failure very high.

Waking from NREM will generally be accompanied by a groggy mental fog, a lack of dream recall and possibly the memory of being in deep thought.

This is a poor time to immediately return to sleep for an induction attempt; whilst there is a chance that REM is just around the corner, it could equally be a whole sleep cycle away. In this scenario, it's best to awaken and delay your attempt until later.

Should you find, upon awakening, that you do need to delay your attempt, the question next is, for how long? Here, things become a little harder to define. The truth is there is no absolute answer, as the jury is still very much out on this topic.

In the magazine *NightLight* (6(3), 1990), Dr Stephen LaBerge et al. shared an article called 'An hour of wakefulness before morning naps makes lucidity more likely'. In their experiments, they found that waking up an hour earlier than usual, remaining awake for that hour, and then returning to sleep was the optimal timing for inducing lucidity. However, their results also showed that 30 minutes of wakefulness also resulted in a high proportion of lucid dreams, only marginally less than that of an hour's wakefulness.

There are so many different factors at play here. In this study, the participants were waking up an hour early. Would the results be similar if they had simply woken at their normal wake time? What if they had been woken even earlier? Was there a correlation between the stage of sleep woken from and the success rate when returning to sleep? These are questions for which there are currently simply no clear answers. However, the very basic and tentative consensus in the lucid dreaming community is that a period of wakefulness of between 30 and 90 minutes prior to returning to sleep is generally beneficial for increasing the likelihood of lucidity.

The truth is, this is an area in which there may not be a single answer that works for all dreamers. Experimentation and documentation of your own experiences is the only way to truly answer these questions for yourself.

On a positive note, many lucid dreamers (myself included) report developing an intuition. They get to know the 'feeling' that indicates when returning to sleep will most likely result in REM. Personally, I find that if I awaken early in the morning, and wish to make a lucidity attempt, I will get up and wait for that certain familiar mindset, a specific feeling that indicates REM is inbound.

Speculatively, it may well be that, after awakening, your mind continues working on a similar cyclical system to that of the sleep cycle. Should that be the case, given the right period of time spent awake, you should eventually hit a point when returning to sleep will most likely result in entering REM directly.

My personal sign that the timing is right, that REM is on its way, is that my thinking takes on a more abstract feel. I find my thoughts becoming somewhat more poetic; I find myself making unusual connections between ideas; I daydream a little more. I also feel a slight mental tiredness, the feeling that going back to bed would be pleasant (this is not the same as feeling burnt out, or mentally drowsy). This helps me realise that, should I return to sleep, I would likely rapidly enter an REM phase. I make further tests to ensure I'm correct in my assumptions.

When returning to bed, I keep an eye on how I start to drift into sleep; if it's a dulling of the mind, I generally abort or delay the attempt, realising that non-REM sleep is more likely. If, on the other hand, hypnagogia is strong, I can be almost certain that I shall soon be in full REM.

It is probable that you, too, will have similar experiences. It takes time to develop a strong familiarity with your own personal signs, but it's worth becoming observant and making notes as to how your differing mental processes are clues as to which sleep stage you are likely to enter should you return to sleep. This will take time and experimentation, but this kind of familiarity with your own mind is a good sign that you're becoming an experienced lucid dreamer.

As you can see, the subject of timing is intricately woven with the subtleties of your sleep cycle. There are, of course, more elements involved than simply choosing the correct time to perform an induction attempt. One particularly relevant area is that of REM rebound. Our hands are not tied to only influence the timing of our attempt, but we can also, with adjustments to our sleeping cycle, impact the intensity and duration of our REM period.

REM rebound is the lengthening and increased frequency and depth of REM sleep after a period of REM deprivation. Many of you may have experienced the effect alcohol, drunk late at night, can have on your dreams. This is predominantly due to REM rebound. Alcohol suppresses REM; however, due to the limited duration of its effects on the mind and body, this REM suppression normally only takes place for the first half of your night's sleep. Once out of the system, your brain, deprived of its normal levels of REM, attempts to correct this imbalance through REM rebound. As a result, the occurrence of REM in the latter half of your sleep is greatly increased, giving long and intense dreams.

Of course, I'm not suggesting developing a pre-sleep drinking habit to improve your morning REM levels. The same effect occurs naturally, should your previous night's sleep have been cut short or of poor quality. What this means is that a careful shortening and regulation of one's sleep cycle (to reduce time spent in REM) on nights prior to an induction attempt will lead to REM rebound once your sleeping pattern returns to its normal duration.

Attempting lucidity induction on a morning where REM rebound is in occurrence, will greatly improve both your chance of entering REM directly and the duration and depth of REM itself. Of course, caution and common sense are advised here, as sleep deprivation taken to extremes can be hazardous, unhealthy and would also create a scenario where your brain is simply too tired for induction to be a success. Small changes are best; waking a few hours earlier for a couple of nights prior to an induction attempt should create a mild REM rebound that will sufficiently improve your chances.

Another relevant factor on the subject of timing is when, for whatever reason, your sleep is disturbed. Outside noises, the need to use the bathroom, a fidgeting partner, or any of the many ways we can be awoken or roused from sleep can, on occasion, be great serendipitous moments to attempt a spontaneous lucidity induction. We discussed earlier, in the bare essentials, the need to minimise disturbances in our sleep, and this advice still holds true. However, if for some reason beyond your control your sleep is disturbed, consider it an opportunity rather than a nuisance.

A very good friend of mine, with only a passing interest in dreams, experienced his very first lucid dream as a result of such a disturbance. Whilst on a camping holiday, one plagued by the inevitable rain of an English summer, the noise of sudden heavy rain on the metallic roof of his caravan offered just enough of a disturbance in his sleep to briefly wake him. Remembering a discussion of ours earlier, he decided to 'give lucid dreaming a try', resulting in a long and vivid lucid dream.

Other factors will have been at play here, too. His brain chemistry would have likely increased in alertness due to the unusual surroundings and the sudden unfamiliar noise. Should you find yourself with similar disturbed sleep, take note of the stage of sleep you've awoken from and proceed in the appropriate manner as we've previously discussed.

To sum up, the subject of timing is complicated. So many factors are involved that personal experimentation is the only reliable way to learn what works for you. On the most basic level, simply aiming to make lucidity attempts after five hours of sleep will increase the chances of your induction occurring when REM is most prevalent. Noting the stage of sleep you have woken from will give you a good indication of how next to proceed, either directly returning to sleep or remaining awake for a period of time until making your attempt. Should you remain awake, an interval of wakefulness between 30-90 minutes before returning to sleep will improve your chances of lucidity.

Experiment to find your personal optimal time. Experimentation will also help you develop a familiarity with your own mindset and how that relates to when you should return to sleep.

Most importantly, whatever technique you use to induce lucidity, you should always be taking into account whether the timing of your attempt is optimal.

Pillar Three: Brain Chemistry

Of all the three pillars of lucidity, it is fair to say that, until recently, the chemistry of your sleeping brain was one of the least addressed areas of lucid dream induction. As it stands, there is currently very little discussion on the subject in much of the literature relating to lucidity. Even so, improving your brain's chemical environment in order to enhance your rational abilities and clarity of thought is equally important to your potential success, as are timing and psychology.

The advent of chemicals such as galantamine have shed light on this area, proving that your brain chemistry is very much a relevant ingredient to the success or failure of a lucid dream attempt. However, regardless of this, the discussion seems to revolve mostly around those external agents, the supplements themselves, and there is still little to be said in regards of improving the chemistry of your brain naturally.

As you will most likely notice as you read further, there is considerable overlap between some of the methods employed to enhance chemistry and those for improving the timing of your induction. As with all things in lucid dreaming, a holistic approach to your practices is ideal, so using techniques that cover multiple needs is generally the best strategy.

It takes a certain kind of humility to accept that we, as humans, are very much at the whims of the chemical makeup of our brains. We like to believe that we are special, that we can 'think our way out of anything'. However, if truth be told, thinking can only ever get us so far. You need only to spend a little time considering those afflicted with mental illnesses to realise that a brain that is chemically imbalanced can powerfully affect the mental functioning and rational abilities of the individual to whom it belongs.

This is an extreme example, but to be frank we must all accept our own biological basis and come to terms with the fact that, whilst we are (hopefully) the owners of healthy brains, our brains and the mental abilities that rely upon them are equally subject to the subtle nuances of chemistry.

A more familiar example of our reliance on brain chemistry is the insomnia that can follow a strong coffee drunk too late at night. Anyone who's experienced this kind of insomnia can testify that no amount of willpower or mental trickery is going to override the effect of the caffeine in our system. You simply won't be able to think yourself to sleep.

When external chemicals are not part of the picture, and to play devil's advocate, there is also a certain 'chicken and egg' logic to this issue. It could be argued that it is difficult to tell if a state of mind is the result of brain chemistry, or if brain chemistry the result of a state of mind. It's likely, however, that both are equally true.

The problem here is a classification or language issue. We define our thoughts as separate from our brain chemistry, creating the logical illusion that one needs to lead to the other. The more likely truth is that brain chemistry (including neural activity) and thoughts are one and the same. If seen this way, the problem then vanishes.

Philosophy aside, we're all very aware that the sleeping mind is running on a very different system to that of the waking mind. It only takes being suddenly woken in the middle of the night and being required to perform a complicated or important task, especially during NREM, to realise just how powerfully different the chemistry of the sleeping brain is. Our job, then, is to attempt to create a fine balance in the brain where conditions are equally as conducive to sleep as they are to rational, critical thought. Should we get this balance wrong, we'll either find ourselves lying in bed suffering a form of self-induced insomnia, or falling asleep with a fuzzy uncritical mind that fails to notice it is dreaming.

Just as walking a tightrope is a difficult skill to master, one which takes time and perseverance, so too is the skill of balancing one's state of mind for the task at hand. You will surely initially experience both failures and frustrations in this undertaking, but this is all very much part of the learning experience. The skill of developing mastery of lucid dreaming is a journey, so be equally prepared for the highs and lows of such an adventure. The destination will be worth it.

Let's first look at our primary tactic for naturally improving our brain chemistry, namely mental stimulation. Here is where timing, brain chemistry and psychology all somewhat overlap. The simplest way to move your brain out of the fog of its sleeping state is to get up and engage yourself in an activity that requires your critical and logical faculties. Our brains will naturally shift their chemical balance in the direction of an activity it is required to achieve.

The act of waking itself sets into motion a whole series of changes in our brain to prepare it for the day ahead. We simply need to get this process underway without reaching the point of no return, where returning to sleep will become impossible. We may also be required to expedite this process should we have woken directly from REM and plan to return to sleep shortly to hit our window of opportunity.

Whilst I hope it is obvious, the following suggestions are designed for use upon awakening and during the time prior to returning to sleep for a lucidity-induction attempt. Here, we can employ all manner of tactics to sharpen our wits and oil the cogs of our rational thought. Many of the possibilities you will already be familiar with, as they'll most likely be part of your morning waking routine.

Open the curtains and allow a little light (should the sun have risen) to stimulate your mind. Open your window, take a few deep breaths of fresh air. Splash your face with a little cold water. Have a refreshing drink (ideally caffeine-free, unless your tolerance is high). Essentially, anything that you find makes you feel 'more human' and clears your head. These activities vary from person to person, but the idea here is to send the signal to your mind that it's time for conscious activity to commence.

It's important to note, however, that eating at this point is a poor choice; there is evidence that the first meal of the day plays a role in resetting our circadian rhythm, which could set you down the path of waking regularly at this time, which isn't our goal. Physical exercise is also a poor choice, as you will rapidly push yourself past the point of no return.

Also, for those of you to whom a morning coffee or cigarette are an integral part of your routine, I would highly suggest avoiding coffee, as it is likely to simply stop you returning to sleep altogether. However, do feel free to experiment if you really feel you can't engage your mind without it. I, myself, have a rather high tolerance to caffeine and find that a cup of tea rarely affects my ability to return to sleep, but the general rule is caffeine is probably not wise.

Whilst I cannot condone smoking, should you be a smoker and it already is part of your morning routine, it is unlikely to interfere with your attempts to return to sleep. Indeed, nicotine is one of the many substances used by those who experiment with chemical induction of lucidity (the nicotine molecule is very similar to the neurotransmitter acetylcholine. When nicotine enters the brain, it attaches to nerve cells in the same way that acetylcholine would, creating the same effects), so it is actually likely to help your attempt. If you don't already smoke, however, it would be the height of foolishness to use this as an excuse to start; in the long-run, regular nicotine use will likely decrease your general ability to become lucid due to the desensitisation of your nicotinic receptors (one type of acetylcholine receptor).

Details aside, the goal is to use whatever works best for you to shake the mental fog you awaken with, just enough to allow for clear thought whilst still maintaining the possibility of returning to sleep. Experimentation and recording your results to compare against future attempts is the approach required here.

Alongside the more familiar procedures for sharpening your mind, it is also wise to partake in activities that specifically focus on engaging your critical and logical abilities. These can really be any of a number of tasks that (depending on your own personal tastes) will achieve the desired result. Word or math puzzles are a prime example, reading through your dream journal with the aim of spotting previous missed or subtle dreamsigns is also a great activity. Meditation is a popular and often cited pre-induction activity, especially any meditative technique in which the focus is to retain a witnessing alert consciousness. Caution, however, is advised when using meditation to not simply let your mind drift, or risk falling asleep cross-legged!

Computer games, especially puzzles that require rapidly recognising and logically responding to events, are also very handy; indeed, the more cerebral the better. Tetris or games of that ilk are ideal. One benefit of using a computer for such puzzles is the scoring system. You can use your score (judged against a game played during a time of day when your brain is fully active) to establish the extent to which your mental abilities have been activated. A numerical score gives you tangible data to work with and should, over time, help you easily establish where your 'sweet spot' for lucidity induction lies.

Whilst these activities and others may, on the surface, appear to be employing a psychological approach, the logic behind them is to engage the circuitry of the mind that is required for lucidity. This appears to take us back to the chicken and egg dilemma; however, as we've already established, there are in reality no hard and fast distinctions between psychology and the chemistry of the mind.

We are choosing to use these definitions for convenience, as it helps us create a framework in which to work. If you focus on a task that requires clarity of thought, you set into motion the cascade of chemicals and activity in your mind that will eventually set the stage for a mind that is capable of achieving lucidity.

Another way we can influence the chemistry of our sleeping mind is to take advantage of our natural tendency to slip into a regular sleeping pattern. As we near our usual waking time each morning, our brain is likely to adjust its chemical balance in preparation for waking. A perfect example of this process is when those with a regular working schedule wake up at the weekend at the time they'd usually be getting up for work.

For those of us with an interest in increasing our alertness whilst sleeping, this can be used to our advantage. Back in 2004, I released online a method with this goal in mind called the Cycle Adjustment Technique, or CAT for short. We'll look into the details of CAT when we look at specific techniques themselves, but the principle in essence is of adjusting your morning wake time earlier for a limited period, then returning to your previous later waking time once the new schedule has taken hold.

Essentially, what this is attempting to achieve is to set in motion the chemistry for wakefulness at an earlier time than is actually required. Hopefully, this will result in an increased alertness during sleep itself (and hopefully REM) once you've returned to your routine of sleeping for longer. You can experiment along these lines yourself, assuming your sleeping pattern is regular. Bear in mind that adjustments like these need to be made not only to the hours you wake up, but also the time you retire. Sometimes, simply going to bed earlier or later can result in a spontaneous lucid dream (presuming you've got the bare essentials covered) due to your routine being thrown out of balance, thus creating a scenario where your brain chemistry and the stages of your sleep cycle may be in a different alignment from that of your usual routine. As with many of these suggestions, experimentation is your friend here, so find what works for you.

One of the few rampant areas of experimentation in influencing lucidity through brain chemistry is that of dietary changes. Online lucidity forums are often full of topics with suggestions for which food or vitamin supplement is the most effective for improving induction techniques. Supplements such as galantamine are the extreme end of this field, and a topic that is large enough to warrant being considered a complete technique in its own right. So, rather than discuss it here, we'll be outlining it in detail once we reach the specific techniques themselves. Needless to say, galantamine and its kin absolutely and unquestionably fall under the third lucidity pillar of brain chemistry, being the most distilled and direct approach for brain chemistry alteration.

For the more familiar and readily available foods and supplements, there is little hard evidence to back up many of the claims made online. Generally, reports are subjective and success rates incredibly varied among individuals. Of course, the substances themselves are equally varied, ranging from apple juice, milk, chocolate, peanut butter, many and varied vitamins, etc. The list is growing daily.

Whilst, our diet can have a profound effect on our mental state, it is often difficult to pinpoint which changes in our diet, or lifestyle, are having the effect. The placebo effect comes into play here, also; a belief that something can work can often be all it takes to increase our chances, especially when dealing in matters of the mind. Almost certainly, a healthy balanced diet will be beneficial.

Of course, I am not claiming that different foods or vitamins cannot improve our chances for lucidity by improving the environment of our brain chemistry, only that it's wise to take reports on the subject with a pinch of salt. That said, a good place to start if you wish to experiment with dietary changes would be to experiment with foods rich in Choline and vitamin B5 (otherwise known as Pantothenic acid).

As we've seen, the purpose of those experimenting with galantamine is to increase the levels of acetylcholine (Ach), which is proven as an effective aid to lucidity and prolonged periods in REM. Vitamin B5 and Choline are the substances required for the body to produce ACh. ACh is created by adding an acetyl group to a choline molecule. B5 is the precursor to the acetyl group. In simple terms, without B5 and Choline, your body would not be able to produce ACh.

Regardless of whether we choose to experiment with galantamine or not, it is almost certainly beneficial to equip our body with foods that help it generate ACh. Vitamin B5 is present in most diets, so it's likely you already have more than enough acetyl groups available in your brain to produce ACh. Foods rich in B5 include liver, bran, sunflower seeds, whey powder, mushrooms, cheese, sundried tomatoes, and fish, to name a few. There is certainly no harm in adding some of these into your diet.

Choline, on the other hand, is a substance that can be lacking in your diet. Those especially at risk are vegetarians, vegans, endurance athletes and those who drink a lot of alcohol. Also, if you're not in the habit of regularly eating whole eggs, you may also be at risk of low choline. It is good practice to make sure you're achieving a minimum of your daily levels. The adequate intake levels of Choline are considered to be 425 mg a day for adult women (higher if pregnant or breastfeeding) and 550 mg daily for adult males.

For our requirements, it may well be that we wish to do more than simply achieve the adequate daily level. Some foods high in choline are raw beef liver, whole boiled eggs, cod, chicken, milk, spinach, tofu and wheat germ to name but a few. Of course, I'd advise research into the exact levels of choline by weight and calorie intake of these and other foods. In practice, regularly eating whole boiled eggs is a good way to improve your daily choline levels. Equally, both B5 and Choline are available in most health stores as supplements.

An important factor to bear in mind when experimenting with dietary changes and supplements is the time that they are ingested. Obviously, it is not as simple as eating an egg and expecting your choline levels to immediately improve. A good rule of thumb for dietary changes is consistency; a regular balanced diet will keep bodily levels of the required chemicals at a relative constant.

If you wish to be more precise in your timing, you will need to take into account the amount of time it takes for food to be digested, enter the system and for the nutrients to become available for the body's needs. Not forgetting how long it may take for certain nutrients to be transformed from one state into another, and how long those elements remain present in the body.

It's a complicated business and perhaps you can see why it is such a difficult area in which to experiment. Keeping a record of when you eat certain foods (and experimenting with different timing) and their apparent effects on dreaming is the best way to edge your way towards an understanding of whether or not they are beneficial in your dreaming attempts.

Supplements are slightly less complicated as we're dealing with purer substances in regulated doses. For example, two popular forms of choline supplement available for lucid dreamers are Choline Bitartrate and Alpha-GPC. Both have different peak plasma times (when concentrations are highest in the plasma of the blood) and elimination half-life (the time it takes for the body to eliminate or break down half the amount of a substance in the body).

These are important factors. The peak plasma time helps us decide when best to take a supplement, as we'll want to be dreaming during this peak (or prior to the peak). The elimination half-life is relevant because it lets us establish how long the substance will be effective following this peak. For Choline Bitartrate, the peak plasma time is 1 hour with an elimination half-life of 1.5 hours. For Alpha-GPC, peak plasma time is 3 hours and elimination half-life is 1.5 hours.

What this means in practical terms is that, when taking Choline Bitartrate, we need to be sure we'll be dreaming within the hour before the effects begin to fade. With Alpha-GPC, our levels will be gradually increasing towards their peak over the course of three hours, giving us a much larger window of opportunity. As such, Alpha-GPC is generally the supplement of choice for lucid dreamers looking to take it prior to an induction attempt, and is generally taken after 4-5 hours of sleep before returning to bed.

A few other additions to your diet deserve a mention, as they are often experimented with and discussed among online lucid dream enthusiasts. Often, however, the logic behind the claims stem from very small-scale research that is optimistically extrapolated upon by enthusiastic dreamers, sadly without any firm evidence. Unfortunately, this can lead to a case of Chinese whispers, resulting in big claims eventually being stated as fact. It's always worth being cautious in these regards, and it's best to research the source of any claims before simply assuming they are correct.

Apple juice is often suggested amongst enthusiasts for apparently improving lucidity attempts. However, we only have anecdotal evidence of its benefits for lucid dreaming. Animal research from the University of

Massachusetts Lowell (UML) suggest regular consumption of apple juice may boost levels of ACh - well, at least in mice on a restricted diet!

There were plans to perform further studies with humans but, as yet, I've been unable to find reports on whether these studies have ever taken place (or their results). It's also worth bearing in mind that this research was sponsored by the U.S. Apple Association and the Apple Products Research & Education Council. Whilst I'm by no means ruling out apple juice being potentially beneficial, it's important to understand that research into its effects on the brain are so far very limited indeed.

Vitamin B6 is also often widely claimed to have potential dream-enhancing abilities. This idea probably stems from what seems to be the sole research into this area: a very small-scale study performed in 2002 at the City College of New York (so small that it involved only 12 university students). The study hinted at improved dream recall using B6.

A single study with just 12 participants is far from solid evidence; however, being quirky enough, journalists loved it and proceeded to report it widely and with undue exaggeration on the results. This is probably the source of the widespread belief that B6 improves dream recall. The truth is, there simply isn't anywhere near enough evidence to support this claim, nor to suggest that it is worth supplementing your diet with B6 to improve dream recall. Also, it's important to be aware that an overdose of vitamin B6, which can happen at surprisingly low levels, can cause irreversible nerve damage.

Omega 3, fish oils and vitamin B12 are all regularly suggested as beneficial for lucid dreamers. Whilst no specific research into their effect on dreams has been conducted, all are generally accepted as beneficial towards maintaining a healthy brain, so it's certainly plausible that they could be of use in our endeavours. It's worth remembering here, though, that the positive effects of such supplements are normally only seen with regular long-term use and are mostly aimed at preventing or countering deficiency. It is unlikely that any of these supplements could directly affect your dreams - unless, of course, you're already suffering a deficiency or are particularly susceptible to the placebo effect.

A final element that can have an influence on the effectiveness of inductions, and which is likely to be related to altered brain chemistry, is the position in which you sleep. Considering the amount of shifting in position that occurs during a normal night's sleep, this approach is unworkable for

DILD attempts that don't include awakening. However, for DILD and WILD attempts following a period of waking, the position in which you sleep may have an impact on your level of mental arousal.

Reports from the lucid dreaming community seem to suggest that positions that leave more of your vital organs exposed (lying on your back or side) tend to result in lighter sleep and higher mental arousal, ideal for improving chances of lucidity. More defensive and covered sleeping positions such as the fetal position tend to result in deeper sleep with low mental arousal.

The familiarity of the environment you're sleeping in can also be a factor here - familiarity promoting deeper sleep, with unfamiliarity resulting in lighter sleep. Logically, this seems to make sense, as the more exposed we feel the higher our mental arousal remains. This is most likely a piece of primal evolutionary programming, a result of the gritty dangerous lives of our distant ancestors, when predators were a much more immediate danger.

Another primal instinct, eating, seems to have much the same kind of programming. Fast food chains have been rumoured to spend a great deal of money researching environments that create the fastest customer turnover. The long and short of the findings were supposedly similar to our conclusions on sleep position, in that the more exposed diners feel (even if on a subconscious level) the faster they eat and leave (making room for new customers). Take note the next time you're eating out - restaurants with higher prices who prefer their customers to stay longer (and spend more) often have enclosed areas in which to eat, seats with high backs, often against walls. Gaps between customers' dining areas are often wider. They want you to feel secure. In fast food chains, the opposite is often true - customers are squeezed together, tables are out in the open and seats are often just stools with no back support at all. You generally have a sense of being out in the open and, as such, eat much faster.

Step back into our distant past and such eating habits would have been the difference between life and death. It's not surprising that, in both eating and sleeping (and other primal activities), we prefer to feel well-defended and secure from intrusions (or danger). The logic seems reasonably sound, so it's certainly worth experimenting with your sleeping position to find the results you find most effective. To experiment with an unfamiliar sleeping environment in your own familiar bedroom can be slightly harder to achieve, but often can be as simple as lying in your bed in the opposite direction (head feet reversal).

In conclusion, brain chemistry is a vital element that should be taken into consideration whenever you attempt lucidity induction. It's a somewhat complicated subject (and a relatively new line of research) that will undoubtedly grow over time, but absolutely worth investing your time and efforts into. Both behavioural and chemical methods can be called upon to achieve our aims, and whichever method you decide to use is entirely up to you and your opinions on the subject.

Should you decide upon the latter, however, then research into any claims for the various foods, supplements and vitamins before deciding to experiment is vital, as there is a good deal of well-intentioned yet misleading information available out there. Also, any dramatic changes in your diet, or experimentation with supplements, should be discussed with a medical professional before proceeding. Many of the behavioural methods involved in improving chemistry have considerable overlap with those used for timing, so try your best to achieve your goals by using tactics that cover both timing and chemistry.

Pillars in perspective

By this point you'd be forgiven for feeling a little overwhelmed, as we've covered a great deal of information and we're yet to reach the specific techniques themselves. To put things into perspective (and hopefully put your mind at ease), what we've covered here whilst discussing the three pillars are the principles involved, various examples of how to apply those principles, hints and tips including useful information and details on mistakes that are worth avoiding.

The level of detail here is by no means an exhaustive list of every possible option available. There is a great deal more that could be said and much to be discovered. However, I've included what I feel are essential points that will hopefully save you time and point you in the right direction of experimentation that will be of value.

You don't need to be performing all of these tasks each time you make an induction attempt. Instead, when choosing an induction technique, pay careful attention to its strengths and weaknesses; consider if it has a rounded balance of psychology, timing and chemistry. If you find it lacking in any of these areas, then refer back to this section and consider how you could use the suggestions here to create a more balanced technique.

Consider, also, if any of the other techniques that follow can be combined to increase their overall balance and effectiveness. It may be that, in time, more elements other than those of the three pillars will be discovered and come into play. For now, hopefully you have a good understanding of the importance of a balanced strategy for inducing lucid dreams. Experiment! You're on a journey of discovery; experimentation is just one of the many joys ahead.

Induction techniques

Now for the individual techniques themselves. At the beginning of each you'll find two quick reference points. The first establishes which type of lucid dream (DILD, WILD or both) the technique is designed to initiate. The second is a rating system to establish the strength of the method in regards to each of the three pillars. Should you find it lacking in any of these areas, then you can consider combining it with a suitable method that addresses this balance, or refer back to the pillar section for suggestions. Following each method will be a review of the strengths and weaknesses of the technique to further clarify these points.

Wake Back To Bed (WBTB) Technique

To achieve: WILD, DILD
Pillar rating
Psychology: Zero/Low
Timing: Medium
Brain chemistry: Medium/High

The concise but awkwardly-named 'Wake Back to Bed' technique (WBTB) is one of the most popular, effective and flexible of the well-known methods for lucidity induction. It is used for induction attempts aiming to achieve either DILDs or WILDs. The technique itself is difficult to trace in origin and seems to be one that has emerged organically from the community of lucid dream enthusiasts themselves. However, the seed of the idea was possibly inspired by Dr Stephen LaBerge's research into the effectiveness of early morning naps following a period of waking (discussed earlier).

WBTB is rarely used as a stand-alone induction technique. Whilst used independently it may (with the groundwork outlined in the bare essentials in place) result in lucidity, more often than not it is combined with additional techniques (generally those of a psychological nature). When discussed among lucid dreamers, it is normally the assumption that when mentioning the use of the WBTB technique, that it was used in combination with another method.

The technique in its basic form, and as is often published, is simplicity itself:

1. Retire to bed. Retire to bed as normal, setting an alarm to wake you after a minimum of five hours[1] sleep (assuming your regular night's sleep lasts eight hours or more; should you sleep less than average, reduce these five hours by an appropriate proportion).

2. Wake at the preset time and remain awake for a short period. Upon waking from your alarm, get out of bed and occupy yourself for 30-90 minutes

1 Five hours is the common suggestion as it ensures you'll be returning to sleep during a period of intense REM. However, in both my own and others' experiences, it is worth occasionally experimenting with a much shorter WBTB timing, even as short as 2 hours (I myself find 3½ hours is my premium for these reduced WBTB attempts). In doing so, you may find yourself able to induce lucidity in an early REM phase, which can often result in a very stable lucid dream in which you are unlikely to awaken. Often, these dreams last much longer than would be expected for an REM period occurring at this stage of the night.

(as discussed in the three pillars section, you will need to experiment to find your optimal time). Do whatever is required to make your mind alert and active, but without going as far as to make returning to sleep impossible.

3. Return to bed. Return to bed with the firm intention to recognise that you are dreaming once it occurs. Allow yourself to relax and fall back into sleep (generally at this point, dreamers will also be employing a second psychological technique to improve their chances of success). Continue to sleep until your usual waking time.

As you can see, this is a bare bones technique, aimed squarely at increasing your mental alertness prior to returning to the most prevalent period of REM of the night. The technique is vague in its focus for both timing and brain chemistry improvements, leaving a lot to chance. As such, it requires fine-tuning with the suggestions discussed in the three pillars section. It also lacks any specific psychological approach, so combining it with a suitable psychological technique is a wise choice. These issues are all easily addressed, making WBTB a great framework on which to base a more complete and effective lucid dream induction strategy. It's important to note that the premise of WBTB is an essential element for a great deal of WILD induction techniques.

Pros

- WBTB is a very simple technique that requires little effort to implement.
- Its simplicity gives you space to experiment with technique combinations, tweaks and improvements.
- Even in its simplest state, it still has a reasonable chance of inducing lucidity.
- Occasionally, an unplanned disturbance in your sleep can lead to a spontaneous opportunity to perform WBTB.
- Its wide use among the lucid dreaming community means there is already a great deal of discussion and hints available for ways in which to improve its effectiveness.

Cons

- As you are required to disturb your sleep, it may not be suitable for regular use or for those who share a bed.
- The basic method itself is lacking many vital elements for success, so requires additional thought and adaptations.
- Without adaptations, this method produces unpredictable results.

Mnemonic Induction of Lucid Dreams (MILD) Technique

To achieve: DILD
Pillar rating
Psychology: High
Timing: Medium/High
Brain chemistry: Low

The Mnemonic Induction of Lucid Dreams Technique (MILD) is perhaps one of the most oft-mentioned lucidity induction techniques. It was devised by Dr Stephen LaBerge whilst working on his PhD dissertation, which explored the possibility of inducing lucid dreaming at will. Since being published in his 1985 book *Lucid Dreaming* and, again, in his very popular 1990 book *Exploring the world of lucid dreaming* (both of which I highly recommend), MILD has become a commonly used technique for many an aspiring lucid dreamer. For the record, the term 'mnemonic' refers to the use of memory, or that which aids the memory, which is, unsurprisingly, the premise of MILD.

The core principle is to use your ability to remember to perform a future task (prospective memory) in order to prepare yourself to recognise you are dreaming whilst dreaming. LaBerge advises developing your waking skills in prospective memory before expecting success using MILD, which is clearly sensible advice. If you can't do something whilst you're awake, there's absolutely no reason to expect you'll be able to in your sleep!

To perform MILD, LaBerge suggests you should retire for bed with the intention to recall your dreams clearly for the night. Should you wake from a dream, clearly and single-mindedly set the intention to recognise you are dreaming the next time you are dreaming. As you do this, also review the previous dream in your mind's eye, only this time with the addition of imagining yourself realising and noticing that it is a dream. Continue this motivation and visualisation process as you fall back to sleep.

Now, it would be rather uncouth of me to explain in too fine a detail another author's work in my own book. So, instead of elaborating on the intricacies of the MILD technique further (the above outline is the basic premise of the principle), I would suggest for a more thorough explanation of this particular method to read Dr LaBerge's excellent book *Exploring the world of lucid dreaming* or visiting his website (search for MILD at the lucidity Institute's website.)

However, to put MILD into the context of the three pillars system, its strong points are psychological (the visualisations and mnemonic preparation) and timing (the advice to perform shortly after awakening from REM; however, it is important to consider the duration of the REM period you have woken from, for reasons we've discussed earlier). When performed correctly and with the addition of tactics to improve your mental alertness, and consideration of the length of the REM period you have woken from, this can be a pleasantly simple and reasonably effective technique.

Pros

- A popular technique that has been tried and tested by many.
- Simple psychological principle, so is easy to undertake.
- Can be combined or adapted to be used with other techniques.

Cons

- Requires waking directly from REM to perform.
- Ideally requires good dream recall upon awakening.
- Requires adaptations to improve reliability.

False Awakening Through Expectation (FATE) Technique

To achieve: DILD, WILD
Pillar rating
Psychology: High
Timing: Medium/High
Brain chemistry: Medium/High

The False Awakening Through Expectation technique (FATE) is one of the more involved techniques and requires a little preparation. However, as with many things in life, the investment of a little effort and preparation is often repaid with the increased chance of success. FATE is an invention of my own and designed to create a natural balance between the three pillars required for a successful induction attempt.

It is likely others have stumbled upon similar techniques in their own experimentation. Indeed, FATE shares some similarities to the FAST technique (False Awakening State Test) published in 1982 by Dr Keith Hearne. However, whilst both techniques approach induction using a similar logic, their tactics differ in important areas. I feel FATE is perhaps a little more practical for the average dreamer in its application (it can be performed alone) and addresses the balance of the three pillars more thoroughly. FAST, however, is an ingenious method and can be read in Dr Hearne's book *The Dream Machine*.

As the name suggests, the FATE technique attempts to induce a false awakening (a dream in which you falsely believe you have woken normally) through the power of expectation. The idea here is that if you develop the strong habit of performing a thorough reality test each time you wake up; then, by generating a false awakening, your habit of performing a reality test upon awakening is highly likely to occur. In other words, if reality testing is a firm habit when you normally wake up, then a dream in which you believe you have woken normally should also include a reality test.

The question here is how do you generate a false awakening? The trick, it would seem, is to create the expectation that your sleep is likely to be disturbed. You may have experienced related phenomena on nights prior to an important event, especially those that required waking early. Before an exam, job interview or the need to be awake at a certain time to travel for a holiday, you are highly likely to dream of the experience in advance.

When our minds are strongly predisposed towards focusing on a definite upcoming event, it is likely that our dreams will rehearse that event the night before it occurs. Similar dreams of running late for work are common for those who use the snooze function on their alarm clocks (if used too often, such dreams quickly become a reality!). It is the strong sense of expectation of an event that generates such dreams. If we can create a strong expectation that our sleep will be disturbed, our resultant dreams should be of waking up.

Normally, when we sleep there are certain expectations that are a default. We expect that we will wake up in the same environment in which we retired. We also have an expectation of the approximate time we will awaken and the series of events that will likely unfold as we get up. These basic assumptions are the stuff upon which normal false awakenings are built. On top of these assumptions, we will be creating further expectations of disturbed sleep and the habit of reality testing. Normally, however, false awakenings are a relatively rare occurrence, triggered mostly through unplanned disturbed sleep. Our goal is to create the conditions in which they shall become commonplace, where we shall be purposefully disturbing our sleep.

To effectively disturb our sleep, we need a device that is capable of generating random alarms within a set period of time. Fortunately, most of us will have such a device available, namely the smart phone. Admittedly, this generally isn't a default function on most smartphones, but there are plenty of Apps (software applications) that can be downloaded, either for free or for a small price, that will give your phone this alarm functionality. These can generally be found by searching the app market of your smartphone for 'random reminder app' or 'reality test reminder' or something similar.

Essentially, the functionality you are looking for is software that can be set to perform a random number (within a set range, under 10 for example) of randomly timed audio alarms during a fixed period of time (between 7am and 8am, for example). Personally, I use an Android application called 'Sleep Check Reminder' as it offers the above functionality. However, there are almost certainly other applications on the various smartphone platforms available that offer the same functions. Should you not own a smartphone, there are also watches and clocks available that can be set to generate random alarms during a set period of time.

It will be much easier to understand the processes and logic behind them if we first look at how to perform the method step by step.

The following is the FATE technique in full.

1. Retire to bed. Before retiring to bed as normal, set your standard alarm clock to wake you after a minimum of five hours sleep. Also, set your alarm app to give random alarms for a 90-minute period, starting shortly after the time you have set your standard alarm clock to wake you. Place both of your alarms some distance from your bed, enough so that you have to leave your bed to switch them off, but not so far that they will be ineffective at waking you. Also, be sure that any clocks or devices clearly showing the time in your bedroom are covered, so you are unable to judge the time simply by looking around your room. Once complete, go to bed.

2. Wake at the preset time. Once awakened by your standard alarm, get out of bed walk, over to where you have placed your alarms and switch off your standard alarm, making sure its face is now covered so you cannot read the time (your random alarm needs to remain active for obvious reasons). Pay careful attention to everything you do as you walk over to the alarm, how it feels, the lighting, your bodily feelings.

3. Perform the nose pinch reality test. Once your primary alarm clock is switched off, and its face covered, making it impossible to read the time, slowly and carefully perform the nose pinch reality test. Once you have firmly established you are awake and not dreaming, return to bed.

4. Visualise the reality test whilst returning to sleep. Whilst you return to sleep, run over in your mind the process you have just performed. Imagine how it felt to walk over to the alarm clock, and imagine yourself performing the nose pinch test. During this visualisation, imagine yourself performing the nose pinch test but discovering you can breathe, that you are indeed dreaming. Remind yourself also that soon you will be awoken by a random alarm and will be required to perform the same test.

5. Awaken to the random alarm. During some point during the next 90 minutes, you will be awoken by the first of an unknown number of random alarms. When this occurs, get out of bed, walk over to the alarm (paying attention to your environment and how you feel), dismiss the alarm if required by your app, then once again thoroughly and carefully perform the nose pinch test. If you establish that you are awake, return to bed.

6. Repeat tasks 4 and 5. Continue to perform tasks 4 and 5 until you achieve lucidity or wake for the day.

There are several factors at play here, and several possible outcomes. The first important factor is that you must attempt to remain unaware of both the time and the amount of alarm calls you are likely to receive. In doing so, your brain will never be given the chance to fully relax. It will stay constantly in an increased alert state, not knowing if an alarm is imminent or not. This is the logic behind covering your clocks (so you will be unaware when the 90-minute phase is over) and also for setting a random number of alarms. This keeps your expectation high. Our ability to judge the exact time in the morning can become easily confused. It is likely that, even when the 90-minute alarm phase has passed, you will remain uncertain of the exact time and continue to expect further alarms. The random number of alarms is designed to heighten this uncertainty.

In this scenario, the nose pinch test is our choice of reality test, but you could equally use the morphing text test. The digital watch test should obviously be avoided as we do not wish to be reminded of the correct time.

By repeating a very structured waking, reality test, then return to bed cycle, you continue to enforce the expectation of it reoccurring, enhancing further the chances of a false awakening. Also, the repetition of this behaviour, with the instruction to pay attention to your environment and feelings, also increases the chances of noticing you are dreaming should you suddenly find yourself performing the task with an inconsistency.

Getting out of bed to perform the reality test is designed to both increase your alertness and to create a repetitive cycle of experience, which should influence the content of your dreams.

Should this induction go to plan, there are two likely routes into your lucid experience. The first is the more obvious DILD. Here, you will simply dream of following the waking procedure of getting up and performing the nose pinch test, at which point you should find yourself able to breathe and become aware you are dreaming.

Secondly, a WILD is also possible here, during stage 4 of the technique.

There is a chance that, during your visualisation, you will discover you are no longer simply visualising, but instead suddenly dreaming, resulting in a WILD. Should things not go quite to plan, and your dream be of something other than a false awakening, the level of mental alertness created by the continued disruptions and reality testing should greatly improve your chances of attaining lucidity.

The most likely difficulty you will encounter is the possibility of finding it difficult to return to sleep. Should this be the case, in future attempts experiment with simply sitting up in bed to perform your reality test (rather than fully getting out of bed). Whilst this may potentially lessen your mental alertness for your attempt, should you be a light sleeper this may be the best compromise.

Undoubtedly, this comes across as a rather involved and somewhat complicated induction technique. But I believe its complexity is balanced by the increased odds of a successful induction.

Pros

- Well rounded technique that covers the requirements of the three pillars.
- High chance of a successful induction attempt.
- Lucidity is likely to be initiated in a familiar environment (the dream version of your bedroom) allowing for the chance to plan dream experiments in advance, especially those that require certain items.
- Lucidity is likely to be of a high level of mental alertness.

Cons

- Requires disturbed sleep, so may not be suitable for regular use or for those who share a bed.
- There is a chance that early lucidity induction will be disturbed by an alarm.
- Additional tools (smartphone) are needed to perform.

Catching the Butterfly (Butterfly or CTB) Technique

To achieve: Primarily WILDs, DILDs are possible
Pillar rating
Psychology: High
Timing: Medium
Brain chemistry: Medium

The Catching the Butterfly technique is a very simple, yet powerful, WILD induction technique. This technique has strong personal significance for me, being my first ever induction technique and the 'invention' of my 5-year-old self, in an attempt to (successfully) gain control over my regular and disturbing childhood nightmares. Its simplicity is somewhat misleading as, when performed correctly, this is a potent technique and possibly the purest form of induction method.

Of course, what follows is a polished and refined version of that early method, with additions and adaptations to enhance its effectiveness. Similar methods abound in lucid dream literature, so it would be foolish for anyone to claim authorship to such a simple and fundamental premise of lucid dreaming. However, being my own first successful induction method, and essentially the founding principle of all WILD techniques, I believe it is absolutely worth sharing.

Butterfly, in its most basic state, is a psychological method. Should you have asked my 5-year-old self how he managed to become conscious in his dreams, he would have most likely answered 'I just try to catch the moment I fall asleep'. That really is the essence of the whole method. Of course, there are many other elements that need to come into consideration here, and they shall be outlined below. However, keep in mind the basic premise: consciousness, as you fall into sleep, is like a butterfly flitting from flower to flower, from one thought to the next, difficult to keep track of and easy to lose. Your goal is to keep track of your mental butterfly and catch him at the point he flits from the flowers of thought into the garden of dreams.

Anyone who practises meditation will be more than aware of how difficult it is to remain present and aware among the constant chatter and distractions of the mind. Buddhists refer to this as the 'monkey mind' as, like our butterfly, the monkey is prone to jumping from tree to tree clutching wildly at anything around it, never satisfied. Catching the butterfly, like meditation, is a process of learning to calmly return your focus upon your goal, even when it has jumped temporarily out of control and in a direction away from your intentions.

There are many tricks that can be employed to help aid you in this process. LaBerge suggests counting yourself to sleep: 'One I'm dreaming, Two I'm Dreaming…' and so on, until eventually you find yourself aware that you are indeed dreaming. Others suggest a more meditative approach, focusing on your breathing, calmly returning your focus should it drift. Tibetan Dream Yoga suggests visualising a flame in a lotus flower or other esoteric symbols.

What matters here is not the mental ploy you use, but the intention and focus to remain present and aware, looking to catch that elusive moment when you transition between two worlds. For my 5-year-old self, the focus was upon a single question to which I'd continue to return: 'Is this a dream?' I would monitor my thoughts, distractions, feelings, etc. Each time anything of note passed through my mind, I'd ask myself 'Is this a dream?' Eventually, of course (conditions prevailing), the answer to the question would be 'Yes, this is all a dream!'

One common mistake for those attempting meditation or CTB is to try too hard. Consciousness, if you try to grasp at it, too often will simply become more erratic, flying faster and further out of reach in order to escape. The trick here is to let it do what it does naturally. Like a butterfly, let it dance between the flowers of thought as it wishes; as you do so, you will find that it rests more often, making it easier to observe. Simply keep aware of where it lands and continue to ask with each new mental experience 'Is this a dream?'

Of course, without the correct conditions, your mental alertness (brain chemistry) may be too sluggish to keep up with your observations. Or, if your timing is off, the dreams you are waiting for may be preceded by the void of NREM sleep, a void that is all but impenetrable. So, with these considerations in mind, the technique that is outlined below is designed to allow you to attempt your butterfly-catching with all three pillars of lucidity firmly in place.

1. Retire to bed. Go to bed at your normal time. Either set the intention to perform CTB should you awaken from a dream during the night, or alternatively follow the procedure outlined in the WBTB technique.

2. Upon wakening, establish your likely sleep stage. Should you have performed WBTB, continue to follow the WBTB technique and employ section 3 of CTB upon returning to bed. If, on the other hand, you've woken naturally during the night, establish which stage of sleep you have woken from. Should you have woken from a brief dream, remain still and, with your eyes closed, adjust your body position only minimally if required for comfort. If you feel your mental alertness is lacking, continue with the following suggestions, otherwise continue to stage 3. Should you have woken from NREM or at the end of a long dream, you will need to get out of bed and increase your mental alertness. Follow the suggestions outlined in the brain chemistry section of the three pillars. Once you feel your mental alertness has been improved, aim to return to sleep within 30-90 minutes of awakening, Follow the suggestions in the timing section of the three pillars to establish the best time to return to sleep.

3. Return to bed. You will now either be returning to bed, or remaining still, preparing to re-enter sleep. Ideally, you should be lying on your back, with your eyes closed. Allow yourself to relax back into sleep.

4. Observe your thoughts. Pay attention to your thoughts. Each time you find your mind wandering, rein your consciousness back towards awareness by asking 'Is this a dream?' Observe the thought and genuinely question if what you are experiencing can be classified as a dream. Alternative mental ploys for awareness can be used here (counting yourself to sleep, focus on breathing, etc.). However, the premise remains the same. You will need a light touch here, as too much awareness will result in insomnia, too little and consciousness will slip out of reach. Should you become distracted, either by an outside disturbance, physical discomfort or simply just getting lost in thought, do not chastise yourself, but merely return to the question and ask 'Is this a dream?' Assess if the distraction or sensation is genuinely external, or if the thoughts are still simply 'just thoughts'. Remind yourself that, at any point, any sensation, apparent distraction or thought could indeed be the start of a dream.

5. Continue step 4 until dreaming. Continue the mental exercise in step 4 until you enter REM. If the process seems to be taking too long, again do not feel disheartened; the longer you maintain this exercise, the higher the chance of success. Remind yourself that your brain wants to return to sleep, and all you need to do is wait for it to occur. If you truly feel you cannot return to sleep, you are perhaps trying a little too hard. Give your thoughts a longer rein on which to run, and lengthen the duration between asking 'Is this a dream?'

Should all have gone to plan, you should find yourself eventually slipping consciously into a dream. The exact experiences you'll have during this process can be tremendously varied, so it is impossible to say with any real certainty what you'll experience (however, we discussed certain possibilities earlier in the section on WILDs).

The second option is that you may have lost a grasp on consciousness during the procedure. Often in this case, should you have been motivated and alert, your mind will suddenly remember its task mid-dream, cueing a DILD. Should you fail, don't worry, as this is a learning process. You will have gathered important information and developed a greater understanding of how your mind works and where you need to be more vigilant. With practice and experience, you will soon find CTB to be a very useful practice and a great way in which to induce lucidity.

<u>Pros</u>

- Simple technique that can be combined with others to increase effectiveness.
- Can be performed spontaneously upon awakening from a dream or as part of a planned induction attempt.
- Requires no external tools to perform.
- Increases in effectiveness with practice.

<u>Cons</u>

- Can be difficult to achieve the desired balance. Practice may be required.
- Like many WILD techniques, it may not be suitable for those who have difficulty returning to sleep.

Electronic lucidity induction devices

To achieve: DILD
Pillar rating
Psychology: Low
Timing: High
Brain chemistry: Low

Anyone with a passing interest in lucid dreaming will most likely have stumbled across discussions on, or adverts for, electronic devices that are designed to help induce lucid dreams. More often than not, these come in the form of a (rather expensive) sleep mask containing circuitry that monitors your sleeping eye movements waiting for rapid eye movement (REM). Once REM is detected, these devices will give generally either a light or sound cue (normally flashing lights and beeping) that is designed to be incorporated into your dream and act as a signal to perform a reality test.

There are also a growing number of smartphone apps with similar aims in mind. Often, these are designed to monitor your sleeping movements and, upon establishing if you are likely to be dreaming or not, they then play a pre-recorded MP3 of your choice (which, again, is designed to be incorporated into your dream and cue lucidity).

In general, these apps are far less precise in judging REM sleep than the specifically designed sleep masks. The use of electronic lucidity induction devices should be considered as a technique in its own right. Whilst I am aware readers of this book are unlikely to have access to these devices, I believe it is important that the principles and effectiveness of them are understood, giving you a fighting chance of making an educated decision as to whether or not they are worth your investment.

The first ever lucid dream induction device was developed by Dr Keith Hearne in the early 1980s. Hearne's 'Dream Machine' is on display at the London Science Museum. Hearne's device was often featured in the media at the time, but a commercial device was never produced or made widely available. During this same era, albeit slightly later, the Lucidity Institute (founded by LaBerge) produced the DreamLight, another lucidity induction device.

The DreamLight was shortly replaced with the more compact and commercially viable NovaDreamer, which became the first widely distributed lucid dream induction device. The NovaDreamer was a reasonably popular device; however, for reasons unknown, it became unavailable for purchase sometime during the mid to late 90s. From the time it had been discontinued, up until the present (time of writing 2012), the standard line from its producers was that the NovaDreamer 2 was 'coming soon'. However, the NovaDreamer 2 is still currently unavailable for purchase, although apparently is being used during Dr LaBerge's Hawaiian Lucidity Retreat classes. Only time will tell if it will be publicly available.

The gap left in the market by the NovaDreamer spurred a good deal of independent companies to produce their own similar lucidity induction devices, many of which offer superior functionality and more regular updates to that of the original NovaDreamer. These are widely available, perhaps the best-known and most easily available being the REM Dreamer produced by Pawel Herchel of Poland.

The birth of smartphones and their 'apps for everything' is the latest chapter in the saga of electronic lucidity induction. There are many applications available that work on a similar principle, if somewhat limited, to that of the lucidity induction devices. However, the limitations of the sensor ability of smartphones means that they can only infer the likelihood of entering REM, rather than monitor it directly, rendering their functionality somewhat less precise. However, what they lack in precision is perhaps balanced by the vastly lower financial outlay required to purchase and experiment with them.

Whichever device is being used, the principle behind them is the same: to create a guaranteed external cue that will be incorporated into your dream (becoming a dreamsign) during REM itself. The logic is that this should remind you to reality test. These devices, by and large, are aiming at solving the issue of timing by producing a signal exactly when it should be required, during the dream itself.

This, however, is not without its problems. The first and most glaringly obvious issue is that the signal itself (the flashing lights or recorded MP3) can just as easily wake you as much as be incorporated into the dream. The second issue is that, even should the signal be incorporated into the dream, for example the flashing light of the sleep mask becoming the glinting of sun on a dream lake, the dreamer still has to recognise this signal for what it is and remember to perform their reality test.

Given that simply using an electronic induction device by no means prepares you either psychologically or has any impact upon your improving your brain chemistry (although the interruptions may improve alertness), this second point is very important to consider. What is vital to remember here is that these devices will require just as much psychological preparation and training as any other lucidity induction technique, and you will still need to train yourself to notice these electronic dream signs. They are absolutely not a quick fix solution for easy and effort-free lucid dreaming, regardless of what the adverts claim.

You may also want to consider that your dream world is already full of dreamsigns. Whilst these devices may guarantee a dreamsign of a certain type (light or sound-based) at the precise time of dreaming, the very act of dreaming itself already guarantees dreamsigns. Therefore, the addition of one more is unlikely to improve your chances, especially if you've not put in the training. If you have put in the training, and are already able to spot dreamsigns, then the question is, why would one more dreamsign in an environment full of them be required?

I believe the effectiveness of these devices, when they do work, is more likely to be due to the regular disturbance in one's sleep and the additional mental motivation that accompanies using one, rather than the addition of an external cue into the dreamworld itself.

It may seem that I am coming across as being rather negative here, and that perhaps I'm not a big fan of these kinds of devices. This is certainly not the case. I feel that all avenues of exploration into lucid dream induction are worthy of investigating. However, the above observations here are an attempt to counterbalance some of the often exaggerated claims in the promotional material that advertises such devices. I, myself, have experimented on and off with a NovaDreamer for quite some time and have enjoyed such experiments (though have found it to be of limited success). I am rather fond of these devices. However, the fondness is less related to their ability to induce lucid dreams and more an appreciation of their place in the history of lucid dream induction. However, it is worth bearing in mind that these devices have been available on the market in one form or another for around 30 years now. If the claims made about them were true, they would have almost certainly been rapidly integrated into popular society, with its constant search for new forms of entertainment, and this simply hasn't occurred.

Perhaps the greatest uses for these devices are as alarm clocks that are able to awaken you just as REM occurs. This would allow for a far more precisely-timed way to induce lucid dreams using the more familiar methods.

It's likely that these kinds of devices will come into their own and increase in effectiveness when combined with the use of supplements such as galantamine. Sufficient psychological training would still be required, but I can imagine that, with the combination of all three areas of the lucidity pillars in place, you could create a potent induction technique. However, such a technique would be utterly reliant upon external chemicals and devices, which seems at odds with some of lucid dreaming true benefits. For those who appreciate lucid dreaming for being a genuinely natural and free phenomenon, such a path would be counterproductive.

My advice to those who are interested in using these devices is to approach them with low expectations. If you're looking for a way in which to avoid the hard work involved in lucidity training, then you will be sorely disappointed (indeed, lucid dreaming is probably not for you at all). If, on the other hand, you have a good deal of expendable income and are interested in experimenting with the concept and owning a piece of lucid dreaming history, then these devices are interesting curiosity items that will certainly give you some unique sleep experiences.

Pros

- The ability to awaken you directly from the start of an REM phase.
- Possibility of disturbing your sleeping mind enough to improve its alertness.
- Guaranteed cue during REM.
- Devices may be made considerably more effective in combination with a supplement like galantamine.

Cons

- Devices are often expensive and do not live up to their claims.
- Reliance on an external device.
- Sensors are not always well-calibrated and can generate cues on false positives, causing excessively disturbed sleep. Also, being woken during the middle of a lucid dream by a badly timed cue is likely.
- Low success rate.

Partner Assisted Lucidity (PAL) Technique

To achieve: DILD
Pillar rating
Psychology: Medium/High
Timing: High
Brain chemistry: Medium/High

The Partner Assisted Lucidity technique (PAL) is, as the name suggests, a method that requires two participants (and also one of the few techniques in which the acronym hints at the procedure). This sets it distinctly aside from the majority of techniques that are performed alone. This requirement obviously imposes certain limitations as to who it can be used by and when it can be performed. However, regardless of this, it is an especially effective and enjoyable induction technique which can teach you a great deal about your own personal sleeping habits and gives you (rather uniquely among available techniques) the possibility of observing another person's dream from the outside. Consider it your own personal sleep laboratory.

This technique is ideal for those who are fortunate enough to share an interest in lucid dreaming with their partner, or for those with a close friend (or pal) with whom you are comfortable enough to sleep in each other's company. Its casual and intimate nature means it is ripe for experimentation and fun, allowing you to attempt all kinds of variations and experiments that you would otherwise find absolutely impossible alone.

Despite its seemingly obvious nature and high level of effectiveness, this technique seems oddly missing from a good deal of literature on lucidity and also the various lucidity enthusiast forums. Indeed, it is a technique I myself stumbled upon almost 20 years ago, purely by chance and simply out of curiosity and experimentation. I can only assume that the requirement for an interested bed partner has limited its usefulness, or restricted its independent discovery more often. It's certainly a shame that so few bed partners share an interest in lucid dreaming. Regardless of this, should your partner ever express an interest in lucid dreaming, this technique is simply the best and most immediate method for giving them a taste of what lucid dreaming is all about.

1. Daytime Practice. During your daily lives, decide upon a key phrase that you and your partner/friend will occasionally and randomly mention to each other, one that will cue you both to perform a reality test. 'Are you dreaming?' or 'You're dreaming' are possibly the simplest and best phrases to use for these purposes. Try to have fun with this. Turn it into a game. Regularly try and slip the phrase into conversation in an attempt to catch your partner out; should either of you miss your cue, then the other must inform them they have 'lost' and remind them to perform a reality test (don't forget to perform one yourself). Try to make this a regular part of your interactions, remembering always to both reality test when the phrase is mentioned in conversation. You could increase the stakes and each other's awareness by agreeing to some kind of forfeit or payment should either of you miss a cue (cooking dinner, buying the other a coffee, etc.).

2. Perform WBTB. When planning to use this induction technique, choose a day when you can both wake up early and where there is no need to rush (a lazy weekend is a good time). Obviously, choose a day you'll be sharing a bed. Follow the WBTB procedure of getting up after a minimum of five hours sleep but earlier than your usual wake time. Once you are both awake and have taken 30-90 minutes to improve your mental alertness, return to bed.

3. Choose an observer and sleeper. Upon returning to bed, it will be time to decide who will be sleeping and who will be observing. Remember to be fair and diplomatic here, for whoever sleeps first will become observer on the next attempt. The sleeper should aim to sleep on their back, so that their face (especially their eyes) is visible to the observer. The observer should ideally sit by the bed in such a way that they will cause minimal disturbance to the sleeper. Be sure to agree in advance any additional experiments or criteria that will be relevant (we'll discuss those after outlining the technique).

4. Sleeper sleeps, Observer observes. The sleeper should now return to sleep. The observer should carefully and silently observe the sleeper, waiting for the tell-tale signs of Rapid Eye Movement that signifies the initiation of dreaming.

5. Upon REM, observer starts cueing. Once the observer notices that the sleeper has entered REM, it is time to signal the sleeper. This can be performed in all manner of ways, but in its most basic form the observer simply repeats your prearranged reality test cue phrase 'Are you dreaming?' or 'You're dreaming' at short intervals. Start with a whisper and slowly increase volume as required. Should you notice your cues arousing the dreamer, simply stop and remain silent until it is clear that they are once again settled and back in REM. When settled, start cueing once again, being careful to avoid the volume that roused the sleeper on the previous occasion.

6. Wake the sleeper when REM ends. Once it is clear that the sleeper has finished their REM cycle, attempt to wake them as quickly as possible. Try to avoid being too abrupt as this may destroy their dream recall. The easiest way to do this is to repeat at increasing volume 'Wake up, what were you dreaming?' Repeat this until they awaken.

7. Discuss results. Discuss your results and observations with your partner, being sure to record the details of the dream. After this, if time permits, it will be time to swap roles and start the process once again.

As you can see, this can be a fascinating and fun way to explore the dreamworld together. The technique as outlined above is also open to all kinds of variations and additions. One idea is to have the observer film the sleeper; this gives the sleeper a unique insight into their own process of falling asleep, perhaps giving them useful data that will help their own future personal lucidity inductions. It may also be useful to decide upon a prearranged eye movement signal that will inform the observer to stop cueing; this needs to be simple and clear, such as the sleeper's eyes moving up-down-up-down-up-down to demonstrate they are lucid and no longer need to be cued.

Practise your signal whilst awake and with eyes closed. Let the observer watch so that they are prepared to know exactly what to look out for during REM. In addition to the vocal cue, you may wish to experiment with others, touch, scent, light - anything that takes your fancy. The key here is to have fun and be creative with your experiments. This can be a very effective method and offers a unique opportunity to collect data that would be impossible using other methods. If you are currently not in a position to give this technique a try, I'd highly recommend committing it to memory and attempting it at the next possible opportunity.

Pros

- Highly effective induction technique.
- Allows for unique experimentation and data collection opportunities.

Cons

- Requires a partner to perform.
- Observer may find the process slow-moving.

Anchor technique

To achieve: WILD, potential for DILD
Pillar rating
Psychology: Medium/High
Timing: Medium
Brain chemistry: Medium

The Anchor technique is a very simple addition to the WBTB technique designed to improve your chances at successfully achieving a WILD. Anchor is one of a large group of techniques that work synergistically with WBTB to increase the psychological focus during the returning to bed phase. Whilst primarily to be used alongside WBTB, Anchor could equally be used at any point where you believe REM to be imminent (such as during a nap, or returning to sleep after a short dream). The premise here is very simple and needn't be outlined in excessive detail. The pillar rating above is assessed assuming Anchor is used alongside WBTB.

The premise of Anchor is to create a mental connection to the waking world, something that your consciousness can focus upon whilst falling back into sleep. It is your 'anchor to awareness' so to speak. In practice, it is little more than choosing a piece of music to your tastes (something relatively calm and ideally without lyrics) that you will play on repeat as background music during the returning to bed stage of WBTB. Music has a fantastic ability to engage us mentally and to absorb our awareness, often helping keep mental chatter to a minimum.

When returning to bed, pay close attention to the music playing; tell yourself that it is your continued reminder to remain alert and aware. Simply let the music and sleep wash over you, attempting to remain aware of the music at all times. Look out for periods where you lose focus on the music, or perhaps even fail to notice hearing it at all; these are signs that sleep is drawing you in and that dreaming is close at hand. Should you lose focus, simply return your awareness to the music and remind yourself of your intention to recognise you are dreaming.

When Anchor is used successfully to induce a WILD, it is often accompanied by an unusual sensation of falling through a long tunnel, with the music becoming more distant as you fall. It's a very peculiar experience, but also fascinating and exhilarating.

That's about all there is to it. It's a simple and often effective technique if used with careful consideration towards the timing of your induction and with the practices designed to increase your mental alertness (brain chemistry).

Pros

- Very simple technique that is reasonably effective.
- Adds the required psychological element to WBTB that is otherwise lacking.

Cons

- May be unworkable if sharing a bed, or with easily-disturbed house-mates.

Impossible Movement Practice (IMP)

To achieve: WILD
Pillar rating
Psychology: Medium/High
Timing: Medium
Brain chemistry: Medium

The Impossible Movement Practice (IMP) is another simple method that is designed to work in tandem with WBTB. IMP is designed purely to aid the transition between waking and dreaming and, as such, is a technique for inducing WILDs only. Once again, it is to be initiated at the point of returning to bed during WBTB, but could also be used at the start of a nap or as a stand-alone technique should you have awoken and the chances of returning to REM be high. Again, the pillar rating is assuming WBTB has been used.

When entering a WILD, one of the first transitions you'll be likely to experience is the shift between your physical and dream body, or the mental reproduction of your physical body (with which you interact with the dream world). The focus of IMP is to expedite this transition, or at the very least to catch it happening. To do so, we need to shift our mental focus away from the physical and towards the mental. If conditions prevail, this can be a relatively easy process.

The procedure is simple and need not be laid out in distinct stages, as the working is somewhat organic. Essentially, once you have returned to bed and have assumed the position in which you are likely to fall asleep (ideally lying on your back), you need to establish any physical movements that would be impossible to perform in your current position. For example, should your hand be flat beneath your head, it would be physically impossible to form a clenched fist. There are countless variations possible here; you just have to decide which position you wish to lie in.

Subtle and easily imagined movements are best, hand movements are ideal; however, larger movements, such as the bending of your arms or legs, are simple enough to imagine to be effective. The best choices are those movements that are completely restricted, either by another part of your body, or the bed itself prohibiting the action. Movements that could be performed but would place your limbs in a slightly different position (such as when lying on your back, the bending of your leg could simply raise it off the bed) should be avoided; instead, choose only those that, if they were to occur, would truly be impossible (in our bent leg example, a suitable choice would be to imagine bending your leg at the knee only, where to do so would cause it to pass through the mattress). The key is to choose a movement that is simple to imagine. I find hand and finger movements are by far the easiest in this regard.

Once you have made your choice, you now need to continue to imagine the impossible movement repeated over and over. Put all of your concentration into this imagining and continue to repeat this process as you fall back to sleep. What you should eventually experience is that the imagined sensation suddenly shifts to a completely realistic and tangible tactile experience; it will really feel as if you have moved in this way.

Once this occurs, and the transition between your physical and dream body has happened, you are dreaming. It is now simply a matter of (leading with the body part that you have just moved) pulling yourself out of the dream representation of your bed. You will find yourself in dreamland, most likely a replica of the room in which you were sleeping. Be aware that the visual element of the dream may not yet be fully formed; however, do not worry, as this should shortly come into force. Also, be prepared to find it hard to convince yourself that you are truly dreaming; if in doubt, perform a reality test.

This simple technique can lead to such a smooth transition into the dream that it can really be very surprising. Its simplicity is also its strongest point, allowing you to use this method virtually anytime you find yourself in a position where returning to REM is likely. If you have difficulty performing the imagined movement, then during your waking hours it is worth taking a little time to practise similar bodily movements and to pay detailed attention to how they feel. This is especially useful if you tend to sleep in a regular position and your choice of impossible movement is likely to be the same very often.

Pros

- Very simple and effective WILD technique.
- Can be performed in a wide variety of pre-dream sleep scenarios (although WBTB is perhaps the best).
- Smooth transition between waking and dreaming can lead to very high level awareness in your resulting lucid dream.

Cons

- May be difficult to maintain the mental concentration required.
- Tactile imagining could be difficult for some, although generally most find this form of imagination much easier to perform than visualisations.

Familiar Scene Visualisation (FSV) Technique

To achieve: WILD
Pillar rating
Psychology: High
Timing: Medium
Brain chemistry: Medium

The Familiar Scene Visualisation technique (FSV) is yet another simple method designed to be used during a WBTB attempt and is aimed at inducing a WILD. As with the previous two techniques, it is to be initiated at the point of returning to bed during WBTB, but could also be used at the start of a nap or as a stand-alone technique should you have awoken and the chances of returning to REM be high. Again, the pillar rating is assuming WBTB has been used.

The concept underlying FSV is to aid the process of visualisation by choosing a scene that is already very familiar to you. You are once again attempting to create a smooth transition into the dreamworld, this time using the power of visualisation. By now, you should have a grasp of the principles involved in initiating a WILD; essentially, you're choosing some form of focus upon which to pin your consciousness, whilst letting the process of sleep and dreaming occur simultaneously. FSV is once again using this principle, whilst at the same time attempting to influence the scene in which you will arrive in the dream world.

The technique itself is the height of simplicity. The first stage is to choose any place you regularly frequent. This can be anywhere from your bedroom, hallway, garden, the path leading to your front door, any place that you are intimately familiar and see on a daily basis. Pay consideration to the kind of dream you'll most likely to be looking to initiate - do you want to start the dream indoors or out? I would suggest, for the sake of flexibility, to choose the path leading to your front door as your choice, as it will keep your options open. However, do choose whatever is easiest for you to remember and visualise.

Once you have made your choice, be sure to spend a little time during your waking hours studying this area, becoming aware of the sights, sounds, smells, and textures of the scene. Be sure, also, that whenever you pass through your chosen environment you perform a reality test. Also, during your spare time, practise visualising the scene in as vivid detail as you can muster. Practice over time will undoubtedly increase your skills of visualisation.

Once you are satisfied with your choice, and you feel you have sufficient skills in bringing this scene alive in your imagination, you are ready to attempt FSV. During your next WBTB session, or when returning to sleep when REM is imminent, start your visualisation. Imagine walking around your scene, focusing especially on the tactile sensations; run your hands against the imaginary walls or hedgerow, feel the ground against your feet. Try to bring every element of the scene alive in your mind's eye. All the while, tell yourself that soon you will be dreaming and you will recognise that you are dreaming.

The procedure from here on should be obvious. Continue this visualisation whilst you fall back to sleep. If you find your mind wandering, calmly but firmly reel it back into the visualisation. If all goes to plan, at some point during your imaginings you will notice that, suddenly, the scene will shift from mere imagination and have taken on the realism of reality. However, at this point you will be dreaming.

This is a very powerful WILD induction technique, but does require a good deal of mental concentration and decent visualisation skills. However, with practice, over time you will find both these areas become much easier, even natural. You will also find that your ability to create vivid visualisations will likely be in direct proportion to how close to the border of dreams you find yourself. The closer to dreaming, the easier you should find your imaginings.

Pros

- Very simple and effective WILD technique.
- Can be performed in a wide variety of pre-dream sleep scenarios (although WBTB is perhaps the best).
- Smooth transition between waking and dreaming can lead to a very high level awareness in your resulting lucid dream.

Cons

- May be difficult to maintain the mental concentration required.
- Skills in visualisation can take some time to master.

Supplements as a lucidity induction technique

To achieve: WILD, DILD
Pillar rating
Psychology: Zero/Low
Timing: Medium
Brain chemistry: High

Disclaimer: Should you wish to experiment with any of the supplements below, it is absolutely imperative that you discuss your plans prior to your attempt with your doctor or a trained medical professional. Your health and safety should always be your first priority. The information and advice on supplements throughout this book is for educational purposes only. I am not a medical professional and cannot guarantee the safety of such an approach. To be clear, I cannot advise or condone the use of any supplements without the express consent from a medical professional prior to any experimentation. Should the reader choose to experiment with these or other supplements, you do so entirely at your own risk.

Ever since lucid dreaming first became widely popular, enthusiasts have been attempting to improve their chances of successful induction by experimentation with various foods, vitamins, herbs, etc., generally with unsatisfying results. However, it wasn't until 2004, when news quickly spread of Dr Stephen LaBerge's application for a patent on Acetylcholinesterase inhibitors (AChEI) as a tool for inducing lucidity, that things really took off. News of the patent spurred a whole host of experimentation; small businesses selling these supplements popped up overnight and a good deal of data on their effectiveness started to appear in the community. Finally, lucid dreamers had a reliable chemical aid for lucid dreaming, and the use of supplements was now a serious and effective approach.

Skipping forward to the present day, these supplements have become a standard topic of discussion and experimentation among a sizeable portion of the dream community. It's fair to say the star of the show, the supplement that is the central focus of this revolution, is the AChEI by the name of galantamine (named after the plant from which it was first extracted, the Snow Drop, or 'Galanthus' from the Greek *gála* 'milk', ánthos 'flower'). The use of galantamine and its kin have most certainly become a firmly-established technique for inducing lucid dreams.

As we have covered earlier, galantamine inhibits the enzyme Acetylcholinesterase, which itself breaks down the neurotransmitter Acetylcholine (ACh). ACh levels are at their lowest during NREM and return to near waking levels during REM. Reduced levels of ACh are associated with poor memory, confusion, distraction, inability to think clearly, etc., essentially all the traits we associate with our usual non-lucid dreaming mind (and also the illness Alzheimer's, for which galantamine has long been used as a treatment).

It's safe to assume that, during REM, our levels of ACh, whilst higher than NREM, are usually likely still below those required for the level of mental clarity we experience whilst awake. This low level, combined with the very low levels during NREM, likely explain most of the amnesia and confusion associated with a normal night of sleep and dreaming. Galantamine essentially helps raise our ACh levels by preventing it from being broken down. This elevated level of ACh results in clearer, more rational, thinking and an improved memory, all traits required for lucidity.

Another important effect of increased ACh is its ability to prolong our time spent in REM. Of course, it almost goes without saying that extended periods spent dreaming are hugely beneficial to those interested in lucid dreaming. It is important to remind ourselves here that it is not galantamine itself directly producing these effects, but the already naturally present neurotransmitter ACh. Galantamine is simply, by proxy, creating an environment in which ACh levels can remain high.

This is a useful point to remember when considering the alternative of non-chemical induced methods for producing the same effects. Inducing lucidity isn't about adding chemicals that our body doesn't already have; rather, it is choosing or creating the correct brain chemistry environment in which to make our attempts. Galantamine is just one method for achieving this goal.

Galantamine is rarely used alone. Most commonly, it is combined with the supplement Choline, which is a precursor (one of the building blocks) to ACh. By ensuring our body has enough Choline with which to generate ACh, our chances of improving our mental environments are further improved. Choline supplements come in several different forms, but it's currently believed that Alpha-GPC is the most effective for our requirements.

There is a whole array of other supplements also used by those wishing to experiment along these lines. 5-HTP, the precursor to Serotonin, is also often used. If taken before retiring to bed, 5-HTP is believed to help suppress REM for the first half of the night; this creates an REM rebound effect for the later hours of sleep, when an induction attempt with galantamine will be made.

5-HTP, Nicotine, Choline, Piracetam, Mucuna Pruiens, Melatonin, Yohimbine and a growing list of other chemicals and supplements are all also used in combination or alone for their various effects, ranging from increasing confidence levels during a dream (Mucuna Pruiens), to helping combat the desensitisation that can occur with regular use of galantamine (Piracetam).

It's a huge topic and requires its own book to cover everything in detail. Fortunately, such a book already exists. Published by an old online acquaintance of mine, and fellow lucid dreaming enthusiast Thomas Yuschak, his wonderful book *Advanced Lucid Dreaming - The Power of Supplement*s, is absolutely vital reading for anyone who is curious about attempting this form of lucidity induction, or is simply interested in expanding their knowledge in this field. I cannot recommend it highly enough.

Despite the additional use of these other supplements, galantamine still remains the go-to supplement for such experiments. Galantamine is quickly absorbed by the body, reaching its peak plasma level in 60 minutes. However, once ingested it can take about 48 hours to completely leave your system. This rapid absorption means that, to use galantamine effectively, it must be taken shortly before a period of intense REM, so commonly it is taken after 5-6 hours of sleep before returning to bed, essentially as a chemical addition to the WBTB technique.

Taking galantamine at the start of your sleep cycle (when you first retire to bed) is counter-productive and very unlikely to aid in lucidity induction. More likely, this approach would result in either insomnia or restless sleep with little of the restorative NREM stages of sleep. Also, due to the long period it remains in your system (48 hours), desensitisation and tolerance issues are likely.

Regular daily use of galantamine is unwise. In practice, many who use this technique leave an absolute minimum of two days between attempts, though an interval of a week or longer is both the best and most effective practice. An effective dose of galantamine is between 4mg and 8mg. It is always advisable to start with the lower of the two doses, simply to avoid both wasting your money and putting needlessly high levels of the substance in your system. Therefore, 4mg should be sufficient. Taking more than 8mg is not advisable, as a dose over this amount makes no noticeable improvement on its effectiveness and is more likely to lead to tolerance, desensitisation, side effects and insomnia.

As is most likely clear, the use of supplements such as galantamine can be a complex process that requires a good deal of research before embarking upon. Under no circumstances should this approach be taken flippantly or without the required considerations for your health and safety. That said, it is undeniable that galantamine and the related supplements are powerful tools to aid the induction of high level lucidity.

However, whilst effective, there is also no reason to believe that these effects are unique to this form of induction alone. We can, albeit with more effort, produce similar beneficial brain chemistry environments through behavioural means. The question that is most pertinent to ask yourself is, Which do you value more, lucidity as a natural and free state of mind that requires a little effort? Or lucidity that may come easier but is reliant upon the availability of an external substance? Personally, I prefer to sit on the fence here, as I believe both approaches have their merits and disadvantages. Whilst supplement-induced lucidity may not be for everyone, it is certainly surely positive to have the option available.

Perhaps the greatest benefit that came with the discovery of chemicals such as galantamine has been to remind us that our brain chemistry is such a vital element in lucidity induction. We can now take this knowledge into account whenever we attempt lucidity, with or without the use of supplements. We must also remind ourselves that, whilst effective, galantamine alone will not produce lucidity, and still requires both timing and psychological training. There is no 'magic pill' for lucidity, which is most probably a good thing. Developing skills in lucid dreaming is not simply about the sole aim of achieving lucid dreams, but also the many more subtle benefits and skills that come with such training.

Supplements legality varies from country to country. Always check the legality of any supplement in your own country, especially when purchased from overseas. Desensitisation and tolerance are very real concerns and may require the use of other supplements or chemicals to counter these effects.

Pros

- Guaranteed to improve brain chemistry for increased chances of lucidity.
- Can lengthen time spent in REM.
- Reduces or eliminates need for behaviour attempts to improve alertness.
- Allows sleep researchers a quantifiable and reliable means to achieve lucidity.

Cons

- Reliance on an external chemical.
- Still requires good timing and psychological elements, is not a 'magic pill'.
- Creates a financial cost for lucid dreaming.
- Long-term use of the effects of galantamine for healthy individuals is still questionable, as most research has been focussed on the long-term effects of those suffering with Alzheimer's.
- Abuse or misuse could cause safety issues.

Cycle Adjustment Technique (CAT)

To achieve: DILD, WILD
Pillar rating
Psychology: Medium
Timing: Medium
Brain chemistry: High

The Cycle Adjustment Technique (CAT) is, as the name suggests, a technique that requires the adjustment of your sleep cycle in order to improve your chances of inducing lucidity. The principle is straightforward. As we near our usual time of waking, the chemistry of our brains begins to change, moving away from its inebriated sleeping state and towards that of waking alertness. If we can adjust our sleep cycle accordingly, we should be able to train our minds to enter this heightened state of alertness earlier than usual, and during a period when REM is likely.

I first shared CAT back in 2004 during an online discussion on the now defunct Lucidity Institute forum. This was at a time when supplements such as galantamine were very new on the scene and discussion of altered brain chemistry for inducing lucidity was a popular and heated subject. CAT, a method I had developed many years earlier and subsequently tested with members of my workshops, seemed to be a natural and effective alternative for improving the environment of our brain's chemistry without the use of such substances.

The outline of CAT as shared on those forums was incomplete, covering only the basic principles; this was mostly due to being written during a 6-month holiday retreat in India, whilst sitting in a power-cut-prone cyber cafe. The limited Internet time, combined with the appeal of returning to the beach, meant that my involvement in such online discussions was less comprehensive than I would have liked.

Regardless of this, and as is the nature of the Internet, the technique proved to be both popular and successful for those who tried it. It gradually took on a life of its own online, becoming widely shared in its basic, but incomplete, form. As such, it seems right to share CAT in its more complete form.

Cycle Adjustment Technique refers to a number of strategies for attempting to manipulate our sleep cycle in order to optimise the biochemical environment of REM in favour of mental alertness. Essentially, the technique is aimed towards those who already have a strict sleeping schedule and have difficulty using other techniques that require sleeping later than usual, such as those who have regular working hours and need to get up at the same time each day. CAT, like WBTB, is also open to adaptation and additions, meaning that it can be used in tandem with many of the various psychological techniques available.

The sleep cycle can be adjusted in several ways: the time in which you retire to bed, interruptions during the cycle, and the time which you wake. In many ways, WBTB could be considered a Cycle Adjustment Technique as it focusses on the interruption of the sleep cycle. CAT, as it is widely known, focusses on the adjustment of your waking time, although is not limited to this alone.

For convenience, let's look at the most well-known CAT strategy, after which we will discuss the logic and possible adaptations available.

1. (Optional) For one week (or more) retire to bed 90 minutes early. The first and optional stage of CAT is to increase the time you spend sleeping by 90 minutes. This is a precautionary measure for those who wish to use CAT without losing vital hours sleeping. If you choose to follow this option, you will be retiring to bed 90 minutes early throughout the entire technique.

2. For one week wake 90 minutes early. Whatever your usual wake time, for one week wake up 90 minutes earlier. This is the primary adjustment phase of your sleep cycle. The plan here is to train your mind to believe this new earlier wake time is now your standard time of waking. Should, by the end of the week, you find yourself struggling to wake at the earlier time, then continue this stage until you feel your sleep cycle has adjusted and that waking early feels natural. Remember, you will not be returning to bed, so simply go about your daily business as usual (enjoy the extra time!). It would also be advisable to develop the habit of performing regular intense reality tests during this extra 90 minutes.

3. Cycle between early waking and normal waking times. Once you have completed the week required to adjust your waking time, you will now be alternating daily between your regular waking time and the earlier waking time. It should hopefully be apparent that it is the days in which you wake at your regular time (sleeping later) in which lucidity will occur. Continue this practice until you find its effectiveness waning, in which case move to stage 4.

4. Occasionally repeat the adjustment phase (stage 2). It may be necessary to occasionally repeat the week-long adjustment phase (stage 2) to maintain the effectiveness of the method. Should you find the method becoming less effective, or you have had an unforeseen disturbance to your regular sleeping pattern, then this is a sign to return to stage 2.

As you can see, the plan here is to transform your normal waking time into a period of extra sleep. The additional sleep during this 'lie in' should also be accompanied by an increased mental acuity and awareness (as your brain believes it should have already woken), hopefully resulting in an improved chance of lucidity. An intense period of REM is also likely, possibly further intensified by a mild REM rebound effect due to the decreased sleep on the days you wake early (more so should you have skipped stage 1).

The concept is really very simple. Should you continue to sleep past the period in which your mind believes you should have woken, then the chemical environment of your brain should be much closer to that of waking, hopefully improving your reasoning and critical thinking abilities while dreaming.

You may find that, on the normal waking days, you will still naturally wake up at the earlier time. This is no problem at all and a great sign that your adjustments have been effective. On these days, I would advise choosing a WILD technique such as IMP and attempting to perform a WILD induction. Indeed, you may even wish to continue to set your alarm for the earlier time, even on your normal waking days, then simply return to sleep after a brief awakening, giving yourself a perfect chance to perform a WILD induction. I regularly use this adaptation of CAT and refer to it as WILD-CAT.

Of course, for any of this to be effective you do need to keep a rigid sleep cycle; any deviation from the plan will throw your sleep pattern off target, greatly reducing the effectiveness of the whole technique. Such a strict sleeping pattern isn't suitable for every lifestyle and, as this is also a technique that requires a considerable investment of time, it's very much worth establishing if you'll be able to stick to your schedule before starting out. For those to whom a regular sleep pattern is already a part of your daily life, then CAT should be relatively easy to incorporate into your life.

As I previously mentioned, CAT is open to experimentation. The technique as outlined above is a suggestion of just one possible strategy. Should you find the adjustment of 90 minutes to be too extreme, then feel free to experiment with a shorter time scale. Also, should you invest your time in using CAT, then please do try the WILD-CAT variation, as it can be an incredibly effective means for inducing WILDs. Whilst CAT is an involved technique that requires a degree of discipline, the rewards of regular high level lucid dreams can be well worth the effort.

Pros

- Ideal for those with regular sleep cycles, who struggle with finding the time for additional sleep sometimes required with other lucidity techniques.
- Easily combined with psychological induction techniques.
- A good way to enhance your brain chemistry to aid awareness during dreaming.

Cons

- Requires a strict sleeping pattern to remain effective.
- Not suitable for all lifestyles.
- Planning and determination make this a rather involved technique.

Techniques and beyond

Now we've come to the end of our journey through our selection of induction techniques. With the information we've covered, you should now have ample knowledge with which to become a proficient and regular lucid dreamer.

Of course, the methods outlined here are just the tip of the iceberg; the field of lucidity induction is a constantly evolving and growing area, with new methods being developed almost daily. It's safe to say that there are likely as many techniques as there are lucid dreamers, and it is ultimately up to you to discover the technique that works best for you. The sheer volume of information and ideas shared, especially in online communities, can be somewhat overwhelming at times; but, with your understanding of the principles underpinning the three pillars of lucidity, you will now be able to make a logical assessment of the likely effectiveness of any new techniques you come across.

You will also be in a position to invent and experiment with your own techniques or to make adaptations to those which already exist. Remember, becoming a lucid dreamer is a journey, a journey which requires dedication, creativity and motivation in equal parts. Do not be disheartened if your first attempts fall flat, nor should you throw in the towel too soon; many of the skills and training required for lucidity take a good deal of time and practice to become fully integrated into the person you are. As with learning any new skill, you will not become a virtuoso overnight; but should you throw yourself wholeheartedly into the subject, it really is only a matter of time before you, too, will eventually find that inducing a lucid dream becomes second nature. Indeed, you will most likely forget many of the difficulties you experienced in your early days.

That said, should you follow the advice given, especially that outlined in the bare essentials, it is likely that you will experience your first taste of lucidity within a very short period of time (depending on your level of motivation), often within as little as the first few weeks of your attempts. This 'beginner's luck' that many experience is an interesting quirk of the subject, the only danger it presents is in creating an overconfidence, possibly resulting in a reduced future effort. Be careful not to fall into this trap, as it could easily hinder your progress. Be thankful for this early glimpse of your destination, but treat it as fuel to motivate you to step up your efforts, not to lessen them.

As you follow the advice given here, you'll find that, over time, lucidity will become increasingly regular, your confidence in the dream world will increase, and your adventures and explorations grow in breadth and depth.

Your journey is only just beginning. It is one thing to learn how to play an instrument, but it is another thing entirely to play with a passion and a deep understanding of music. Eventually, you will, of course, reach a point where you will compose your own symphonies. Now that you are taking your first few steps in learning to play the subtle and enchanting instrument of your mind, your abilities will also grow. Eventually, as you progress, the symphonies of your dreams will soar, carrying you with them to worlds that never were, and to places you could truly only ever have dreamt of.

6

Awake in Dreamland

As we wander through the doorway of dreams, a new world opens before us. This is a world of wonder and enchantment, a place in which the myths and legends of old have been forged. We find ourselves in a familiar, yet strange, land. There are fewer rules here; the laws of physics (for example) do not apply, nor do the customs or expectations of society. But there *are* rules; certain constraints do still apply, be they purely the confines of neurology, or the limits imposed by the ever-flowing sands of time. Here, you will discover that you have powers unlike those in waking life, powers that allow you to shape this world according to your will. But you must still be careful, for this world and its inhabitants are, in the most fundamental way, part of you.

For those who have yet to experience your first taste of lucidity, you must be prepared for what is, in essence, a deeply profound event. To find yourself standing fully cognisant in another world, a world as tangible as the one in which you currently find yourself, can raise in you some of the deepest philosophical questions, questions that humanity has wrestled with since the dawn of time.

You must also be prepared for the immediate sense of excitement and shock you'll encounter. After all the preparation you will have put into arriving in dreamland, to suddenly find yourself actually there, combined with the sheer realism of the experience, can be quite overwhelming. Shortly, we'll be looking into ways to help control this excitement in order to avoid the common problem of shocking yourself awake.

There is, of course, no right or wrong way to explore the world of dreams. However, there are certain tricks and tips that have been hard won by previous explorers, methods that will save you falling into frustrating pitfalls that may have otherwise hindered your progress. We shall be covering these also.

Did I experience a lucid dream?

One of the most frequently asked questions by those new to lucid dreaming is whether or not the dream they have recently experienced can be classified as lucid or not. This is a perfectly reasonable question, and not surprising for those who are trying desperately to achieve lucidity (it's also common for those without an understanding of lucid dreaming to assume they've had the experience, when all they've really experienced is a very vivid dream). The answer to this question is really very simple: you will know with absolute certainty when you have experienced a lucid dream, not only after the experience but equally during it. However, there are degrees of lucidity, much as there are degrees of mental clarity during waking hours.

There is a tendency among those new to the subject, before having experienced their first lucid dream, to attempt to classify non-lucid dreams, or very low-level lucid dreams, as the full-blown experience. This is understandable, and a combination of impatience and overzealousness is normally the reason behind such claims. However, there is one simple way to judge whether your dream was indeed lucid and also the level of lucidity achieved. This can be summed up in a single sentence:

Lucidity can be best measured by the appropriateness of one's emotions, thoughts and behaviours to the knowledge that one is dreaming.

This statement is the very heart of assessing your level of lucidity. Let us take a look at a couple of examples to clarify this point. To do so, we shall look at three versions of the same dream, demonstrating the difference between the behaviour, thoughts and reactions of the dreamer when non-lucid, in low-level-lucidity, and with full lucidity.

Non-Lucid: I'm at a busy train station. I'm late to catch my train. The platform is full of people. I struggle to make my way through the crowd and worry about being late. The crowd bustle and hold me back. I start to panic that I'll miss my train.

Low-level lucidity: I'm at a busy train station. I'm late to catch my train. I notice a dreamsign and perform a reality test. I discover to my delight that I'm dreaming. The platform is full of people. 'No problem' I think to myself. 'I'm dreaming, so I can simply fly over these people and reach the train.' I fly quickly, rushing to reach my train, all the while worrying about missing it.

Full lucidity: I'm at a busy train station. I'm late to catch my train. I notice a dreamsign and perform a reality test. I discover, to my delight, that I'm dreaming. The platform is full of people. I realise that the need to rush to the train is no longer relevant because I don't need to get on the train. This is all just a dream and such concerns are just illusions. I consider what I would really like to experience now that I am conscious in dreamland, and proceed to follow my own wishes, not those of the dream.

As you can see, there is a distinct difference between the depth of realisation between a low-level and fully-lucid dream. Whilst both can still technically be classified as 'lucid', it is only the fully-lucid dream that offers the full extent of freedom, power and enjoyment of a true lucid dream. Simply being aware that an experience is a dream, is not the same as the deep understanding of what this knowledge implies.

To discover one is dreaming, only to then still respond as if the events and emotions of the dream are of genuine importance, is to have not fully understood the implication of your discovery. In a true and fully-lucid dream, you will have established and understood that all you experience is an illusion, that whatever dramas unfold around you are the creation of your mind and have no consequence outside of the dream or beyond what you give them. It is your choice to either choose to play along or to control the dream in the direction you wish.

It is this realisation that gives lucid dreamers the true freedom of dreamland. Lower-level lucid dreams, whilst still entertaining, can very easily slip back into a non-lucidity and can also be frustrating once you awaken, only to realise that you have not explored the experience to its full potential.

It is also important to note that the level of control you will be able to exert over the dream (such as ability to fly, to change scenery, etc.) is in direct proportion to your comprehension and awareness of the implications of knowing you are dreaming. The higher your awareness of what it means to be dreaming, the easier you will find it to control the dream world around you.

Increasing and maintaining awareness

To avoid falling into the trap of experiencing only low-level lucid dreams, there are several techniques that allow you to enhance your level of mental clarity during the dream. It is easy for both beginner and experienced lucid dreamer alike to forget to perform these simple tasks, but it is wise to really put the effort into making them the standard procedure for all of your lucid dreams. In doing so, you will ensure a smooth and enjoyable experience with the highest mental clarity and most potent dream control.

Ground yourself

Once you have established that you are dreaming (generally immediately after performing your reality test), take the time to take stock of your situation. Look around, appreciate the realism of the scenery before you; remind yourself that everything you are witnessing is a dream and, therefore, a construction of your own mind. Verbalise this thought, as there is something especially powerful about clarifying your thoughts in a dream by speaking them out loud (of course, I mean speaking out loud within the dream, not with your physical sleeping mouth). Tell yourself 'I am dreaming, what I am experiencing is all a product of my mind. Nothing is real. I cannot be hurt. I am in control.' Use your own words, and genuinely take the time to let this realisation sink in. Remember not to simply rush into the dream, as doing so will only lessen the experience in the long run. Consider this your 'pre-flight check', a task that must always be undertaken before you embark upon your adventures in dreamland. It is useful to also practice this behaviour during your waking hours, so that it becomes second nature before you find yourself required to perform it in a dream.

Verbalise your actions

This is a particularly useful technique for those that are new to lucid dreaming. However, there is no reason why it cannot be used by more experienced lucid dreamers, as it is a powerful way to remain fully present in the dream. As you go about your dream, regularly verbalise what you are doing, what you plan to do and continue to remind yourself that you are dreaming. This can be as simple as just talking out loud as you go. For example, 'I am walking down a dream street. I am looking for a dream character to talk with. I am dreaming and aware I am dreaming. None of this is real.'

The act of speaking out loud helps solidify your intentions, helps you remember your goals, and acts as a constant reminder to remain lucid. There is something uniquely powerful in the process of verbalising your thoughts in the dream world, perhaps because we so rarely do so in waking life. As such, the very act of continually speaking out loud is in itself enough to be a clear reminder that things are different here, that this is not the behaviour of the waking world and that you are dreaming.

Speculatively, it may also be that, by engaging the verbal centre of your brain, you are somehow helping maintain conscious awareness. Whatever the case, it simply works. Should you wish to have more fun with this process, singing your way around dreamland is equally as effective.

Detach yourself from intense emotions or situations

During almost every lucid dream there will be moments when your emotions or the events around you become so intense that you risk losing your mental clarity. This 'getting caught up in the dream' is one of the biggest dangers for lucid dreamers; they are moments when the chance of slipping back into the mental fog of a non-lucid dream is a very real risk. There are two options for countering this danger, both are forms of detachment.

The first is to simply 'physically' disengage from whatever activity you find yourself in. Depending on the circumstances, either step back, move away or simply stop fighting the tide of events. As you do so, it is also a good time to verbalise your lucidity once again. Say to yourself 'This is a dream, nothing is real. I cannot be hurt. I am in control.' If, for example, a dream character is hurling verbal abuse at you and you can feel your temper flaring, simply walk away, do not allow the emotion to take the reins of your mind. Or, perhaps you may be flying and suddenly find yourself struggling to remain aloft, or perhaps a panic sets in about falling; if so, cease your struggles, remind yourself that you're only dreaming and cannot be hurt in any way. Simply let yourself fall to the ground (more often than not, this thought alone will result in an instant reinstatement of your control).

Not all events are necessarily frightening or unpleasant, as intense positive experiences can also overwhelm your awareness. Should you feel that any experience is engaging you too strongly, you must simply detach yourself from it.

The second approach is that of mental detachment. This is a slightly more advanced practice and likely suitable only for more experienced lucid dreamers. Here, when you experience intense emotions or situations, the goal is to maintain a level of mental detachment whilst still being involved in the experience. You can use the same kinds of psychological exercises that are successful in waking life. We've all been told to 'count to ten' should we feel angry, and this advice works just as well in a lucid dream. Instead of simply counting, perhaps a revamped version such as 'One I am dreaming, nothing matters. Two I am dreaming, nothing matters…' is a good starting place.

The technique isn't limited to anger, either. The reality here is to just treat the dream as a dream, letting nothing reel you too far into the drama or intensity of the experience. However, as a world of caution, this is a subtle balancing act; to remain lucid, one needs to have a level of detachment, yet to remain dreaming one needs to maintain a level of engagement. Finding this balance is something that takes both time and experience, so with the knowledge that such equilibrium is both required and achievable, it will be your responsibility to find your own inner balance. Over time, you will find that such behaviour will become second nature.

The shock of realisation

As previously mentioned, for those new to lucidity (and, even occasionally, for more experienced lucid dreamers), the immediate shock of discovering yourself standing consciously in dreamland can be somewhat of a problem. The issue here is that such a high level of mental stimulation and emotion is likely (if not quickly put under control) to rapidly wake you. Such a frustrating experience of achieving lucidity, only to be immediately thrown back into the waking world, can be incredibly disheartening to beginners. Fortunately, such an event can be avoided with the correct preparation.

The first and foremost counterattack to this issue is developing a mental preparedness for the inevitability of experiencing a lucid dream. What is meant by this is simply to approach every night's sleep, every attempt at lucidity, with the expectation that you will be successful in achieving your goal. Assuming success will go some way to reducing the initial shock of lucidity (it will also help improve your motivation which, in turn, further increases your chances of success).

However, this alone may not be quite enough for some, so there are a few other additional tactics to help avoid shocking yourself awake. Whilst it may seem a somewhat obvious approach, the old British WW2 affirmation to 'Keep calm and carry on' is just as pertinent in the war against premature waking. Staying calm when becoming lucid is vital. We all have our own personal methods for relaxing in the face of shock or stress, so rather than patronise you with suggestions on how to do so, I'll simply ask you to do whatever you find works best for you. Of course, it would also be wise to develop and practise your skills for remaining calm in your waking hours also.

Another more concrete approach to this dilemma overlaps with the principles involved in increasing your awareness. The method for grounding yourself outlined previously in the section 'increasing alertness and awareness' is an ideal technique and focal point to move your mental energies away from the surprise of lucidity and onto practical matters.

Finally, the last tip when faced with the shock of lucidity is to physically engage with the environment. This is another technique which has several uses, so shortly we shall explore it further in the section on prolonging dreams, where it is of equal importance. In short, physically engaging with your dream environment using your sense of touch is a fantastic way to keep a firm grasp on dreaming and to avoid waking.

Controlling your dreams

The topic of dream control is one of the fundamental areas of lucid dreaming, often eliciting the most interest as it is the premise with which we interact with and build the dreams we wish to have. Control needn't be considered as purely a direct act of manipulation of the dreaming environment, or the events that take place.

Many lucid dreamers enjoy merely letting the dream play out on its own terms, barely altering the flow of events at all. However, even in such lucid dreams, the dreamer is exerting a mild form of control, if only a control of his or her dreaming body and the directions in which it moves, the interactions that it makes, or where it places its attention. Therefore, we really must conclude that every lucid dream is a process of conscious control, even those in which we temper our manipulation to a bare minimum.

At the other end of the spectrum are the extreme manipulations of the dreaming environment. These major changes in the dream world are normally the sales pitch for the less than savoury lucid dreaming products available; those that are aiming to make a quick buck rather than genuinely educate. They often oversell just how much control a lucid dreamer is likely to initially experience, for obvious reasons; the more astounding they can make lucid dreaming appear, the more of their products they can sell.

That said, extreme lucid dream control is absolutely possible, but it certainly is nowhere near as immediate as you may have been led to believe. The reality is very much that your skills with dream control often start out rather limited and grow with both experience and time. The more experienced the lucid dreamer generally, the more control they are likely to have achieved in their dream lives. In addition to this, the level of conscious awareness during the dream, combined with how developed the understanding of what it really means to be dreaming, are both directly in proportion to the level of control a dreamer will be able to exert. In other words, the more you understand that the entire experience is a mental construction, the more you can alter and play with it. On the flip side of this, and as is experienced nightly in non-lucid dreams, the more you believe the dream to be reality, the higher the chances that the dream will be in control of you.

To understand dream control, one first needs to understand the nature of dreaming itself, the foundations upon which dreams are built. As we have touched upon in earlier chapters, dreams are mental models, models that are untethered from the constraints that are placed upon them during waking hours by the information afforded by our senses. Without the stability of sensory data to hold these models in place, our minds whilst dreaming are able to 'free associate' and so what we are left with is a model of the world that is fluid, unstable and built from the thoughts, memories and beliefs of the dreamer.

In a non-lucid dream, this free association runs rampant, with our conscious mind playing a very small role and also making the incorrect assumption that what it experiences is reality. The dream becomes a series of feedback loops; dream events lead to expectations which, in turn, create the expected outcome of these events, and those outcomes lead to further expectations and so on. It is these feedback loops and associations that create the seeming story, the narrative of the dream.

Dreams have storylines because our minds already have within them a series of neatly structured associations (called schemas) covering just about everything you have ever experienced, including their relationships to other experiences. Using our past experiences as a template, our brains are endowed with a fantastic capacity for predicting the likely outcomes of events. Therefore, if given free rein in a world unhindered from the stability of reality, our predictions about what is likely to happen do indeed happen and, of course, the results of these predictions lead to further self-fulfilling predictions. So, the feedback loop continues, and the story is written.

Also (and for those of you asking why dreams can often be so bizarre), we must bear in mind that not all of our associations and expectations are logical, nor do they make a great deal of sense at first glance. For example, if you were to word associate (which is a form of association but with much less depth and fewer dimensions than that of dreaming), let's say starting with the word 'tree', your associations may go something like this: *tree, branch, fruit, apple, banana, monkey,* etc. However, let's say, for example, you have a good friend to whom you have given the nickname 'Monkey'; your associations at this point could go off on a completely and seemingly unrelated tangent. Let's say your friend is also a photographer, who enjoys photographing rainbows; thus, your associations may continue: *monkey, camera, rainbow, pot of gold, myth, leprechaun*.

So, as you can see, in a very short series of associative steps you have moved from a tree to a leprechaun. In such a way, the associations in dreams can flow in equally peculiar ways; so, to dream of a monkey dressed as a leprechaun photographing a rainbow-coloured apple may not be as bizarre as it first appears.

To add further surreal spanners into the works, it may well be that, during dreaming, our brains are also undergoing some kind of process to integrate new information into existing schemas. Or perhaps they are engaging old and rarely used neural pathways (and their schemas) in such a way as to keep the data contained within them alive. Such processes may throw further unusual elements into the dreaming mix.

In essence, our dreams are built upon our lifetime of accumulated knowledge about the world we inhabit and our expectations for likely or possible outcomes to the events in which we find ourselves. In lucid dreams, the process is exactly the same. However, we have one piece of information that allows us to break the cycle of expectation, or at least to be able to focus the direction of its flow. The information I am referring to is the knowledge that what we are experiencing is not the waking world, that the rules that apply to the real world are no longer valid here. It's such a simple piece of information that it could almost be mistaken for being trivial; however, like an onion, there are multiple layers to this understanding, with each layer taking you to a deeper comprehension of its meaning and a more profound ability to transform your dreaming experience.

The simplest grasp of this concept allows us to use our lucid dreams to give us the freedom to escape social conventions, the (more obvious) rules of physics and the consequences of our actions. Examples of this are behaviours such as flying (gravity is an expectation that no longer needs apply), kissing a stranger, walking through walls, crushing or breaking expensive items, dancing or singing in public, breathing underwater, etc.

Knowing that we are dreaming and that the obvious rules of the waking world no longer apply is where most lucid dreamers first express their control. Generally, the scope of this level of understanding is very broad and an area for which many lucid dreamers can spend years, if not their entire lifetime, exploring. There are limitations here, though. Whilst offering a much wider scope of freedom than waking life, certain more ingrained assumptions and expectations can limit the dreamer from experiencing the more complicated and impressive aspects of dream control.

As an example, let's look at a very simple procedure in more depth.

Imagine you find yourself lucid, standing in the hallway of your home. You wish to get outside, ideally to a completely different environment. Whilst you are aware that the dreamworld is an illusion, you may still walk (or fly) down the hallway and open the door; or, perhaps if you're thinking a little deeper, you may skip opening the door and walk straight through it instead. However, in both examples, you are expressing an assumption, or an expectation, that there is an 'outside' that you need to physically move yourself towards to experience.

This is an absolutely fair assessment, considering that, for the majority of life, you have lived in the waking world where this is indeed a concrete fact. However, here in dreamland, there are no physical places to visit, there is absolutely no physical distance between you and anywhere else in 'the dream universe'. All there ever is in dreamland is the current moment and the immediate environment as it expresses itself. When you walk through the hallway, you are not moving, you are not getting 'closer' to the outside; you are simply morphing[2] through a series of expected occurrences that express themselves in the moment with the appearance of walking down a hallway (much in the same way that the images on a TV screen do not move, but are simply a rapid change of frames all occurring on the same flat screen).

When you find yourself 'outdoors', you are no more outside than you were indoors a moment ago. All that has happened is that your immediate environment has transformed, morphed around you, in such a way to create the illusion of the smooth and logical transition of walking down a hallway and out into the open. You could have just as easily immediately transformed your environment to that of the outside, or any other scene for that matter. Equally, you could have stood still and moved the environment around you, rather than you through the environment. Also, simply making the entire building vanish is another option, as is teleportation. However, because of the deeply ingrained belief that physical movement is required to take you from one place to another, and the equally as persistent belief that there is distance between two places, you have limited your dream control to a set of rules that have no need to limit your experiences in dreamland.

There are millions of other such assumptions that are so deeply ingrained in our psyche that we take them for granted. The more obvious are those such as our gender, age, even species. Less obvious are those things such as

2 Morphing is a very apt word to use here, related to the word 'Morpheus' who was the Greek God of dreams. Indeed, the name Morpheus itself means 'shaper of dreams'. It's perhaps a useful reminder that the control and traversing of the dream environment is a process of shaping, rather than 'physically' moving.

the direction of time (whilst our brain, dreaming or not, does still exist in a world that requires our continued movement in one direction through time, the experience of the dream needn't move in a linear fashion, nor should it be limited to one period in history), the use of verbal language (we needn't 'talk' to dream characters, we can equally simply communicate telepathically - after all, you and your dream characters are sharing the same brain!), or requiring a physical body (again, there is no need for a body in dreamland, it is simply a convention we are used to).

Even deeper still, we can start to get to a level of philosophical deconstruction that can really start to boggle your mind. For example, are the thoughts we experience in a dream genuine, meaningful thoughts, as real as those of waking? Or are they simply dreamt thoughts? Are the emotions we feel in dreams real?

As you can see, our human minds are full to the brim with assumptions, rules and expectations about what is real. None of these need necessarily apply to the world of dreams. How far you wish to explore the notion of the insubstantial nature of dreams, and explore deprogramming yourself from your deeper assumptions about reality, is up to you. However, doing so will greatly increase your understanding of dream control and help you break down some of the psychological restrictions that may stand in your way of achieving certain dream goals.

Yes, you can experience a distant galaxy, or travel back in time. No, you do not need to move a muscle to get there. No effort is required on the part of the dreamer. All you need to do is to genuinely expect and believe such things to be possible (and this is the hard part, which takes a lot of practice and rewriting of your mental programming).

There are tricks to speed up the process of developing dream control long before we develop the philosophical mindset with which to approach dreaming. Essentially, most of these are 'mind hacks' and use the concept of reframing our expectations or the dream experience itself into something we find easier to believe possible. If nothing else, remember:

Expectation, or belief, is the key to controlling your dreams.

Let's look at a few different techniques that are commonly used for controlling the dreamscape.

Wishing/Magic

This is perhaps the most basic of all dream control techniques. Unfortunately, it is also the most unreliable for the beginner. The process is to simply attempt to wish or magically transform the dream to your will. Here, once again, expectation is king; unless you truly believe that what you are doing is possible, the chances are the results of your wishing/magic will be the same results as if you performed this action in the waking world. Whilst a basic technique, ironically, it is also the technique that is used most effectively by advanced lucid dreamers, those whom (as we have previously discussed) have developed a genuine deep understanding of the malleability and nature of the dreamworld. This said, many new lucid dreamers do find simply wishing to be successful, so it is absolutely worth attempting.

Reframing

Reframing is one of the most potent mind hack techniques for dream control. Essentially, what you are aiming to do is to alter your view of the dream away from the default assumption that it is operating within the same, or similar, rules as the waking world (whilst we all understand, on an intellectual level, that the rules of dreams really need have no relation to the waking world, it is such a profoundly ingrained habit, being our default assumption that 'all realities are the same', that finding ways around this is a useful place to start). How we go about this will vary greatly depending on the interests and beliefs of the individual. Those of you who are science fiction, fantasy, or computer gaming fans have somewhat of a head start to others in this regards. It's not the easiest process to explain, so perhaps the best place to start is with an example.

As a teenager, I was a big fan of the TV series *Star Trek: The Next Generation* which, other than developing in me a fondness for Earl Grey tea, also had a positive side effect on my lucid dream control. Those of you who are familiar with the series will be well aware that, in this particular science fiction show, the *Starship Enterprise*, which was the primary setting for the show, had what was called a 'holodeck'. For those of you who are unaware of what this is, let me explain.

The holodeck was a room on board the *Starship* in which crewmembers would be able to create realistic virtual representations of any environment, people, or period in time that they wished. So convincing were these virtual realities, that entire episodes of the show were often set occurring purely on board the holodeck. In short, it was a plot device for exploring the concept of 'what is real?' It was also probably intended to give the writers a little more freedom with settings.

Anyway, as you may have already guessed, a holodeck experience was essentially a fictional computerised version of a lucid dream. In the show, the users of the holodeck were able to manipulate the environment in any way by simply speaking commands to the ship's computer. For example, when walking down a virtual street the user could say 'Computer, pause', in which case the scenery and all its characters would freeze. Or, should they wish, they could say 'Computer, generate Sherlock Holmes' drawing room, complete with butler' and suddenly the scene around them would change to their request.

Of course, as a teenage boy with an interest in lucid dreaming, at the time this was absolutely tantalising stuff. It occurred to me that lucid dreaming, being a natural version of the holodeck, should offer the same level of control. So, I set myself the goal to treat my next lucid dream as if it were taking place in a holodeck.

Now, it may be that our subconscious minds are less picky between reality and fiction than we are aware, and that even experiences seen in a fictional TV show may go some way to convincing our minds that such events are possible. Whatever the case, during my next lucid dream I dutifully made commands such as 'Computer, freeze programme' and, indeed, the scenery around me froze. Next, I tried 'Computer, generate a beach scene' and yes, just like in the TV show (with the same visual transitions also) the scene changed.

What I had done was reframed the lucid dream and convinced my mind that I was experiencing a holodeck, rather than its usual assumption of a waking reality clone. I'd developed in my mind the ability to control the lucid dream in profound and extreme ways with just a voice command. Of course, without knowing it, I'd always had the potential for this level of dream control, I just needed a way to convince my mind that it was possible. I had managed to do by this by unwittingly rewriting my own inner expectations. (For the record, up until this discovery my level of lucid dream control had been relatively high, but I'd regularly come up against situations where I would find it hard to convince my mind that what I was attempting were possible. As such, I'd be frustrated when this inner doubt influenced the outcome, when essentially the expectation of failure won out.)

As you can hopefully gather from this example, you do not have to be a *Star Trek* fan to achieve the same outcome. Whatever fiction you find yourself drawn to, be it film, TV, gaming, or reading, look out for technologies, belief systems or magical abilities within them that you could potentially use in your own lucid dreams. All you are trying to do here is to give your brain an excuse for why your attempted dream control and manipulations will work. The holodeck was perfect, as it was such a close match to the lucid dreaming experience, and the ability to simply verbalise commands made it so much more practical.

However, the power behind all of this was that, as a teenager, I genuinely bought into the reality of the show; it almost felt as if these characters and their world were real. It was that belief that was the force behind the technique.

There are, of course, alternatives to fiction for building a reframing technique around. Throughout our lives we use technologies, software, etc., that allow us to quickly and consistently alter various media. For example, those of you who regularly use video or digital photo editing software will already have a mental framework in which certain commands perform certain tasks. These can be used to reframe your approach to the dreamworld. All you have to do, in this case, is to attempt to use variations on the control framework you are already familiar with, only in the dream world itself; but again, do so in such a way that you can find the idea plausible.

A very simple example of this would be to imagine the dream you are experiencing to be a video recording on a very realistic projector. Simply believe that you can fast forward, rewind, pause the 'video' of the dream, just as you can during your experience with waking world video editing software (or even a DVD player). If you believe it will work, then it shall. The trick is simply to find whatever framework is most convincing to your own mind.

In the simplest terms, reframing is viewing the dream world within a new mental framework, one in which your attempts at control are more believable, where they make more sense to you. There is a good deal of room to experiment here, and what works for each individual can be very different. As you progress and become successful with reframing, you will eventually find that you no longer require the process. Your belief in the malleability of the dream world will have been proven on enough occasions that you will have instilled in yourself a deeper understanding of the nature of dreams, and a belief in your control of them.

Behind closed doors

Another fantastic technique that is especially useful for beginners is to use your own expectations to manipulate that which is unseen. In dreamland (and quite unlike our waking experience), that which isn't seen, simply does not exist. In other words, what lies behind a closed door is just empty potential - there really is absolutely nothing there. When you open the door, the only reason you are often faced with what you assume you'll see is simply because you expected to see it. In fact, the same applies for everything that is out of your field of vision. There is no world behind you in a dream; all that 'exists' in dreamland is whatever falls in your immediate field of view, within your current perception.

Once you understand this principle, you are imbued with the knowledge that anything can lie behind a closed door, anything can be behind you. This understanding gives you the power to use your expectations to transform the dream world. By controlling using your beliefs, you can create whatever you wish in these empty spaces of potential.

With this in mind, should you wish to visit a completely new scene, or to conjure a specific character into your dream, all you need do is to genuinely believe that they (or it) are somewhere within your immediate vicinity, but currently out of view. Closed doors are clearly ideal for this purpose.

Experiment with this the next time you find yourself in a lucid dream. Remind yourself that the door you see before you is not the same doorway you would experience in waking life (should it be familiar), and that absolutely anything you wish could be behind it. Choose where you would like it to lead, or whom you would like to discover behind it. If your expectation is strong enough, and you have truly grasped that this is possible, then you will discover exactly what you intend. Equally, remember the same can be true for anything that is out of your immediate perception. If you want someone to appear, just believe they are already standing behind you, then just simply turn around. If you genuinely expect them, then they will be there.

To reiterate, all that exists in the dream world are your immediate perceptions. Other than this, there are no stable objects; indeed, there isn't even a ‘world’ to speak of at all. If you can break the mental habit of assuming that objects, places or even the world itself have an independent persistence beyond your experience of them, then you can start to set yourself free from the limitations of your own ingrained assumptions dictating the direction of your dreams. In the dreamscape, every doorway you encounter is potentially a portal leading to anywhere or anyone you can imagine.

Schema linking

As we have already discussed, dreams are built upon associations. A useful technique, especially for those who are initially struggling with using the power of expectation, is to manipulate the dream through a more subtle process of association. The trick here, when attempting to manifest a goal within the dream, is to look for aspects of the dream that are already somehow linked to our desired outcome, and then to place our focus upon them. Such connections can at first appear a little difficult to make, but generally we can always find some part of the dreamscape that is at least vaguely related to our desired outcome. The reason for doing so is to attempt to tilt the balance of the dream in the direction of our goal, to create associations which will hopefully act as seeds from which our desired outcome will grow. Let’s look at an example to help clarify this concept.

Imagine that your dream goal is to talk to an old friend, someone you have not seen in a long time. You find yourself lucid, yet all of your attempts at more direct manipulations seem to be failing. Let’s assume that the scene in which you find yourself is that of a street in a busy town. The task is to look for anything in the dreamscape that has an association with your friend.

A good place to start would be to look at the crowd around you; try and find any dream character that shares a vague resemblance to this friend. A particularly good method is to look out for those characters with their backs facing you, as generally it’s much easier to find someone who has a similar appearance from behind (for the obvious reason that there are simply less distinguishing characteristics at this angle). In this example, once you’ve found a suitable character, you could simply start calling your friend’s name. Should you have chosen a close enough resemblance, it is likely that the combination of your association and belief will transform the character and, as they turn around, you will find they have indeed become the friend you were trying to invoke.

Let's look at a slightly less ideal scenario. Assume the dream environment is empty, that you do not have the luxury of dream characters to work with. In this case, you will need to look for associations in the environment. Is there a particular cafe, shop or social area where, during your waking life, you would be likely to run into your friend? If so, head in its direction. At this point you will need to perform another little mental trick; concoct a storyline, a little white lie, to your subconscious. Tell yourself that you'd forgotten that you had arranged to meet your acquaintance there. Really try and act as if you believe what you are saying; play the part putting on your best Oscar winning performance.

What you're attempting to achieve is essentially to fool yourself, so really get into the role. Again, if the association is appropriate and you've done a good job at playing your part, you will greatly increase the chances of meeting your friend once you arrive at your destination. If you are still having trouble at this point, try using a more direct dream manipulation (such as the above doorway technique), as these methods are often more prone to success once your dreamscape is more closely associated with the goal.

If the dreamscape in which you find yourself has little in the way of suitable environments to work with, you may want to make an even more vague association. Look around the dream, searching for anything whatsoever that could in some sense remind you of your companion. Consider their interests, personality traits, clothing or any other pertinent details, then search for anything in the dream world that shares a link, however subtle, to your friend.

For example, perhaps they are a sports fan and you notice a tennis ball amongst a pile of items. If so, then be sure to pick up the ball and try to conjure a memory of when you may have seen your friend playing tennis. Or maybe you spent time with them whilst they watched a televised game? Really try and make any mental association you can find. Continue around the dream, looking for any other props, places or people that could also help aid your connection. Once you feel that you've found several links relating to your friend, then it is once again a good time to attempt a more direct dream control technique.

Of course, this kind of schema linking, or dream manipulation through association, is not limited to just the appearance of specific dream characters. Every concept in our minds can be linked to any other, even if only tenuously. All we are trying to achieve here is to focus our attention only on the areas of the dream that remind us of our goal. In doing so, we are giving the process of expectation (which, as we have learnt, is the foundation upon which the dream is built) a chance to work with and develop upon these themes. The more we gently guide our dreams in the directions we wish, the higher the chances we can use the more direct methods of dream control effectively.

Solving dream control problems

Should you ever find yourself genuinely struggling with your ability to control the dream, the most probable cause is likely to be a diminished level of lucid awareness. As we've discussed earlier, there is a world of difference between simply knowing that you are dreaming, and grasping the full implications of this knowledge. Without this grasp, you may find yourself in the odd position of believing that 'I am dreaming', whilst treating the dream world around you as if it were something other than a dream.

The experience of a lucid dream is shockingly convincing and the levels of detail and realism are truly phenomenal. No wonder, then, we find it so difficult to convince ourselves that the world we are experiencing isn't just as solid and real as that of our waking experience. However, the knowledge of its insubstantial nature is vital for our ability to control it.The very first thing to do, should you be struggling to control your dream, is to ground yourself. You can use exactly the same procedure outlined in the section on increasing and maintaining awareness. All you need to do is simply allow the realisation of the situation you find yourself in fully sink in. It is useful to take regular pit stops during a lucid dream to allow yourself a moment of reflection and awareness. Doing so maintains your own mental alertness and the understanding that there is nothing other than your own beliefs and expectations standing between you and your dream goals. However, even the most experienced lucid dreamers will admit that there are occasions in which the dream simply doesn't seem to want to play along, no matter how aware we may believe ourselves to be. We can only speculate why this may be the case. Perhaps we have come up against some kind of neurological limitation? Or maybe the process behind dreaming requires us to dream of a particular series of events? It may even be a case of hiding a bruised ego? Perhaps us, more experienced, dreamers are slightly ashamed to admit that, on occasion, we may not be quite as aware as we should have been, and to hide our shame we instead blame the dream rather than ourselves for our lack of control.

Regardless of the reasons, there may be occasions when you will need to temporarily give up on a particular dream goal or attempt at control. This needn't be for long; perhaps return in a minute or two and try again, or maybe simply wait until your next lucid dream. However long you decide to wait, you may find that it is simply a better option than risking frustrating (and possibly waking) yourself. Personally, I believe that in such moments when our dreams refuse to budge, we are experiencing a case of expectation reinforcement. The more we attempt something, only to discover it fails, the more likely it is for it to fail the next time we make an attempt, creating a vicious circle. This is exactly why taking time away can be beneficial.

Another option would be to attempt the same goal or control with a different approach. For example, if you're struggling to walk through a wall, try instead walking through it backwards. Or, if you're having problems with flying, try swimming through the air (which is an example of reframing). As with waking life, sometimes all you need to do is simply take a break from a problem, or approach it from a new angle.

Prolonging the dream

However much power we develop in the dream world, the sands of time will always remain a concern. Whether we like it or not, a period of REM can only ever last so long. In practice, lucid dreams can last anywhere from a few seconds to as long as several hours (realistically, few people experience dreams that last longer than an hour and a half - or, perhaps if they are particularly lucky, maybe two hours; more often than not, the duration of a dream falls somewhere between 5 to 30 minutes in length). Various factors come into play, one of the most prominent being REM rebound.

As we have discussed, REM rebound is the process in which, should your body have been deprived of REM sleep the previous night, or even in the early half of the current night's sleep (as can be the case if one has been drinking alcohol before sleep), then it will attempt to redress this balance by increasing the amount of time spent in REM once the opportunity arises. As such, REM rebound can be a powerful way to influence the amount of time you will spend dreaming. However, the process of creating rebound the natural way is a little too unpleasant for most, as obviously you are required to disturb or cut short your sleep on the previous night to create the effect.

Rebound can also be induced through artificial means, as mentioned alcohol being a familiar example (although I would strongly suggest against developing a drinking habit to induce REM rebound). A method used by some is to take the supplement 5-HTP which, being the precursor to the neurotransmitter serotonin, can help suppress REM during the earlier half of the night whilst, at the same time, promoting the deeper stages of sleep (for the record, those who would prefer to avoid taking supplements, food such as bananas, papayas and dates all increase the ratio of tryptophan to phenylalanine and leucine, which can also increase our natural levels of serotonin). Such supplements and foods must be eaten before sleep to be effective.

In the case of 5-HTP (and likely also with the foods previously mentioned), what can supposedly be achieved is a reshaping of the pattern of the sleep cycle. In a normal pattern, NREM is dominant in the early part of the night, but still with the occurrence of REM, followed by the reversal in the latter half of the night (REM dominance, but still with NREM). Instead, during the first half of the night, when our serotonin levels are high, we will experience only NREM sleep. Once our serotonin levels have dropped (roughly after 4-5 hours), then the REM rebound effect occurs, and the majority of our sleep will be REM.

It's certainly an interesting theory, although still somewhat in the speculative stages. However, I see no harm in attempting eating a few bananas and dates before sleep in an attempt to experiment with their effectiveness.

Other factors, which are sadly almost completely out of our control, are those natural disturbances in our sleep. Outside noises, a fidgeting bed partner, etc., can all be enough of a distraction to wake us in the middle of a lucid dream. The only real way to deal with these issues are those methods mentioned in earlier chapters, such as the use of earplugs, a sleeping mask, or simply only making attempts at lucidity when we know we'll be alone in bed.

The most powerful method for prolonging a dream is the behaviour we exhibit whilst in the dream itself. There are several popular techniques among lucid dreamers for attempting to prolong the dream, all of which share one essential factor: to engage the dream with as many of your senses, especially the tactile sense, as possible. Techniques include behaviours such as spinning around, rubbing one's hands together, stamping your feet, touching your body or the environment surrounding you - in other words, really using any method to completely focus on the experience of dreaming, rather than allowing your mind to focus on your sleeping physical body.

The logic here is to create a 'sensory overload' within the dreamworld, making the experience as intense as possible so that, by comparison, the relatively dull input from your sleeping body pales in comparison. Of course, such behaviours are initiated within the dream (and with the dream body) when the dreamer believes that waking is imminent, normally through signs such as the visual aspects of the dream fading. This tends to exhibit itself as the visual aspect of the dream taking on a less tangible quality, either becoming blurred or even cartoon-like in appearance. Personally, I favour the hand-rubbing and spinning techniques as they can be easily performed at a moment's notice.

An interesting point to note is that, even after the visual element of the dream has faded, often the physical and tactile elements remain. So, by 'feeling your way around the dream' you can often remain dreaming long enough for the visual element to re-establish itself.

Essentially, should you feel your dream is coming to an end, come out kicking and screaming, literally. Engage in the dream with all your senses, touch, grab, feel the environment; shout, sing or scream, so that your dream ears are full of these dream sounds. Look at interesting and vivid scenery - put your full focus onto it. Deeply breathe in the dream 'air', notice the smells and tastes in the environment. Also, and this is very important, *expect* this behaviour to work. *Believe* you will remain in the dream.

One final point of special importance is the experience of false awakenings. Often, when a dreamer is attempting to remain in the dream, and believes they are waking, they do indeed succeed in maintaining the dream; however, their doubts may manifest in such a way that the dream transforms into a false awakening. This can be a very convincing experience, so be sure that, once you believe you have woken, to make absolutely sure that what you are now experiencing is indeed reality, and not a false awakening. Always, always perform a reality test once you have woken from a lucid dream, especially those in which you've attempted to prolong. Never simply assume that you have woken, as the dream may simply have changed form.

Waking at will

For most lucid dreamers, the idea of being able to wake up at will is rarely going to be of much use, as more often than not the battle is not waking up, but staying asleep. However, there are a few occasions in which it may be beneficial. The first and most obvious is when you find yourself in a particularly unpleasant dream, especially one in which you find yourself with an insufficient level of control and you are unable to escape the situation. This is incredibly rare, and more often than not the healthiest course of action is to attempt to improve your dream control (by methods such as grounding yourself) and to simply face your fears. However, should you genuinely wish to just escape back to the safety of your bed, it is possible.

A second reason for wanting to awaken at will is when you have achieved what you have set out to do in your dream, and wish to wake, so that you can record the details of the dream whilst they are still clear in your mind (and avoid potentially falling into NREM and losing these memories). This is especially relevant for those who are using lucidity to perform specific experiments, when the specific details of the results are more important than the duration of the dream.

In essence, in order to awaken on command, the process is the exact opposite of that which has been previously discussed regarding prolonging a dream. Instead of engaging with the dream, you will be actively attempting to disengage your senses and emotions from the environment, and reminding yourself that your true body lies asleep in your bed. The best approach here is to simply stop doing whatever you are doing, fix your attention on a single and unimportant area of the dream (or even just close your eyes), stop moving, or avoid interacting with the dream altogether. All the while, you will also be reminding yourself that you are shortly going to awaken in your bed.

Another popular tactic is to 'fall asleep in the dream', which is exactly as it sounds. Lie on the dream floor and follow the usual process you would undergo as you prepare to sleep. This can occasionally have the odd side effect whereby, rather than waking, you instead create a 'dream within a dream'; essentially, you 'fall asleep' in the dream, only to find yourself in yet another. However, the most likely scenario is that you will genuinely awaken. Again, there is the risk here of experiencing a false awakening, so be sure, once you believe you have awoken, to perform a reality test. Should you find yourself in another dream, continue the process of withdrawal from the experience until you do indeed wake up. A final tactic, which we've already covered in the section on sleep paralysis, is simply to hold your breath within the dream. As our dreamt rate of breathing correlates to our physical breathing, holding one's breath can shock the body into waking up.

Dream Pegs - A notebook for multiple realities

I'd like to finish this chapter with a personal technique that I've used for some time to enhance memory within the dreamworld. The method itself is a variation on a much older memory technique; however, I believe it has yet to be used to bridge the memory gap between waking and sleep. The text below was originally written as a short article for a publication on the topic of dreaming, although it never quite saw the light of day. It has, however, been shared during my workshops for students looking to improve their memory between worlds. I believe this is an incredibly useful technique that is well worth putting the time and effort into learning. Rather than rewrite the method, I have included the text as it was originally written.

The dream peg system

The dream peg system is a supplemental technique for lucid dreaming that helps increase the clarity and quantity of your lucid dreaming recollection. I have found it to be a unique new way for increasing lucid dream recall, even for those dreams that are seemingly forgotten upon awakening. Before delving into the technique itself, I'd like to share with you the journey and thoughts that led to its realisation.

Ever since a child I have wished to be able to bring something tangible back from the dream world, perhaps to pick a flower in a dream meadow and awaken with it still in my hand. Of course, as I grew into adulthood and my understanding of the psychological basis of dreams developed, I soon realised that such thinking was just a fantasy, the wishful thinking of a child's mind. It could sadly never be (though to this day I do still secretly hope to wake up surprised one day!). However, from the seed of my childhood wish, the concept of the dream peg system was founded. In many ways, it is as close to that original idea as can possibly be within the bounds of reality. It is essentially a notebook that you can carry between worlds.

Throughout my lucid dreaming practices, from the early days and even to this day, I have found that dream recall is a slippery beast. Some nights I'd have blindingly vivid dreams, remembered as clearly as if I'd stepped directly from one world to the next. Others would be as if a thick fog had fallen between dreams and waking. I'd be lucky on these mornings to pluck even the vaguest notion of the events that had transpired, or even the faintest whiff of the emotional content from my night's dreaming. Of course, keeping a dream journal helped greatly, but even with the strictest regime of journal-keeping, there would still be the occasional mornings where I would awake with nothing but a blackness where my dreams should have been.

This was true of both lucid and standard dreams, normally much less with lucid dreams due to the intensity of the experience, yet the fact it happened at all was unconscionable. After all the effort involved in developing my lucid dreaming skills, to succeed in becoming lucid only to promptly forget upon awakening seemed criminal. There were many nights when my lucidity occurred in the early REM stages (early in the sleep cycle), followed either by a brief awakening (and quickly dozing off again without finding the will power to write physical notes) or simply continuing into dreamless sleep.

Obviously, such lucid dreams are prone to be, at best, only vaguely remembered by the morning, and sometimes (as I discovered, to my surprise, after using the dream peg technique) not remembered at all. Most surprising was just how many lucid dreams were falling through the net of memory.

On a side note, as one becomes a more seasoned lucid dreamer, whilst the intensity of the lucid dreaming experience remains, the novelty factor lessens due to familiarity. This makes the recall of certain lucid dreams harder than it was in your earlier days, due to the nature of memory favouring the novel. This, combined with an increase in lucidity in earlier REM stages (which are followed by the uncanny memory-erasing nature of deep, dreamless sleep), can create a lethal cocktail of forgetfulness.

From my own experience and discussions with many other dream enthusiasts, I knew I was far from alone in this occasional waking amnesia; indeed, it was possibly the most frustrating and common aspect of dream study. So, not being one to give up easily, it became a private nightly battle to overcome this limitation. Luckily, much of the work had already been done for me, only it had yet to be applied to the problem at hand.

For centuries, humankind has sought to improve its shortcomings, with waking memory concocting any number of techniques and tricks. Perhaps the most famous is the 'Roman Room', a mnemonic system in which one visualises a room (this can either be a real or fictional room, it simply has to be unchanging and vivid in the mind's eye). In order to remember a list of items, you simply imagine entering the room (you ideally have a set route around the room) and you place the items to be remembered in specific places within that room. When the time comes to recall the list, one simply mentally returns to your 'room of memories' and (hopefully) will find the items where they were left.

Whilst such a technique is incredibly handy and effective whilst awake, it is almost impossible to utilise in the environment of a lucid dream. Such detailed visualisations tend to corrupt or change the dream environment, or, worse still, brings the dream to an abrupt end with a loss of lucidity. It simply takes too much time and mental effort. Lucid dreams can, at times, be quite fleeting and, in truth, you never really know exactly how much time you have to explore. Time is, indeed, doubly precious when lucid. You simply don't want to be wasting valuable seconds on the dream clock in complicated memory techniques.

A method was required that would quickly and simply burn key moments of your dream (or key words representing those moments) into your memory, whilst you get on with the important business of dreaming. Such a method would allow you, once awake, to use these key moments, or mental notes, as memory triggers, allowing you to piece together the dream (should it be poorly remembered or even forgotten) much like a mental jigsaw.

Fortunately, a method that fits these criteria had already been developed for quickly and concisely improving one's waking ability to remember lists, only so far it had not been used to bridge the dreaming-waking divide. The method in question is called the 'Mnemonic peg system'.

In order to use the peg system, one needs to pre-memorise a list of words that are easily associated with the numbers they represent. In our case, these will be the numbers 1-10. These associations become the 'pegs' of the system upon which our memories can be hung. Once you have established these pegs, it becomes easy to rapidly memorise a list of arbitrary objects/thoughts as each one is associated with the appropriate peg. Once a memory is attached to a peg, it remains in place up until a new association replaces it (this can be anything from days to years). The original peg list only needs to be developed and memorised once, after which it becomes a lifelong tool that can be used whenever you need to remember a list of items. For those of you to whom this all sounds a little daunting, trust me, for it is all incredibly easy to master, as you'll soon see.

Hopefully, by now the practical applications for this, as a dreaming tool, are obvious. The question was, would such a method function reliably in the dream world and offer us a non-physical note-taking system? (or, as I like to call it, a 'multiple reality notebook'). Fortunately for us, I can confirm that, after repeated and thorough testing, the answer is most certainly 'yes'.

So, without further ado, let us get to grips with the basics of the dream peg system, after which we will explore how you will be able to use your newfound skill to enhance your dream life.

Building your own peg system

To develop your own set of pegs is an incredibly simple process that should take very little time. What we'll be doing is creating a set of associations unique to yourself for the numbers 1 to 10. There are two approaches to this, visual similarity and rhyme associations. For the sake of simplicity, I shall be outlining the first of these, though it is important to remember that the latter rhyming peg system can be used alongside a visual system (they work independently without interfering with one another), doubling your notebook capacity from 10 items to 20. Once you understand the principles involved and have experimented with the visual system, it will be up to you to decide if you need to expand your capacity and create a second rhyming peg list. In my experience of using the system to recall details of a lucid dream, a list of 10 items is more than sufficient (although I shall explore further uses for an expanded system later).

The most important point to stress before going any further, is that any examples I give should be seen as simply examples. Please make sure your associations are unique to your own psychology and are those that come easiest to mind. Firstly, what you will need to do is make a list of the numbers 1 through to 10 (written as numerals not words), as if you were making a shopping list. Now that your blank list is ready, it's time to create the pegs. Let us walk through it (once again, my examples are from my own peg list - you need to make your own).

Take a look at the shape of the number one. Then, as quickly as you can, make the very first visual association that springs to mind based on its shape. What does the number one (viewed as the numerical 1) look like to you? For me, my first association was that the numeric one looks similar to a cigarette. A friend of mine, who also uses the system, instead uses the image of a carrot.

Choose something that has the most obvious association you would make if you were faced with a situation where you had forgotten your original choice, and were to have to do this again. This way, you will almost certainly be able to recall the peg should the need arise. If possible, add a little humour to your connection (feel free to be silly or saucy; indeed, many people choose a penis, so don't be embarrassed by what you choose, just make it memorable). Choose something striking or vibrant.

This is the basic principle for the creation of a peg. Now that you understand what it is you need to do, work through the remaining numbers, making similar-shaped based connections. I have included below my own list of connections:

1 - Cigarette
2 - Swan
3 - Bottom (derriere)
4 - Sailboat
5 - Pregnant woman pointing
6 - Golf club
7 - Cliff top
8 - Snowman
9 - Sperm
10 - A thin man standing next to a fat man.

For variety and to emphasise the point, here is the peg system a good friend of mine uses:

1 - Carrot
2 - Duck
3 - Ear
4 - Chair
5 - Running
6 - Spoon
7 - Building
8 - Peanut
9 - Sunflower
10 - Playing Football

Take your time when developing your peg list. If you struggle with finding a visual association with a particular number (I found numbers 4 and 5 difficult) then play with the shape in your mind; use humour, surrealism, or whatever works best for you. As a rule, the first idea is generally the best.

Once completed, put the list aside, face down, then try and rewrite the list on a new sheet following the original procedure, without referring to your first list. Are your associations the same? If not, review the differences and decide which association (from the first or second list) are more natural. Which is the more default choice of your mind? Make this your final choice of peg for that number. Test yourself several times, working on committing them to memory. Try choosing random numbers, or recall the list backwards and be sure you can recall the peg for each number. It should be simple if you have chosen a solid and predictable association. Once you have finished, congratulate yourself - you've just created a system that you will be able to use for the rest of your life. That's the hard work over. Now let us put it to the test.

How to use pegs

Now that you've done the groundwork, you may be wondering how exactly to use the system. Once again, it's a very easy process that, once you've mastered, is incredibly handy, both whilst waking and dreaming. I would advise getting familiar with the daytime use of the method, so it becomes second nature; this way, when you do first come to experiment with it in a lucid dream, you'll know the process inside out. Firstly, we need to generate ten random ideas/ objects to remember. In keeping with the idea that you will eventually be using this whilst dreaming, let's do a little dream role play so that we start as we mean to go on.

Find yourself another blank piece of paper and, once again, write the numbers one to ten in the format of a list. What we are about to attempt will be much the same process you would follow whilst dreaming. Of course, in dreamland you would not be making physical notes, but we need these for the time being to assess how successful you are in implementing and remembering using the dream peg technique. Look at the numbers on your list. By now, each number should immediately be connected with the associations (pegs) you formed earlier. For example, whenever I think of the number two I now always see it as a swan.

In a moment I am going to ask you to take a short walk around your room or house, as if you were dreaming the event. As you do so, you are going to find ten objects in the building that you wish to remember. Using the process I shall outline below, you will peg these items into your memory. But also, in this case (unlike a dream) you shall write them next to the corresponding numbers they have been pegged to on your sheet of paper.

When attaching any random object or thought to a peg, the key is to use as many sensory connections as possible. You need to be inventive, creative and, if you can, add a little humour. At first, this may take a little time, but with practice it will become second nature. For example, on my walk around my house, if the first object I wished to remember was, say, a book, I would do the following. Firstly, I would call up my personal peg item for the number one (the cigarette) in my imagination. I would then imagine a book with cigarettes sticking out between the pages, perhaps with a few stubbed out over the cover. I would imagine smelling the scent of the burnt tobacco, the feel of the ash falling from the pages.This, of course, happens much quicker in the mind than it appears to take when written. However, as this is your first attempt at using pegs, really take the time to visualise and imagine an interesting, funny, vivid connection between the item you find and your peg item. Memory works best when connections are funny, vivid and you are engaging as many senses as possible.

Following the instructions, I would then continue around the house, moving onto each new randomly-chosen item and pegging them in numerical order to the corresponding number (more specifically, the peg symbols for those numbers) until I reached item ten.

Hopefully, this has made the process clear. You are using mental connections to tie a random thought to the stable, consistent memories of your pegs. If you are unsure, please reread the above until you are certain of what you are doing.

Now it's your turn. Imagine you are suddenly dreaming, and you are in a dream replica of your house. Go and explore your surroundings. Whilst you do so, choose random items you wish to remember and peg them in your memory (try and be inventive in what you choose; don't pick things simply because you think they'll be memorable, but challenge yourself). Of course, remember to write the names of these items on your physical list so you can test yourself later. Take your time, and enjoy the process. Go try this now and we'll see how well you've done on your return.

The test

Welcome back. By now, you should have in your hand a list of ten random items from your house and, more importantly, those same items now associated with the pegs into your memory. Place your written list face down so that you cannot read it (cheating here really would be a case of only cheating yourself!).

Then, find yourself a second blank piece of paper and, once again, write the numbers 1 to 10. Run through each number in your mind, calling up your peg symbol for each number. Then write down the associated memory that you have recently attached to this peg next to the corresponding number. Ideally, you will end up with a duplicate of your list you have placed face down.

If you struggle with any recollections, don't worry (although, do try your best). Just move onto the next number and finish your list. If you are unable to recall any particular item, consider why that may be. Perhaps your connection was weak, or you rushed it. Remember where you went wrong for future reference, so as to avoid making the same mistake.

Once you've finished your list, turn over your original notes and check to see how well you've done. If you are missing any items, try to peg them to their numbers again. Do this until you are certain you have each item well remembered. Also, be sure to note any particularly easy-to-recall items. What was it about the connection that improved your memory? Over time, and with practice, you will become more aware of how your own memory works, making your associations and the process of using pegs more efficient and effective.

If you've followed all the instructions as prescribed, you'll probably have done very well. Far better than had you just used conventional memory. You may also notice that you can now remember a list of ten items in any order. Randomly choose a number - let's say seven - and you'll recall the object you attached to this peg. Also, try testing yourself in a couple of hours, or even a few days or weeks. You'll be surprised at just how solid this method is for storing memories.

Expanding the peg system

As I mentioned earlier, if you wish to expand your peg list to 20 rather than 10 items, you can follow the same procedure outlined above to create a second peg list; however, instead of creating images visually similar to the relevant numeral, instead one connects each number (again 1 to 10) with words that rhyme with the relevant number (for example, in my personal expanded system One=Nun, Two=Shoe, Three=Tree, Four=Door etc.). The process is otherwise identical as above. Again, you need to choose your rhyming words so they are the first (or most likely) connection your mind makes. One important factor to remember here is to be sure that the rhyming images chosen are not similar to those for any numbers in your visual system. Other than this caveat, you needn't worry about each peg system interfering with the other, as they can both happily coexist and be used in tandem.

How to use pegs within dreams

Now that you have experimented with, understood, and proven the effectiveness of the system whilst awake, the next step is to use the system within the dream environment. There are several ways in which dream pegs can be used to enhance your lucid dreaming experience.

The primary function, as I am sure you have guessed already, is to simply peg items you wish to recall into your memory whilst within a lucid dream itself. These pegged memories can then be easily accessed when you awake. The key here is to choose details of the dream that you believe will be sufficient to trigger further memories once awakened.

I have found the most practical way to do this is to peg the most striking environmental feature of the dream scene as item one on your peg list, then use the further pegs for more specific details of dream events as and when required. This way, when recalling the dream upon awakening by reviewing what is attached to your pegs, the first peg should generally be enough to trigger other latent memories and 'set the scene'. With this in mind, be sure to peg each new environment (or 'landmark' feature of that environment) as and when you encounter them within your dream.

You needn't feel under pressure to use your entire 10 pegs in every dream. They are tools to be used as and when you need them. Try to think of the technique as your own multiple reality notebook. You're in charge of when you take notes - you'll soon learn with experience exactly how much and what kind of information you need to 'jot down'.

Of course, you will need to develop, alongside your usual morning activity of writing your dream journal, the habit of reviewing your pegs to look for attached memories. I advise doing this after you have written your traditionally recalled dreams of that night. There are two reasons for this. Firstly, it is always good practice to write exactly what you remember from your dreams as quickly as possible whilst the memories are fresh in the morning; any interference between waking and writing in your journal tends to lead to the (non-pegged) memories fading. Secondly, in recording what you naturally recall first and then approaching your pegged memories, you will soon start to build a picture of how many dreams, or details of dreams, you would have missed if not using the dream peg system.

A second, yet equally handy, application for the peg system, is for those lucid dreams in which one forgot to use the peg system whilst dreaming, but have awoken in the middle of the night shortly after a lucid dream with clear recall of the details. Normally in these instances, the dreamer faces the unpleasant struggle of getting up, turning on the light and physically recording the details in their dream journal or voice recorder. This is unpleasant enough if one sleeps alone, but if one shares a bed, it's certainly not going to do your relationship any favours!

With the dream peg system, you can instead make mental notes by reviewing the dream in your mind's eye, and to peg key elements you wish to recall in the morning. All this can be done comfortably without moving, leading to the second benefit that, once finished, you'll be able to fall asleep easily, perhaps even into another lucid dream.

The third application for dream pegs is a complete reversal of the concept. Many lucid dreamers find that the tasks and experiments they choose (whilst awake) to carry out in their next lucid dream, are easily forgotten when they are suddenly (and almost always surprisingly) faced with the shock of discovering they are, indeed, dreaming. Memory is temperamental in dreamland, so you cannot always rely on your normal mental faculties to aid recall of your waking life goals.

This unusual combination of surprise and the (sometimes) inhibited memory in dreams often leads many lucid dreamers to simply improvise their behaviours in dreamland. This, of course, is fun in itself, but far from ideal if you have a specific task you'd been hankering to complete. This can be incredibly frustrating, especially for those who are approaching lucidity for experimental purposes, or those others to whom lucidity is a little more elusive.

To combat this issue, one could easily peg the task into your memory whilst awake, ready to be used as a cue card, easily accessible when you next find yourself in dreamland. Ideally, it would make sense for any pegged 'dream goal' cue to be consistently attached to a specific peg in your system. I would suggest the 10th as, this way, you leave pegs 1-9 free for recording the details of the dream. If, on the other hand, you use the expanded system, you could use the slots on the rhyming peg list for this purpose.

If you do wish to use the system for this task, you will have to develop the habit that, whenever performing a reality test whilst awake, to also immediately check which memory you have attached to your cue peg (in my example, the 10th visual peg or the 1st peg in your rhyming system). This will (ideally) trigger the same behaviour when one finds oneself reality testing within a dream, cuing you immediately to the task required.

Dream pegs are a powerful and versatile tool, allowing you to proactively overcome some of the innate limitations of dream recall. Whilst the benefits may, to some, seem subtle and perhaps a little less appealing than those of the methods for direct lucid dream induction or control, I cannot stress enough the value of developing a familiarity with this technique. You will most certainly find that the small investment of effort required to master the method will be greatly rewarded by the opening of new avenues of dream exploration and experimentation that would have previously been inaccessible.

7
Exploring Lucid Dreams

Once you have developed the skills, understanding and techniques required for inducing and controlling a lucid dream, the obvious next step is to establish how you would like to spend your time in dreamland. It is here that the world really does open up before us and the options are close to limitless.

No two dreamers ever approach lucidity in quite the same way, for the very same reasons that no two personalities are identical. Our experiences, desires, values, interests, knowledge, wishes, etc., are all factors that make each individual's universe of dreams a truly unique place. Your dreamworld is very much a mirror of who you are, reflected in a painstaking and unsurpassed realism.

You will find yourself in a world that is absolutely one of a kind, and respond to that world by making choices that are uniquely the result of your own personal tastes. As such, lucid dreaming could well be considered the epitome of a subjective experience. Clearly, how you spend your time consciously wandering dreamland is entirely up to you, considering you are exploring a world built from the bricks and mortar of your own mind.

However, a guidebook would be of little use if it didn't offer a few suggestions on the sights to be seen, the experiences on offer, or hints at some of the more practical and rewarding ways you could spend your time. In this chapter, we will be exploring just some of the uses and experiences of lucid dreaming. Consider these ideas as food for thought and experiment with them to your heart's content.

Entertainment, pleasure and wish fulfilment

On the most basic level, lucid dreaming is fun. You only need to take the most cursory glance at human society to realise that we are constantly seeking new and novel ways to be entertained. It is unsurprising, then, that for many lucid dreamers pleasure-seeking is their first port of call. Here, we find ourselves in a world where, like some kind of deity, we have an 'all you can eat' buffet laid out before us, containing all possible human (and beyond human) experiences ready for our own personal enjoyment.

There are good reasons to spend time enjoying the pleasures of lucid dreaming, aside from the obvious. When learning any new skill, enjoyment is a critical factor: the more pleasure we derive from any pursuit, the faster we learn and the more likely we are to continue to invest time and energy into developing our skills. Positive reinforcement comes into play as well; the more satisfied and rewarding our experiences of lucidity, the more likely it is that our minds will aid our attempts at inducing them. In short, fun can be considered as a powerful tool for improving our skills in lucid dreaming.

Apart from the role that pleasure plays in improving our skills, perhaps the most important factor is that the experience of enjoyment will positively affect your waking life. The feeling of waking from an exhilarating or pleasurable dream can leave an afterglow that can stay with you for the entire day. Indulging yourself in satisfying dreaming experiences is the ultimate way to ensure that you always wake up 'on the right side of the bed' so to speak. Happiness is healthy and lucid dreaming can go a long way to increasing your general level of well-being and satisfaction with life. To know that there is a world of limitless possibility available to you, at the end of each day, is a wonderful way to keep a happy and positive attitude throughout your daily life.

Lucid dreaming is, in itself, an innately enjoyable experience. The freedom it offers alone brings with it a satisfying sense of being freed from the limitations that restrict our waking experiences. Such a sense of freedom can go a long way to helping you develop a positive mindset, one that can be carried with you as you go about your daily life. Indeed, many lucid dreamers report a kind of re-evaluation of their lives as they become more at home with the experience of unlimited freedom.

What often occurs is that the limiting mindsets that many of us carry when approaching our waking life problems can become loosened, or more flexible. We may start to find that we approach the difficulties of life with a more optimistic attitude, expecting solutions rather than assuming the worst. Our experiences of freedom and pleasure in the dreamworld can slowly filter into waking life, giving us the confidence to try to attempt new strategies for dealing with waking issues that may, before, have seemed unsolvable.

Essentially, we start to see that the waking world, like dreamland, is a place where, whilst a little more restricted, can still offer us a huge amount of freedom and pleasure, if only we allow ourselves to invest the time and energy (and belief) to pursue our goals.

How each individual pursues their wishes and entertainment in the dreamworld is as varied as human tastes. However, let's look at a few of the more common activities that dreamers use to bring themselves pleasure.

Flying

Dreams of flying are intimately entwined with the experience of lucid dreaming. Flying, for most, comes naturally in dreams, although the means by which flight is achieved tends to be rather varied. For many, it's a simple act of flying superhero-style, simply pushing off from the ground and taking flight. Others use props such as flying carpets, magic umbrellas, or any manner of devices.

Others approach the experience as if they are swimming through the air. Perhaps, for these dreamers, the experience of flying in dreams is a mechanism by which the brain practises the skills of swimming albeit in a different medium. Indeed, maybe the reason humans fly in dreams at all is due to our prior experiences with swimming, as the two share many similarities.

Others have speculated that flight dreams are some kind of evolutionary throwback, either related to distant flying ancestors, or - and more likely - our ancestors' arboreal past, when jumping from tree to tree was very much a part of daily life (and a dangerous skill that would have required regular practise, both in dreams and whilst awake).

Another explanation, and perhaps the simplest is, that we experience flight in dreams because it is so enjoyable. Since the dawn of time, humans have envied the abilities of the birds who so effortlessly dance around the skies. Such a longing itself is enough to provide fodder for wish-fulfilling dreams of flight. Whatever the reasons for such dreams, flight is one of the most liberating and enjoyable experiences of lucid dreaming.

It's important at this point to mention a word of warning regarding flight (and which can also be applied to other areas of lucid dreaming). While flying in dreams is hugely enjoyable - and, of course, completely safe - it is wise to develop certain safety precautions regarding how you approach the experience. Whilst lucid dreamers are better than most at distinguishing reality from dreams, none of us can ever be completely sure that we will remain in good mental health for our entire lives.

However unlikely, there may be a point during our lives where our grasp on reality (either through intoxication, or mental illness) may not be as firm as it currently is. It is a wise precaution, in this case, to approach any behaviour in a dream that would be dangerous to perform in waking life, with a cautious approach; we must avoid developing habits that, if performed whilst awake, would be injurious or even fatal.

In the case of flying, I would suggest always initiating flight in a safe way, such as simply hovering above the ground, before risking jumping out of window or off a cliff top. It's a simple concept that does not impede on our experience of dreaming, but one that helps us avoid developing potentially dangerous habits that would, if our mental health were to take a turn for the worse in the waking world, be disastrous. The same approach should be applied to any activities you perform in dreamland that would be dangerous if performed awake. Simply 'test the water' before throwing yourself in at the deep end.

Warnings aside, flying is an incredibly liberating experience and one that I believe all lucid dreamers should attempt. Of course, expectation as always plays its role here. Interestingly, those lucid dreamers who live in cities are more likely to experience issues with their flight being disturbed by overhead wires, such as electricity or telephone cables, compared to their country-dwelling peers. Of course, this makes perfect sense, considering our minds are building the experience from expectations and memories of what is common in our waking life.

Should you have this experience, do not let yourself get 'caught up' either mentally or physically in the dream. Remember, the only power these power lines have over you is that which you give them via your belief. They do not exist beyond your thoughts and there is no reason for them to restrict your flight.

I, myself, have experienced this on a few occasions, especially when living for extended periods in cities. My personal trick was to reframe the role of these cables in the dream. I would tell myself that I would be able to pass directly through the cables (which is obviously true and easily done with enough lucid clarity) and that, when doing so, rather than restrict me, the power running through these cables would act as a boost to my own powers of flying. This simple mental reframing worked as a great tool for flying at turbocharged speeds to the destination I required, and was especially handy for those evenings when I wanted to visit outer space.

Expectation also plays a role in how easy one finds it to fly. If you believe it will be difficult, then indeed it shall be. Again, as we've previously discussed, such difficulties are normally always related to your level of lucidity within the dream. If, at any point, you struggle with flying, then remember what you have learnt about dream control. Take a moment to step back from the experience and enhance your mental clarity, reminding yourself that everything you are experiencing is a mental construct and under your control. As your understanding that 'it's all a dream, all under my control' increases, so too will you discover flying to be effortless and hugely enjoyable.

Reframing can also work here. One method would be to consider that it is not you that is flying, but the ground moving away from you, that the environment is moving whilst you remain stationary. Perhaps you can convince yourself you are in an advanced virtual reality simulation and the environment is simply a projection completely under your control.

In fact, this reframing is barely reframing at all, just a statement of fact. In reality, this is exactly what you are experiencing, the world's most advanced virtual reality, running on the most advanced biological computer known to man: the human brain.

Sexual encounters

In a world of endless possibilities, it is inevitable that many find themselves exploring one of humanity's most basic pleasures: sex. Indeed, whilst some may be a little embarrassed to admit it, sexual encounters in lucid dreams are one of the most popular activities pursued by dreamers. There is perhaps good reason for this.

During the REM phase, both males and females experience the physical changes associated with sexual arousal. In fact, the guaranteed occurrence of nocturnal erections in males is one of the ways in which sex therapists can establish the cause of erectile dysfunction in their clients. Because these erections are a natural physical aspect of the REM phase, should a client believe that the cause of their problem is physical, yet still experience nocturnal erections, it is clear that the source of the issue is psychological.

The mind may boggle at how therapists establish the occurrence of these nightly arousals. However, the truth is rather simple. The client simply wears what is essentially a thin loop of paper around their penis before retiring to bed; should they awaken and the loop be broken (due to the obvious pressure exerted on it during the night), then they can be assured that there are no physical problems 'down below' (and the therapist can then prescribe a psychological solution to the issue).

It may well be that these physical changes associated with REM play a role in increasing the likelihood of sexually-related dreams. Even if this were not the case, the fact still remains that sex is a very popular pastime for dreamers.

Given the consequence-free environment of dreams, and the sheer level of experimentation that can be made, lucid dreams involving sex can be a very healthy way to explore one's sexuality. This may be especially beneficial for those who, due to their circumstances (miners, the physically disabled, oil rig workers, prisoners, etc.), may not have access to sexual encounters they desire in waking life.

Of course, there is no reason to limit yourself to the sexual experiences that are available to you in your waking life. Indeed, why not experiment with something completely new? Some find that changing their gender in the dreamworld can allow them a new understanding of the nature of sex from the perspective of their partners.

Perhaps this may be a little too extreme for some, but there are many options still available that one may not initially consider. The obvious route is to explore one's sexual fantasies. Perhaps these fantasies are simply impractical in waking life, or one feels too embarrassed to share them with their partner.

However, sexual experiences needn't be limited to the physical restraints of waking life; for example, combining flying with sex can be a fascinating experience. I doubt that many of you will need advice on how to explore these matters as, for most of us, inventing interesting sexual experiences is somewhat of a private pastime.

I'll reiterate, however, that it is worth experimenting outside of your normal pallet of tastes. Remember, that whatever (and with whom) you choose to experience in the privacy of your own dreamworld, it is absolutely your own personal business and you really needn't feel ashamed of these explorations. A healthy sex life in your dreams can do wonders to improve your confidence and creativity in your waking sex life.

The dreamworld offers the unique opportunity to be freed from the social constraints of waking sexuality, and an environment safe from the dangers of sexually transmitted diseases. Of course, should you wish to share such experiences with your partner depends greatly on the level of communication, understanding and trust upon which your relationship is based, but this is something only you can judge. One word of warning is required here, however. As with all experiences in dreams, follow your own moral compass of what you feel is acceptable behaviour. Dreams may well be a consequence-free environment, but we all still must live with the knowledge of our own actions, real or imagined. To thine own self be true.

Exploring your senses

Being the creatures of sensory pleasure that we are, indulging our senses in the dreamworld is another wonderful way to bring ourselves enjoyment. Sight, sound, scent, touch and taste are all available to be explored and enjoyed in dreams. The sensory experience in dreamland can be a varied and unusual experience; not only can we experience the more familiar and obvious aspects of our senses, but there is room to experiment with synesthesia, the combination and hybridisation of our senses.

Many lucid dreamers report that their senses seem heightened in dreams, with colours appearing brighter, music conveying more depth and meaning, and physical sensations feeling more direct and intimate. I would speculate that the reason for this amplification of our senses may be due to the more direct fashion in which we experience them.

Rather than being the end result of a process, starting with the processing of input from our genuine physical senses, our experience of these things in dreams all occur in the immediacy of our own brains. There is no processing to be done. If we experience, say, the colour blue in our dream, this is not an interpretation of an external wavelength of light that has required a certain amount of effort by our brains to convert; instead, we are calling up the 'schema' or mental model for blue, which is already a complete entity within our minds, available directly from our own memories. There is an immediacy of perception in dreams that is unlike that of waking experience.

The more obvious senses of sight, sound and touch are relatively easy to explore and enjoy within a dream. Seeking out beautiful scenery (which is often accompanied by intense shimmering electric colours), listening to enchanting music, or enjoying the physical sensations of the body are all generally very common experiences that require little effort on behalf of the dreamer.

Scent and taste seem to be somewhat less apparent in most people's dreams. Whilst we are perfectly capable of experiencing delicious foods and exotic perfumes in a dream, it would seem that often, without turning our attention to these senses, they tend to go unnoticed. However, the most likely reason for this is because, in general, the exact same thing can be said of our waking lives, where we give little attention to these senses unless there is a strong reason to do so (a sudden pungent smell, or bad-tasting food, for example). Our dreams will focus on the same things we give our attention to in waking life. If you wish to experience taste and scent in dreams, then start to make them more meaningful in your waking life.

How we explore our senses is a topic that is incredibly vast, but with a little imagination we can all think of novel, entertaining and useful ways to do so. One perfect example that would be both pleasurable and practical is for those who are dieting. Dieters, starved of the tastes of their favourite foods in waking life, will likely develop a strong desire to enjoy the experience of these foods again, say perhaps a slice of chocolate cake. Of course, in dreamland, you can eat as much as you like without ingesting a single calorie. Why settle for just a slice when you can run riot in the cake shop and eat the whole store!

Such explorations and uses are reasonably easy to conceive, so I'll not overstress the point, although I would advise putting a concerted effort into exploring this concept.

One area that is less often explored by dreamers is the previously mentioned idea of synesthesia. Synesthesia is a reasonably rare condition in waking life where those who are affected experience their senses overlapping; for example, one may 'hear colour' or 'smell sounds'. Dreams, being the realm of the mind, allow us all to explore this unusual phenomenon directly.

There is little in the way of advice I can offer on how to induce this experience other than by simply suggesting using your powers of expectation. If you can bite into a dream apple, believing that, in doing so, you will also hear the 'music of the taste', then you may be able to induce your own synesthetic experience. This is absolutely possible to achieve, only rather difficult to explain the process, as it is entirely reliant on your ability to control your expectations. Reframing is also another way to induce such an experience (for example, you could tell yourself that you are under the influence of an hallucinogenic agent during the dream, one that has the effect of mixing up your senses). As always, experimentation is the best way forward.

Exploring your senses in the dreamworld can be a deliciously pleasurable experience, one that can leave you waking up with a profound sense of satisfaction.

Rewriting history and missed opportunities

A very straightforward and satisfying way to find pleasure in the dreamworld is to rewrite situations from your waking life, in which you would have preferred an alternative outcome. Each of us experience moments in our lives, or missed opportunities, that we often daydream about and wish had turned out differently (and isn't it just always the case that we think of the best things to have said after an event?).

Conversations with attractive members of the opposite sex (or the lack of conversation, should we have failed to gain the confidence, or missed our chance to start one) are a common example. Stressful situations at work, especially discussions with our boss where (due to the restraints of consequence) we had to bite our tongue, are another fine example. Whatever situations you have lived, of which you would have preferred an alternative outcome, you can relive and rewrite in the world of dreams. Why simply daydream when you can relive the experience with the realism of a lucid dream?

Of course, such dreams will not fix our missed opportunities, nor can they genuinely change our past, but they can go a long way to venting some of the stresses and feelings of frustration that may linger. Indeed, using dreams in such a way can help develop in us a level of confidence and self-assurance that may reduce the occurrences of such events in the future. Regardless of this, there is a unique pleasure to be gained by allowing ourselves to re-experience an event exactly as we would have wished it in real life.

Exploring the dream world

There is a lot to be said for simply enjoy the experience of dreaming. Exploring the world around you, taking in the sights and relishing the realism of the event, can be profoundly enjoyable. You may be surprised by the level of detail that the dreamworld can muster, from the lines on the palms of your hand, the clouds in the sky, to the individual cell structures on leaves. All of these things, and a whole world more, are there to explore and experience.

There are limitless ways to experiment here; you can play with reflections in mirrors, feel the sensations of the wind against your skin, explore gravity (or lack of it) within the dreamworld, perform experiments with dream physics - essentially, anything you wish to study will offer up a level of detail and realism that can take your breath away. Each new experiment will surprise and entertain you, whilst, at the same time, teaching you more about the world around you. In many ways, you can approach your dream much as a young child approaches waking life, full of awe, wonder and constantly curious. Become a child of the dreamscape and explore to your heart's content.

Here, you can act like a tourist in dreamland, merely soaking up the sights on offer. Or, you can be more proactive and pretend to be an alien scientist, experimenting and probing, trying to understand the new world you have discovered. It's important to remember here that such behaviour is not purely valuable from the perspective of entertainment; in fact, developing this kind of relationship with the dream is a fantastic way to improve your chances of becoming lucid in later dreams.

The more familiar you become with the nature of dreaming, the more likely you are to notice inconsistencies between it and waking life. These inconsistencies will soon become some of the subtle signs that alert you to the fact you are dreaming. You will start to develop a more advanced knowledge of the dreamscape. Many experienced lucid dreamers are often cued into lucidity purely by knowing how a dream 'feels'.

It is through continued exploration, observation and experimentation that, over time, one develops this ability; it may take some time, but the process of developing this skill is, in itself, incredibly enjoyable. Of course, all activities in dreamland fall under the banner of 'exploring the dreamworld' and, as such, we'll be going into more detail as we journey throughout the various topics of this chapter.

Fiction embodied

In the modern world, we are surrounded by entertaining fiction, be it in films, books, computer games or television shows. Most of us have at least some form of fiction, or some specific story that captures our imaginations. We all have a fictional world we would like to visit. Of course, there is absolutely zero opportunity to do so in our waking lives, as we're limited to waiting for the next episode, the new book, upcoming game or sequel to a film, until we get our next adventure in the world we have grown to love. Lucid dreaming offers us a unique opportunity to visit these 'worlds that never were', places that have only ever existed in the minds of the imaginative people behind such creations.

In many ways, lucid dreaming can become the ultimate form of fan fiction, a place where we can bring whole imaginary worlds to life, interact with the characters, and generally just explore the fantastical worlds of another's imagination. Part of the beauty of such an endeavour is that we can use such dreams to play any role we wish within these stories; we can play the hero or villain, or maybe simply be an independent observer watching the dramas unfold.

This can be particularly satisfying for those shows, books or games that have long since ended. We can revisit these worlds, continuing the stories that have been abandoned and, in doing so, explore the potential of our own creativity at the same time. Here, the concept of reframing becomes relevant once more when, recreating these worlds in our dreams, often the rules of reality are slightly altered by the concepts behind the story.

Perhaps there are superheroes, spacecraft, vampires, fairies, or all number of other elements, that simply do not exist in waking reality. Once we have established a lucid dream that is based upon our choice of worlds, it can become much easier to explore the new rules and 'powers' that are part of the storyline, opening up new ways to explore and control our dreams. Should, for example, you wish to explore space in your dreams, then reframing the dream in the guise of a science fiction universe makes the process so much easier.

We also live in a time where so much of the media we consume is full to the brim of highly convincing CGI and effects, which all work as 'brain fodder'. This helps our minds build a convincing model of these worlds, based on the memories we have developed when viewing these effects on the original media. We shall discuss how feeding our minds with suitable content can greatly enhance the dreaming experience later.

Wish fulfilment

Of course, all of the above ideas can fall under the topic of 'wish fulfilment', but clearly there is a great deal more that can be explored other than just these suggestions alone. Lucid dreaming could be considered as your own personal genie, granting you as many wishes as your heart desires. Exploring our wants and wishes can range across the entire scope of what is (and isn't) possible, from adventures in exotic lands, meeting famous characters, either modern or from bygone times, time travel, experiencing fame and fortune, seeing life through the eyes of another species, travelling into outer space, reliving past memories, erotic encounters, dangerous stunts, adrenaline-filled activities, spiritual and philosophical exploration - the options are as wide open as your imagination.

Indeed, there are likely many more wishes that can be granted through dreams than there are people on planet Earth. Of course, the skills that are required to enable you to use your lucid dreams for such pursuits are not always immediate and it takes time, training and practice to develop a level of dream control that can fully unlock the potential of the lucid dreaming experience. However, indulging in your wishes is certainly a rewarding way to practise and develop these skills. Start simply and slowly work your way towards your more adventurous and complicated goals.

For many, the use of lucid dreaming starts and ends with wish fulfilment, and this is a perfectly valid way in which to use your skills. However, dreaming is not limited purely to pleasure-seeking. Although most experiences in dreamland are by default entertaining, they can be much more. Entertainment is just the very tip of the iceberg, and the subject goes much deeper than this alone. Let us take a look now at some of the more practical uses of the lucid dream.

The practical dreamer

The term 'practical dreamer' may at first glance appear to be an oxymoron; but, in truth, there is no contradiction here. Lucid dreaming can have many practical applications (likely many that have yet to have been conceived). The trick here is to stop viewing the dream state as a passive activity. Whilst non-lucid dreams may well seem to be the equivalent to being strapped to a cinema chair whilst forced to watch whichever film our minds decide to play, lucid dreaming is an interactive pastime where freedom abounds.

Perhaps the best way to view lucidity is to consider it as a place you visit, or, better still, a piece of advanced computer software. The latter is probably a very good analogy. Like a computer system, the brain is capable of multiple functionality; the entertainment options we discussed previously can be seen as the equivalent of playing the latest computer game, the practical applications as the various software tools available.

Once again, we need to remind ourselves that, in a very real sense, what we are exploring is the world's most advanced simulation software (the ability to lucid dream) running on the most powerful biological computer in the known universe (the human brain). Of course, unlike the latest PC or software release, there is no user manual for the human mind, nor are there specific software applications.

We have already looked at how to understand and control the basics of the system. We now need to choose and design the 'software' we wish to use - which, of course, is completely reliant on our own particular needs.

Sticking with the computer analogy for the time being, perhaps the best place to start is to look at the most obvious practical use of dreaming, that of fixing a common issue with dreaming itself. Let's do a little troubleshooting on the software of our minds, roll out the 'anti-virus software' and start with learning how to deal with the common issue of nightmares and unpleasant dreams.

Overcoming nightmares

As we've already discovered, if the studies are to be believed, then approximately 70% of dreams contain unpleasant or stressful content. It may well be that the cultural concept of (non-lucid) dreams being fantastical voyages of the imagination is wrong and, instead, that dreams are a little darker than we give them credit for. Why this should be remains a mystery. However, it could be that one of the functions of dreaming may be as some kind of psychological 'fire drill' preparing and practising our mental reflexes for unpleasant situations.

More likely, however, it is the role of our old friend expectation. As we've covered already, in dreams we often see what we expect to see. For example, let's compare a real world situation with an equivalent dream. Imagine, if you will, spying out of the corner of your eye, a large black spot on the wall; from your limited view, you may also conclude that this spot also appears to have what look like legs. Your mind (in lieu of more information) may try to make a judgement assuming that, perhaps, it's a large spider.

For most of us, dreaming or awake, our initial assessment will be based on the instinct of self-preservation. We assume that, yes, it could well be a spider and react accordingly. In the waking world, our internal assessment has no impact on the genuine cause of the suspected arachnid. It may well be a spider, but equally it could simply be a crack in the paintwork. We may jump away in fear, only to laugh later when we see that it wasn't a spider at all. It isn't until we examine it further, giving our brains more data to work with, that we can make a more informed judgement. Either way, it is reality and not our imagination that decides the outcome. Should we turn and see that it is indeed simply a poorly painted wall, so it shall remain and no amount of belief or willing otherwise shall change this fact.

The objective outside world calls the shots. In dreams, however, there is no outside world from which to gather our data; the spot we see on the wall remains in a state of limbo, being neither a spider nor a crack in the paint, simply an 'unknown'. There is no way for us to objectively establish its true form, because it has no true form. Here, our expectations rule; if we believe that it *is* a spider, when we turn to examine it closer, that's exactly what it will be. Our brains build a story that fits what we expect.

In most dreams, this is the process in which the apparent storylines of the dream are written - expectation leads to outcome, which leads to expectation, which leads to another outcome and so on. As most dreams begin in relatively benign scenarios, this feedback loop mostly produces dreams that dart around from one set of relatively harmless associations and assumptions to others, creating the often surreal and coincidental happenings in the dreamworld.

Because daily life for most of us is generally pleasant, or at least comfortably free from regular horrors, so too are our dreams, as it is our memories upon which they are built. But life is not without its stresses, worries and unpleasant circumstances and these have an equally strong foothold in our memories.

For an unpleasant dream to occur, all that is required is for our series of associations during the dream to stumble upon something that is at least related to a less than pleasant experience. Once this aspect enters the dream, there is now an associative seed from which a tree of unpleasantness can grow.

Most of the time, all that occurs in this scenario is that the dream takes this seed and proceeds to create a situation built around a relatively low intensity series of negative assumptions and associations, such as running late for work, arguments with loved ones, etc. However, every now and then this feedback loop spirals out of control, with each association (based on expectation) ramping up the negativity and unpleasantness of the experience. Once a critical mass of negative aspects enters the dream, the scope for further unpleasant associations grows ever wider, and thus a nightmare begins.

Of course, once this point is reached, it is likely for the dream (now nightmare) to spiral into further dark and fearful places, the environment having turned sour, creating the perfect breeding ground for even more negative associations. As most of us have experienced, the outcome of this process is a rapid increase of the intensity of negativity and panic until, eventually, we find ourselves startled awake by a crescendo of fear.

An understanding of this self-fulfilling and self-fuelling nature of nightmares can go some way to explaining the experience of those who are afflicted with their recurrence. Should we have been (by chance) unfortunate enough to have had a particularly unpleasant nightmare, especially one that is related to something close to our hearts or our current waking situation, then it is likely the memory of such an event will linger, creating a certain unease surrounding our sleep. We may also dwell on the dream during our waking hours.

This combination of giving the dream our thoughts during daylight hours, and with a possible sense of fear as we drift into sleep, acts as a form of dream incubation, greatly increasing our chances of experiencing a similar dream. Of course, should this unwitting incubation be even mildly successful, our previous waking preoccupation will have already created an environment of associations and expectation that will need only the slightest nudge to activate.

To counter this without the aid of lucid dreaming, the majority of sleep therapists will advise a form of daytime dream rehearsal, where one is advised to imagine the nightmare in advance, only rewriting the 'script' into something more positive - essentially, a form of dream incubation. However, with the skills of lucid dreaming under our belt, nightmares can be dealt with in a much more direct fashion. It may be surprising for some, but actually the experience of regular nightmares, especially those with a recurring theme, can be a springboard into lucid dreaming itself.

To accomplish this, one needs to follow several practices. The first, as already described, is to rehearse the dream in your daytime hours. This time, however, when imagining the nightmare, add to the story a scene in which you become aware that the experience is just a dream. Following this, continue to imagine the nightmare (in which you would now, of course, be lucid) with an outcome you would prefer.

Secondly, during your daytime reality test practices, make sure you perform a reality test when anything during your waking hours is related to the nightmare. However weak the connection, always perform a test. It may be somewhat obvious, but reality test whenever thoughts of the nightmare enter your mind throughout the day.

After performing your test, consider what you would do once you realise that the nightmare is just a dream; go over in your mind how you would positively deal with the situation. Later, as you retire to bed, do so with optimism and a positive mindset. Remember that you are now prepared to deal with the dream head on, that you are very likely (with the previous practices) to become lucid at the next occurrence of the dream. If you are feeling especially brave, go over the nightmare (with the added reality test and realisation of lucidity) in your imagination as you fall asleep.

The combination of these practices over time will lead to one inevitable outcome: you will realise during the nightmare that you are dreaming, and you will become lucid. At this point, you must choose how to deal with the experience from within it. The most successful approach seems to be, when dealing with a nightmare whilst lucid, is to face your fears head on.

Such behaviour may seem counter-intuitive and, for many, once lucid the temptation to escape the nightmare scenario altogether and fly off to explore more exciting options can be strong. However, doing so is unlikely to stop the recurrence of the nightmare. Instead, whatever it is that is the subject of your fears should be approached directly with a firm mindset to resolve the issue, once and for all.

Often, when dreamers find themselves conscious in their nightmares, and have the courage to approach their 'demons', something rather special happens; armed with the knowledge they are safe and 'only dreaming', whatever fearful situation they find themselves in can suddenly take on an almost comical quality. The slobbering beasts you have been running from all these years may seem rather pathetic when you finally resolve to turn and face them.

One powerful option is to attempt to open a dialogue with the dream itself, especially if the source of your fear is personified as a dream character. Ask the character what it is they are trying to achieve, or why they are trying to frighten you. Often, you may be surprised by the answer. Some choose to use their powers to 'battle' the source of their fear; whilst this can be effective in some scenarios, it is generally nowhere near as effective as the diplomatic approach. By opening yourself to directly witness your fear and perhaps enter a discussion with it, you can lead the dream towards integration and a sense of empowerment, an outcome that a battle with dream powers rarely offers.

Essentially, the approach here is to find a sense of closure. The best way to do this is to work your way to the seed of your fear and then attempt to understand it. This may take several attempts, perhaps many, depending on how deep the issue is. Eventually, however, as your courage grows and you start to see the nightmare for what it really is, namely an element of your own personality and mind, then you will soon start to see that the fear you are facing is part of your own psyche. As a result, the only true way to deal with it is to integrate it into your personality.

You cannot run from your own mind; instead, the elements inside you must learn to live in peace together. Lucid dreaming offers you the tools to open that dialogue, which will, in time, end the war in your mind.

Solving problems

Finding creative solutions to waking problems is one of the many practical uses of lucid dreaming. The folk saying often used when faced with one of life's conundrums is to 'sleep on it', and it is doubly true here. It seems that the very nature of dreaming, lucid or otherwise, is to aid the consolidation of memories. This rewiring of the brain and the addition of new information into our 'databank' often leads to the development of new and novel solutions.

Many of us have struggled to find an answer to a problem before sleep, only to wake the next morning with new ideas on how to approach the situation, ideas that seem to have suddenly just 'popped' into our minds. Often, we can even wake with fully-formed solutions, as if by magic. It seems as if there were a part of our mind ceaselessly working on our puzzle whilst we slept.

On top of this natural problem-solving aspect of sleep, lucid dreaming offers a more direct means for addressing our issues. For here we have a virtual environment in which to explore problems in more depth, to experiment with different strategies without having to worry about the consequences of such actions.

Problems come in all shapes and sizes, and the practicalities of using lucid dreaming to aid in the discovery of their solutions will vary depending on the particular issue. One thing is certain, however: regardless of what the problem is, the more knowledge you have available, the more information you 'feed' your mind, will vastly improve the resources you and your sleeping brain will have to work with in finding a resolution. Falling asleep, having never read a word on physics, is unlikely to aid you in your physics exam the next day, but doing so after a hard day of reading and research on the topic will.

Sometimes, the only barrier between you and the solution to an issue is not a lack of knowledge, but a lack of creative associations between your current knowledge. In this situation, dreaming can be an especially powerful tool. Dreaming, and lucid dreaming, can be a very potent way of 'thinking outside of the box', giving one a unique access to the creative potential of the mind.

So, how do we go about unlocking this potential? The obvious way to achieve this is to enter a lucid dream with the goal of looking for answers within the dream. How you go about this process is something you must decide depending on your particular issue. For example, should you be struggling with an academic problem, perhaps conjuring up a famous person from this field and asking their advice (such as Carl Sagan for those struggling with a problem related to astronomy) would be the simplest approach. Indeed, using famous or historical figures, as people we respect in a particular field of knowledge, is a great way to quickly get advice on a problem or topic of that nature.

Even more mundane issues, such as the best way to decorate your new house, could be resolved in this manner. Why not simply dream of a famous interior designer or creative mind that you respect and ask them how they would deal with the issue? This tactic is a great way to access areas of creativity and knowledge from within your mind that you may feel are beyond your own reach. Whilst, of course, this knowledge and creativity will come from inside yourself, by projecting this through a famous character your mind is freed from any self-limiting restrictions you may have placed on your own thinking.

Be prepared, however, to receive often cryptic or seemingly nonsensical responses. Occasionally, upon awakening, you may realise that the advice you have been given makes little sense. In this scenario, it is best to take time to ponder what you have been told. Remember, the dreaming mind works in ways unlike the waking mind and, sometimes, the riddle that you face does indeed contain the answer to your question, only spelt out in a more fanciful and imaginative language.

Of course, do also be prepared for the possibility that the response is also simply nonsense. The dreaming mind is a powerful creative tool, but equally it has the power to imbue meaningless nonsense with a false sense of meaning. Use your own judgement in this area.

You are not limited to only specific dream characters for this task. You could, for example, just wander the dreamscape asking your question to anyone you meet. This can be especially effective, as it gives you a more diverse range of responses to work with and also continually focuses your dream towards the specific goal. If you persist in asking the same question over and over, then your dream (expecting this persistence) will be forced to engage with associations that may be more fitting for your situation.

Problem-solving isn't limited to just discussions with dream characters; using the flexible environment of dreamland, you are free to experiment with the problem directly within the dream. Should you be an artist, surgeon, builder, etc., you could use the dreamscape to rehearse or examine your problem in a virtual replica of reality. A simple example of this would be that of preparing for a speech or a discussion with someone; in dreamland, you can live out this scenario on multiple occasions prior to the real world event, trying out variations and seeing how well they are received.

Even issues such as self-confidence can be dealt with in this fashion. Should, for example, you suffer social anxiety, then use your dreamscape to practise talking to strangers. Here, you can deal with the emotions this process brings up in the safety and consequence-free environment of the dream.

Whilst many books on the subject can slightly oversell the possibilities regarding problem-solving via lucid dreaming, it must be said that lucidity can only ever really be seen as a tool to aid you, and is unlikely to be the sole solution to any issues you may have in your life. That said, it is a powerful tool and one which, when used alongside your daily activities, can go a long way towards helping resolve all manner of life's problems.

Accessing your memories

The world of dreams is equally the realm of memories, for it is the information held within the storerooms of our minds from which our dreams are built (even if it is sometimes in bizarre and unusual arrangements). It seems that, during dreams, access to our memory is greatly enhanced, although not in the obvious sense. It is certainly not the case whilst lucid dreaming that we will suddenly find ourselves endowed with a powerful, newfound ability to recall. In fact, quite often the opposite is the case and our memory can occasionally be somewhat limited.

Instead, it is the world of dreams around us that holds the key to our memories. We are, in essence, walking around the warehouse of our minds. Here, we can access seemingly forgotten details from our memories, brought to life in exquisite living detail. Our access here is not through the power of thought and recall (as it is during waking hours), but through the power of exploration and observation of the world around us.

Almost all of us have experienced non-lucid dreams in which we are suddenly face to face with aspects or environments from our past, which we may have long since forgotten we'd experienced; perhaps walking through our childhood home, or re-experiencing the classrooms of schools from decades past. Lucid dreaming allows us to initiate this experience consciously, allowing us to guide and explore these recreations on our own terms.

We all record a good deal more information about our daily experiences than we can generally access with our recall alone. Whilst we may not realise it, details such as the eye colour of the person serving you coffee a month ago are likely still stored somewhere within your mind. When using our waking memories to try and invoke such details - unless we have a photographic memory - almost all of us will struggle. However, should you by chance dream of visiting the very same cafe, it is likely that your mind will serve up a convincing replica of not only the cafe, but a realistic copy of the barista also, which will, of course, include his or her eyes.

With lucid dreaming, we do not have to wait by chance for such a dream to occur. Rather, we can choose to experience it. Not only that, but once we do we can explore and investigate the exact information we require.

The practical uses for this kind of memory access are incredibly wide and should hopefully be reasonably self-evident. Essentially, we can use our lucid dreams as a more direct route into the storehouse of our memories, allowing us knowledge that may have been previously unavailable. A simple use for such a practice would be for nostalgia alone; we can relive our past, recalling details with a profound sense of realism (such as the voice of an old friend, or maybe a departed grandparent).

More practical uses could be those things such as attempting to recall where we placed a lost item, piecing together memories in which details are missing, reliving an important lecture, or any of the many other endless uses for which we generally can only use our waking memories. Caution about the validity of such results needs to be mentioned here, though; sometimes, it is simply the case that we have not stored the relevant information, or the data has long since become corrupt and unusable in our memories.

Whilst dreams are a great tool for exploring memory in a direct fashion, the dreaming mind is also very capable of making a 'best fit' guess, filling in any gaps in our knowledge with suitable (although not necessarily correct) approximations of what may have occurred or details from similar events. Therefore, always treat the information gathered in this way with a critical mind; do not simply assume it is correct. Of course, the same can be said of any form of retrieved memory, dreaming or otherwise.

This is a topic that is ripe for experimentation, and I assume the reader, now well-versed in the skills required for dream control, needn't be given endless examples or suggestions on how to approach this particular use of lucid dreaming. I would advise, however, testing your dreaming memory access against real world facts. For example, why not attempt to explore an environment with which you are familiar, but perhaps have not visited in some time, in your next lucid dream? Make mental notes of as many prominent details as possible during this dream.

Once you have woken and recorded as many of these details as possible, on the next opportunity visit the real-world equivalent and judge how close an approximation your dreaming mind was able to create, establishing the quality of your dreaming recollection. In performing this kind of experiment, you can confirm (or deny) the effectiveness of using lucid dreaming for memory recall, giving you a more realistic sense of how such a process operates, and its capabilities.

Expanding your hobbies

A fabulous practical use of your powers within a lucid dream, which often also falls under the earlier category of 'wish fulfilment', is to use them to enhance or expand upon your existing hobbies or interests. Perhaps the easiest way to demonstrate this concept is through an example, so the following is one of my own personal uses of lucid dreaming in this regards.

For many years now, I have been a passionate amateur astronomer, spending many a night observing the various celestial events and features of the night sky. Armed with my telescope and a little knowledge, it is a humbling experience to witness with my own eyes the vastness of the universe we all inhabit. However, one thing any astronomer will tell you is that, what you see through your telescope (however large and expensive), bears little resemblance to the images of planets, nebulae and galaxies that are often seen in the media or books on astronomy.

These images are taken with very long exposures, processed, and are often taken from very powerful (and occasionally non-Earth) telescopes, allowing for a view that is impossible with the human eye armed with a telescope on Earth. Whilst, during those cold nights viewing beauties such as the Andromeda Galaxy, the Orion Nebula or Saturn's rings, my imagination and knowledge of what I was viewing played a very large role in the pleasure of the experience.

For the uninformed, the images through the telescope would be somewhat underwhelming, often simply a smudge of light, or a pea-sized planet. You can imagine for someone with a passion for the cosmos that such a tantalising experience is also tainted with a little frustration; to witness these spectacles from afar and never being able to experience them up close and in more detail.

Now, it is probably obvious to the reader where this is all leading. Of course, as a lucid dreamer and an astronomer, such an experience is possible! I have for many years combined both interests, using many of my lucid dreams to explore space in the comfort of my own mind. In the world of dreams, limits such as the speed of light, or distances are irrelevant; the only requirement is an ability to control the dream and the relevant knowledge from which the dreamworld can accurately build a convincing model of the experience.

So, to my joy, after a night spent viewing the planets and stars in the waking world, I could retire to bed and visit these places in my dreams. I could enjoy such pleasures as flying through the rings of Saturn, climbing the solar system's largest mountain, Olympus Mons, on Mars, or witnessing the birth of stars in the Orion Nebula. All of these experiences, that were previously the realm of fuzzy daydreams, could now be experienced with the clarity and realism of a lucid dream. Importantly, as my knowledge of astronomy grew (often compelled by my dreaming experiences), so too did the realism of each subsequent dream replica.

As you can see, the combination of lucid dreaming and a personal interest can offer new realms of exploration into your current hobbies that you may not have originally considered. This is, however, not limited to astronomy. If you are a musician, then perhaps you can dream of playing with a favourite band or performer; for the classically trained, why not visit the era in which your music was composed and play in the original orchestra? Maybe your interest is in Martial Arts, so why not then train with one of the greats such as Bruce Lee?

These are suggestions only, and it is up to you to find a way to enhance whichever interest you currently enjoy. The options are vast. One thing you are likely to discover, as did I with my explorations in astronomy, is that this process can create a very positive feedback loop between your waking and dreaming life. As you improve your skills and knowledge in your waking life, so too will the detail and realism of your dreams grow. Furthermore, as the potency of your dreams increases, so too will they inspire you further to pursue and expand your knowledge whilst awake. I needn't say more on this subject, but I heartily recommend this use of lucid dreaming as it can truly bring about some profoundly inspiring experiences.

Living the future you

Skim through many 'self-help' books and you'll more than likely come across a very popular technique for improving confidence and working towards improving yourself. The idea is simple. Firstly, you 'design' the person you want to be in the future, making a list of all those character traits, behaviours and aspect of your lifestyle that you would like to one day achieve. Once you've compiled this 'future you', you are told to spend some time each day, usually first thing in the morning and last thing at night (but also during any spare time), visualising this new you. You are told to imagine every aspect of this improved version of you, how it feels to be them, what their life involves, etc. You are normally also told to set various goals in your life that move you towards becoming more like this future version of yourself, and to compare yourself to this goal daily, making any changes to your behaviour, thoughts or lifestyle that are not in keeping with your goal.

The idea is that this 'positive thinking' works to motivate you into making positive changes in your life; that, by clearly defining your goals, you can more easily work towards making them a reality. This seems like a fair assumption and, whilst I am usually not normally a fan of these kinds of self-help books (as they often contain more quackery and pseudoscience mumbo jumbo than genuine quality advice), it's obvious that goal-setting with clearly defined goals, combined with regular reflection and the relevant lifestyle changes, is a good start for making positive improvements in your life.

Of course, the power of such a technique lies in the ability for the user to clearly visualise their goal, something that most of us find rather difficult. Yes, we can all daydream, but often this is just little more than fuzzy, ill-defined thoughts. Think, then, just how much more powerful and motivating the ability to experience the 'future you' via lucid dreaming would be. You can, of course, use lucid dreaming with the technique as it is outlined above; once you have chosen the person you are aiming to become, you can simply use your lucid dreams to experience this life long before it becomes a reality.

An additional benefit, beyond the powerful realism of lucid dreaming, is that by actually living the experience in this way you have the chance to evaluate and adapt your goal, should you find that the actual experience isn't quite what you originally expected. You may also find that your dreaming mind offers alternatives and improvements, giving you ideas on self-improvement that you had not yet considered.

The options for living future events and exploring future versions of yourself offer plenty of opportunity for exploration. You are not limited to simply enhancing self-help techniques as above, but there are all manner of ways in which the rehearsal of future events can be beneficial. Experimentation is your friend here and many examples of possible uses spring to mind, such as preparation for interviews, testing out planned changes in personal appearance, practising social events before they occur, rehearsing difficult or awkward conversations in advance, etc.

Once again, your own lifestyle and needs in life will dictate how you choose to use this ability. One interesting example is that of expectant mothers experiencing a dream version of motherhood prior to giving birth. Such an experience may help aid the mother in psychologically and emotionally preparing for the event whilst, at the same time, giving her the unusual opportunity to bond with (and 'meet') her baby before its birth. Whilst the experience would, of course, only be a mental model of reality, it should still help prepare the mother for the emotional reality of parenthood (of course, there is no reason fathers cannot also experiment with this idea).

To take this idea one step further, parents struggling with choosing a name for their child-to-be could use the ability of living future events to 'try on for size' various names for their child. Furthermore, as the rules of reality have no sway on what is possible within a dream, why not ask the dream version of your baby which name they prefer? If nothing else, you will have a very interesting story to share with your child once they grow up!

Dreams are a powerful virtual world. Once your ability to control the dreamscape reaches a certain level of accomplishment, the exploration and practice of possible futures becomes a wonderful way in which to prepare yourself for the future events.

However, you must remain level-headed; lucid dreaming is not a crystal ball offering you a genuine glimpse of the future. Instead, it is more akin to a computer simulation offering you the ability to experience a model of a potential future, based on available data. You are free to play with this model, however you wish, but just remind yourself that what you are doing is not a mystical glimpse into the future, but a try-before-you-buy experiment with your available options.

Exploring creativity

Dreams by their very nature are creative. Every night, our minds give us a personal viewing of a unique work of creative fiction - our dreamlands. Throughout history, people of all walks of life and all manner of professions have been inspired by the creativity of their dreams, many using their nightly adventures as inspiration in their daily pursuits, often even finding creative solutions to their problems.

Famous examples of creativity inspired by dreams abound, as history is full of those who credit dreaming as their muse. The novelist Robert Louis Stevenson is one of the more famous examples of dream inspiration, with his now classic novel *The Strange Case of Dr. Jekyll and Mr. Hyde* being attributed to the creativity of his dreaming mind.

It seems, however, that he may have used a combination of hypnagogia and dreaming. In *A Chapter on Dreams,* he describes the central role that dreaming and the twilight states of sleep played in his own creative process. Stevenson claims that many of his stories came to him courtesy of dreamland creatures he called 'Brownies'. He writes 'And for the Little People, what shall I say they are but just my Brownies, God bless them! who do one-half my work for me while I am fast asleep, and in all human likelihood, do the rest for me as well, when I am wide awake and fondly suppose I do it for myself. That part which is done while I am sleeping is the Brownies' part beyond contention; but that which is done when I am up and about is by no means necessarily mine, since all goes to show the Brownies have a hand in it even then.'

In more modern times, another famous example is the composition of The Beatles' famous song 'Yesterday' written by Paul McCartney. Apparently, the entire melody came to him whilst sleeping at his then girlfriend's house (his girlfriend being Jane Asher). Upon awakening, he quickly rushed to the piano to avoid forgetting it. McCartney was worried that he had somehow subconsciously plagiarised the tune, thinking it was something he'd already heard yet had forgotten the source. In his words: 'For about a month I went round to people in the music business and asked them whether they had ever heard it before. Eventually it became like handing something in to the police. I thought if no-one claimed it after a few weeks then I could have it.'

Dream creativity is not limited to the arts, however. Science also has had its fair share of nocturnal inspirations, perhaps the most famous being the inspiration of the organic chemist August Kekulé. In 1865, Kekulé woke up from a dream in which he saw a snake forming a circle by biting its own tail. Kekulé had previously been struggling with describing the true chemical structure of Benzene. The secret to this problem lay within this image of the snake, and it was just enough inspiration to clue Kekulé into realising Benzene's structure was in the form of a ring.

A more recent scientific discovery also inspired by a dream (and which shares much in common with that of Kekulé) was that of the discovery of the structure of DNA by James Watson and Francis Crick. It's claimed that Watson dreamt of a series of spiral staircases, which again was the creative leap needed to push him in the direction of their discovery.

History is full of accounts such as these. All of these creative dreams share one thing in common: they were non-lucid. Therefore, the dreamers were at the whim of chance, waiting for inspiration to visit them in their twilight worlds.

Lucid dreaming offers us the perfect means for initiating creativity within the dreamworld. Using various strategies, we can influence our lucid dreams so as to nudge them in the direction of creativity. Creativity can mean many things depending upon your requirements; for example, a scientist's needs will be very different from that of a musician, as is an artist's from that of a dancer. The key here is to plan your approach to fit your own needs. To do this, let's have a look at a few examples of how creativity can be extracted from the dreaming mind.

As a teenager, I had a passion for art. I was never particularly talented in this regards, but loved the process and thought patterns that went behind the creation of a new piece. At the time, I used several dream creativity techniques as inspiration. The first and simplest (that given thought can be adapted to other creative pursuits) was that of the 'gallery of unpainted pictures'. Here, I would seek out galleries in my dreamworld, telling myself before entering them that I would find within artwork that is unique to the dreamworld, not simply recreations from my waking life memories.

Once lucid and having found a suitable gallery, I would spend my time exploring the artwork on offer, waiting until I found a piece I believed to be suitably impressive. I would spend much time examining my choice, attempting to commit as much of the detail to memory as I could. Usually, once I had found and memorised as much of the painting as possible, I would wake myself (using the technique for waking at will, outlined in Chapter 6) and, depending on the time of night, either make notes, or a brief sketch to capture the information as clearly as I could.

Such a technique is incredibly easy, requiring little more than one's ability to navigate and explore the dreamworld in order to look for a suitable gallery. Of course, dream control can be used here and you could equally create such a gallery in this manner. As mentioned, there is no reason why this concept shouldn't be transferable to other areas of creativity; for example, a musician could visit a dream record store, or seek out musical dream characters performing their pieces live. A scientist could, for example, visit the 'museum of science-to-be'. The idea is as simple as finding suitable environments or characters in your dreams, ones related to your particular interests, and using these to find inspiration.

An important point needs to be made here - for those who are looking for inspiration in the written word, the first idea may logically be to visit a dream library to hunt inspiration. However, as we have seen in our earlier discussions on reality tests, text is unstable in the dreamworld and it is usually very difficult to read. As such, inspiration-seeking writers will need to approach this with a different tactic. Yes, visiting a dream library may well be the best environment in which to place yourself, but you yourself will not be able to read the available books; instead, the best approach is to either find audio books or, better still, have a dream character read sections of the books out loud for you to hear. The result will still leave you with the information you require, only this clever loophole allows us to avoid the inherent limitations of dreamworld.

Indeed, many of the limitations you may be faced with in the land of dreams can be bypassed through similar tactics (often enlisting the help of a dream character to work on your behalf). So, should you come up against similar problems, don't be disheartened - just find a loophole.

The second technique I used to inspire my own artistic creativity was something I called 'Fractal Dreaming'. The process is very simple, but leads to a nice continuity to the creative process. Once lucid, I would seek out the dream version of my own already-painted artwork (or sometimes that of my favourite artists). Once found, I would use these paintings as 'windows' into other 'dimensions' of the dreamworld, jumping through the painting itself with the intention of entering the world within the painting.

More often than not, this would be successful, with incredibly mixed results. Sometimes, the dream scene would shift to something seemingly unrelated to the painting, while other times I would find myself in a far more surreal dream landscape based on the artwork itself (this was especially unusual for more abstract pieces). Whatever the result, I would then seek out a scene or image within this new landscape, something that I believed would make an interesting new painting. Once again, when I had found what I needed, I would examine and commit this image to memory, ready to record it once I awoke.

It is here that the fractal recursive nature of the process takes place. Once I had eventually painted and recreated this scene in waking life, I could then repeat the whole 'fractal' dreaming process once again. I would find this new painting in the dreamworld and jump through its 'window', looking for inspiration for my next painting. Eventually, and after many months of this kind of practise, I would end up with a series of paintings, all of which would be scenes from within the world of the previous painting in the series.

This particular practice may be a little more specific to visual art, but with some thought you may well be able to invent your own self-fuelling creative process within the dreamworld. Often, the best way to inspire creativity within the dreamworld is to become creative in how you approach the dream itself. Experiment with different tactics and ideas; seek out advice and inspiration directly from the environment and dream characters, all the while keeping a watchful eye on what is occurring. Sometimes, the smallest detail can be just the seed of inspiration you are looking for.

8
Delving Deeper

So far, we have taken a look at just a handful of the many possible experiences and uses of lucid dreaming. But the world of lucid dreaming is vast and its potential is much wider than could ever be condensed into just one book on the subject (or even an entire library). In reality, each lucid dreamer is walking a path that is unique to themselves, and the adventures and practical uses you will undertake in your dreamworld will always be for you to decide and for you alone to experience. Your journey will be one of a kind.

However, so far we have only touched the surface. Lucid dreaming is more than simply an amusement park ride or an elaborate computer simulation. Whilst lucid dreaming, we are in many ways approaching some of the deepest mysteries of life; we are exploring what it means to be human, what it is to inhabit a brain. Essentially, we are looking deep within the machinery of who and what we are.

Here, we enter the realm of philosophy and are faced with the same questions both scientists and the spiritually-inclined have been wrestling with for eons. It is neither mine, nor anybody else's place to answer the questions that arise for you; nor would it be possible to do so, as every human life is a unique entity, an individual expression of the universe, a thread woven through time and space.

My personal truths may be very different from yours. Even the objective truths of the universe must be processed and assimilated by each of us in a way that fits with our own knowledge and experiences as we passage through our lives. I can only assume that most curious dreamers will stumble, as I have, upon such fundamental questions about what it means to be alive during their time in dreamland. The very nature of lucid dreaming is such that it can pull the rug from beneath your feet, while those things that you have taken for granted about existence suddenly become questionable, such is the power of the experience of waking up in a world that isn't there.

It is difficult to approach this subject without falling into the trap of preaching. It is common for many books on dreams to attempt to tie these experiences to those of a particular religious or spiritual tradition, or even to dismiss such philosophical concepts altogether in favour of looking at the purely scientific facts.

Whilst I myself am a man with a deep respect for science, I feel that, when it comes to the deeper philosophical questions that lucidity can raise, it is wrong to let my own subjective world view and beliefs, or any other traditional or spiritual concepts, influence the journey and thoughts of others. As such, in this section I shall be exploring a selection of dreaming experiences and the questions that they may raise. Of course, it would be impossible for me to be completely objective in my approach, as much as it is for any human to slip free of their own programming (and every idea must be explored from within a particular framework). However, I will strive to avoid sharing my own personal 'answers' to these questions, and instead let you the reader decide if the questions raised are valid and worth exploring in your own dreams. Consider this section of the book and the following ideas as short philosophical essays with the intention to plant a seed of curiosity in your own mind.

Meeting the people that live inside you

Of all the many events one can experience in a lucid dream, few are nearly quite as fascinating, nor pose as many philosophical questions, as that of meeting the inhabitants of dreamland. From the simplest life forms all the way through to fellow 'humans', the dreamscape can be teeming with entities with whom you can make an acquaintance. Of course, given the boundless creativity and bizarre rules of your inner universe, the beings you encounter can come in any manner of guises, most common (as perhaps you'd expect) being the appearance of familiar faces, friends, loved ones and even pets. The waking rules of life and death hold no sway here, so do be prepared to come face to face with people you'd assumed you'd never see again; be prepared, too, for the emotions that come with such a meeting.

Time, also, is flexible and you may find yourself encountering younger (or older) versions of those you know, or even people you'd long since forgotten about. It can all be quite disorientating. Furthermore, the creativity of our dreaming minds isn't limited by our Earthly rules of biology, nor for that matter is it bound by such trivial things as what-is-possible. Beings can, and do, come in truly any shape, from angels to demons, gods to goblins, aliens, spirits, fairies, dragons, genii, fictional or historical characters, and so on. Even inanimate objects, given the opportunity, can become enchanted with their own spark of life, their own communicative identity.

Such is the nature of exploring a world upon which the very foundation of its existence is consciousness, your mind. Everything you encounter is weaved on the enchanted loom of your own mind. The birds you see in your dream sky are patterns of energy flowing through the neural connections of your brain, as (if you really stop to think about it) are you.

This would all be much easier to swallow if, on encountering such beings, they appeared to be little more than puppets, nearly convincing but flawed facsimiles of their originals. However, whilst on occasion one does stumble upon an inhabitant of the oneirosphere that seems less than cognisant, more often than not the illusion is perfect, *if indeed it is an illusion*. Time and time again in both my own dreams and, as confirmed, in my discussions with (and reports from) other lucid dreamers, the consensus is that dream characters pass all of the criteria we would expect when dealing with any genuine waking life entity.

So, what of this? Why make the statement 'if indeed it is an illusion'? Well, firstly I am not for a moment making the claim that dream characters are indeed independent, self-aware beings (although, with humility, I wouldn't want to completely rule it out). Instead, I am asking you, the reader, to ponder the nature of consciousness, the nature of your interactions with other living creatures whilst awake and, at the very core, the nature of your own consciousness and self-identity. In short, what does it mean to be you?

As I have already alluded to, whilst dreaming; your sense of self, your environment and the apparent entities within that environment all exist within the same neural architecture. From the perspective of an external observer monitoring your brain activity, would it be possible for them to distinguish the neural activity that represents you and your dream identity from that of the neural activity for whichever dream character you are interacting with? The obvious answer is that, to the outside observer, all activity within your brain would be considered you. Yet, from your subjective viewpoint, whilst dreaming you would have a very distinct sense of self (which, upon reflection, would be almost, if not totally, identical to that of your waking sense of self) and you would experience both the environment and characters within the environment as external independent entities. These are important points to consider and can, like Alice, lead us down a very interesting rabbit hole of philosophical thought.

Should you give this thought experiment it's due consideration, you may find yourself asking further questions, such as 'How much of what I experience of others in my waking life is genuinely their external influence, and how much of it do I myself generate?' Or perhaps 'How do my opinions and mental models of others affect who I am as an individual?' Maybe you'd also be wise to consider asking 'Is the person I identify as myself, really all I am?'

It is neither my place nor my desire to answer these questions for you, as half of the fun and value of all this is to explore these ideas yourself. I do believe, however, that it is both healthy and rewarding to dissect and experiment with the assumptions you make about who you are and those things you assume about others, dreamt or otherwise. Lucid dreaming can be the perfect experimental laboratory for your own psychological and philosophical journey, and meeting the people who live inside your dreams can teach you a lot about who you are. Who knows what you'll discover?

There are no graveyards in dreamland

If we examine the idea of dream characters further, we will inevitably stumble upon a rather sensitive subject and one that affects us all, that subject being death. As the title of this topic suggests, in a sense there is no death (at least, not of the permanent variety) in the dreamworld (although there may well be graveyards!). Our dream characters can just as easily be reproductions of the deceased as they can the living. Of course, this is a topic that can be loaded with emotion and so, for those of you who are in the sad position of grieving the recent loss of a loved one, I would advise using your own judgement as to whether or not to continue reading or skipping to the next topic.

The appearance of the deceased in dreams can raise all manner of philosophical and spiritual questions, and is often one of the most intense of all the experiences you are likely to encounter in the dreamworld. Equally, however, we must also remind ourselves that, often in our dreams, we will interact with characters that are most certainly no longer among the living, but have less of a personal emotional impact on us, such as those times we invoke famous historical characters whom we had never known personally. Whoever we interact with in the realm of dreams, one thing remains the same: our brains, it would seem, are very capable of creating a likeness that is uncanny. The dead in dreams seem very much as alive as can be.

Here, we are faced with questions to which there are perhaps no answers. Some may wonder if such experiences are transcending the purely mental process of dreaming and are perhaps tapping into something far deeper. Or, we can be pushed to question what it really means to know others. How much of them are stored in our own minds (and what does that really mean?). Also, just how much have we remembered of them correctly?

Even if we accept the most likely explanation for such dreams, that they are just the products of our minds, we are still faced with some incredibly potent questions about reality. If the 'essence' of a human is only the patterns of energy (or data) living within the architecture of our brains, then what does it mean to know someone else? (and what does it mean for them to know us?).

A deep closeness with another human could be considered, in a very real sense, to be allowing part of them to reside in your own brain. The information they share about themselves (not just what they tell you, but their actions, behaviours, etc.) will all be recorded within your own mind, and a mental model (or schema) for this person will be developed within you. Essentially, part of their pattern becomes part of who you are - part of *your* pattern. In a way, the closer we are to another, the larger their residency in our own mind.

Realistically, when we think of others during our waking hours, we are not truly thinking about them as the objective entity they are, but simply accessing our own subjective models of them. Our models of others are our way of knowing those around us - and it's important to remember that they *are* just models. The difference between the living and the dead, as far as our minds are concerned, is that the living are still able to choose to update their models in our minds (through their actions, etc.), often surprising us with new information.

The dead, on the other hand, can obviously no longer update what we know of them, at least not of their own volition, so they remain 'frozen' in our minds, their models being a record of everything we knew of them up until our final meeting (of course, we may still update our mental models through discussions about them with family or friends, or through our later discoveries about them).

So, what does this mean? Could it be considered that interactions with the deceased during dreams are, in some way, a genuine connection with who they were? We often hear phrases such as 'They live on in my mind' and, in many ways, this could be considered as true; as we go about our daily lives, we are constantly building copies of ourselves in the minds of all those we interact with. Indeed, even the act of writing this book is sharing with you, the reader, thoughts transmitted directly from my mind, at this point in time (my now), to your mind at some point in the future (your now). Part of what makes me who I am will then reside within your own mind, even if this occurs a hundred years after the time of writing.

Such a process and the resultant dreams can be the seed of whole worlds of philosophical thought. We can dissect our own personalities and consider just how much of who we are is built upon who we know. We may question our own mortality and our behaviours in life, how the legacy of our minds may be transmitted beyond our lifespan. Questions about the basis of personality, and the old nature versus nurture argument, may also surface in our minds. We will all inevitably face death, both our own and those whom we love.

Dreams offer us an opportunity to experience the deceased once again and in a way that no waking experience can; we can talk with them, laugh with them, re-experience their idiosyncrasies. It is a beautiful gift of the dreaming mind. Dreams also allow us to experience our own deaths, or our own beliefs about what occurs after death. In exploring these topics, you may well find yourself asking 'What or who dies?' and this is probably a very good place to start. By pursuing such lines of thought, peeling away each layer of the onion of 'self', it may be that you will stumble upon a new understanding of yourself and those around you.

What lies beyond the stars?

Since we first looked up at the stars, humans have wondered what lay beyond. History is filled with myths and legends of magical realms, the world of the gods. Modern science has mapped a good deal of the observable universe and we live in a time where we know more about the Cosmos than ever before. We now know a lot about the universe in which we live, but many people ask the (perhaps meaningless) question 'What lies beyond the universe?'

Whether or not this question is meaningless in the physical realm, in our inner universe of dreams, the oneirosphere, there is an answer to this question - a question that raises further questions about reality.

Earlier in the book, we looked at how our experience of the waking world is indirect. Whilst awake, our bodies feed our brains with sensory information about the outside world; this information is then processed in our minds, resulting in an internal mental model being created, based on what we observe. Our experience is of a subjective model, limited by our senses and the abilities of our brains. Whilst dreaming, we no longer build these internal models based on sensory input, but instead from the contents of our minds, our memories and expectations, etc. Either way, whatever world we inhabit, waking or dreaming, what we are experiencing is a model - a model that exists within our brains.

This information can lead us to a rather strange, but seemingly inevitable, conclusion; Whilst dreaming, whatever we experience, occurs within our brain; therefore, the only correct answer for questions such as 'What lies beyond the stars?', 'What lies beyond the universe?' or even 'What is behind that wall?' is:

'The inside of your skull.'

There is no physical space in which we can traverse in the world of dreams. Every environment in which you find yourself occurs in exactly the same place: in your brain, *within your skull*. Regardless of whether you are sitting in a dream replica of your home, or orbiting a distant dream star, you are in exactly the same place, *inside your skull*.

The same can be said in some respects for our waking experiences. When you look up at the stars, again you are not directly witnessing the stars; instead, you are seeing the model your mind has built based upon the information supplied by your senses. If you look at the wall of your room, it is not the 'real' wall, but your mind's interpretation of the wall. Every horizon, every place your gaze lands and can see no further, occurs in the same place and has the same thing behind it: the *inside of your skull*.

Of course, when waking, our model is a scaled-down replica of the actual place in the universe which your body inhabits. However, you will never experience that universe beyond what your human senses inform you about it. Take a moment to look into the distance - find the furthest point you can see. Now, consider the fact that, beyond that point, is the *inside of your skull* and, beyond your skull, is the real scene expanding onwards into the vastness of the universe. It would seem the human condition is to live in a facsimile of reality, one that is only as good as is required for our continued survival and requirements as intelligent primates.

We live our entire lives within our minds, dreaming or awake. Everything you are experiencing right now is a form of waking dream. Even the words you are reading on this page are occurring within your mind. They are the interpretation of your sensory input. These words, the pages they are written on, the book, your hands and the world around you are all (from your perspective, as an observing consciousness) thoughts within your mind.

Are they thoughts based on reality? Yes. But objective reality itself? No. The book, of course, exists independently from your thoughts, but your experience of its independent reality can only ever be that of the model of the book that exists within your mind, and therefore includes all the schemas, relationships and connections that you hold also within your mind.

Each of us could be considered as a walking, talking miniature model of a part of the universe held within our brain. A truly unique model built from the data we have acquired on our own individual passage through space and time. So, where does that leave us? That's not really for me to say, but it's an interesting thought experiment and one that, I hope, you'll enjoy exploring. Take time, both whilst waking and dreaming, to ponder what this really means - or if, indeed, it does mean anything.

What is real?

Perhaps the core question that can arise through lucid dreaming is that of the nature of reality. How exactly do we define 'real'? In our daily lives, we make many throw-away assertions about what is or is not real, often not giving them the thought they deserve. If something is solid and tangible, then surely (people say) that is more than enough to be accepted as real?

For most people, dreams are not 'real'. Yes, they are a genuine phenomenon, but our experiences within them are 'just an illusion'. But is it really this black and white? The advent of modern science has already demonstrated that, the further you look into the structure of matter, the less solid it appears to be. Reality, it seems, is far more about fields of energy, more than it is about the solidity.

The majority of what we consider to be a physical item is, in fact, mostly empty space. Even without physics, simple thought experiments can disrupt our views on what is real. Take, for example, an orange. Should you hold this fruit in your hand, you are likely to assert that this orange is 'real'. It's physical, it has a weight, it has a name - it exists. Yet, in many ways it is only real as a particular event in space and time. For example, long before the orange in your hand was a fruit, it was a flower; before that, it was sunlight and soil. Also, if you were to peel the orange and share the segments between your friends, where has the orange gone? Is it still an orange, or is it now a series of separate entities?

If we continue along this line of thinking, we must accept that our world is a transient series of events, and the 'real' items we interact with are only a snapshot of reality, a single frame in the ongoing movie. Of course, this does not mean to say that oranges (or anything else, for that matter) are unreal; rather, they are only temporary. However, we so often confuse ourselves into believing that there is some kind of essence to physical items, something deeper that makes them what they are. Instead, we could consider them as patterns in reality, temporary configurations. Our hypothetical orange exists for a time, but the 'reality' or 'essence' we project onto it is not inherent to the item; instead, it is our own label, our own lazy thinking that attempts to define a fluid process into a static entity.

Here, we need to remind ourselves that the mental models we create for everything we come into contact with are essentially stereotypes, simplified and convenient labels and explanations for what are really complicated waves of transformation flowing through the universe. If we mistake the map for the terrain, then we risk falling into psychological traps of our own making; we will experience cognitive dissonance, when the true nature of reality conflicts with the models we have built in our own minds.

As we have already discussed, whether we are waking or dreaming, we seem to live in our own mental model, and our experience of reality is filtered. A dream orange, or a waking world orange, are experientially the same as far as our minds are concerned.

So, what other criteria do we have for judging reality? How does a dreamt orange differ from that of its waking counterpart? The most obvious is the objective nature of waking life events. Items in the real world exist independently from their observers; they also form part of the endless series of cause and effect that we call the universe.

However, dreams are not independent from the universe. As we have already seen, many dreamt experiences in history have influenced the external waking world (for example, the invention of the sewing machine came about after Elias Howe dreamt of cannibals carrying spears with holes at their pointed end, which inspired his invention). So, dream events are not outside of the world of cause and effect, either. Indeed dreams both feed on the waking world and can feed back into this world.

The purely subjective nature of dreams is also arguable. Whilst they do indeed occur within the mind of the dreamer, and are to the dreamer a subjective experience, the dream itself is still a physical event occurring within the architecture of a brain. A dreamt orange may well not be physical in the same sense as a real-world orange, but it still exists physically as the firing of a certain combination of neurons within a human brain.

But the experience of being human is more than simply interactions with objects in the physical world. Few of us would argue that emotions are unreal. In fact, many times in our lives our emotions define our reality; they feel more real than anything else we can imagine. Falling in love, for example, is one of the most profound events in a human life. Music, poetry, religions and even wars have been inspired and waged by the depth of human emotions.

Feelings are intangible; they are as insubstantial as the wind. Yet, like the wind, they are an invisible force that shapes our world. In our waking lives, our emotions and moods can affect us even without obvious cause. Yes, we may be moved and inspired by outside events, but equally we can simply find ourselves in a dark mood, without reason, that can deeply impact the way we behave and how our day unfolds.

If emotions - with or without cause - are 'real', what then of the emotions we experience within the dreamworld? Are they illusions? Are they less real because we experience them in another world, or because their source is considered unreal? It's a very difficult question, and one that deserves thought. The emotions in our dreams can and do (often even without our knowledge or recall of their source) affect our waking lives. Sayings such as 'She's got out of the wrong side of the bed' are a testament to this fact.

So, what does this all mean and where do we draw the lines that define reality? Perhaps there are no solid answers to this question. Maybe, like the physical world, the deeper you delve the more questions arise and the less substantial things become. I will leave you to explore these questions and define your own reality. However, perhaps the words of Henry Havelock Ellis may help you on your way:

'Dreams are real while they last. Can we say more of life?'

Row your boat

'Row, row, row your boat, gently down the stream, merrily, merrily, merrily, merrily, life is but a dream' goes the famous children's song. Like this seemingly simple song, the journey of exploring your dreams can also seem equally simple at first. However (again, like this song), there are hidden depths that lie just beneath the initial veneer of simplicity, depths that can be uncovered with just a little thought. The previous discussions have only touched the very surface of an ocean of philosophical enquiry that you may find yourself exploring. Lucid dreaming can become a powerful tool that aids you, not only in the exploration of your dreams, but also your own psychology, philosophies, relationships with others, the world around you, and your views on what it means to be alive.

When I originally decided to write this book, I had assumed that the philosophical element to this book would be the majority of its content. Yet, as with many things in life, ideas and reality are very different things. Instead, upon approaching this topic, it became abundantly clear that it is not my place to influence too strongly your 'journey downstream'. Life, dreams and reality are, for each of us, very different things. What I may take for granted as 'normal' may well be utterly alien to your existence and vice versa.

Therefore, how you approach the bigger questions that surround lucid dreaming and life should be a private journey, one in which you should make your own discoveries and reach your own conclusions. It is much better, it seems, to offer and teach the tools available to make such explorations, rather than to spoil the surprises that lay in store. Therefore, this section is here to serve only as a reminder that there is more to lucid dreaming than initially meets the eye.

Lucid dreaming can be many things; you may decide to approach the topic as simply a quirk of psychology, something with which to entertain yourself. I, myself, am drawn to the deeper questions it raises, and I believe it is this, more so than any other element of the experience, that has held my attention for my entire life. Fun is certainly rewarding in its own right, but the nature of reality can give us far more than a lifetime's worth of new and fascinating experiences, discoveries and insights into our reality.

As we skilfully row the 'boat' of our minds with a gentle awareness through the stream of life, if we keep pushing and moving forward we can find endless joy in its constantly astounding and mind-boggling complexity and beauty. We may find that lucid dreaming aids us in this process, opening our eyes to the magic that can occur even behind closed eyelids.

Life is full of such hidden secrets and wonders, both dreaming and waking. It may help us to learn, as William Blake wrote, 'To see a world in a grain of sand, And a heaven in a wild flower, Hold infinity in the palm of your hand, And eternity in an hour.' Your journey down the stream of life is for you alone. Hopefully, the wonders of dreamland will help keep you 'merry', but perhaps you may also eventually come to discover that, in many ways, that life is but a dream.

9
Lucid Living

Perhaps the most rarely discussed element of lucid dreaming is the effect it has on the waking lives of its practitioners. The effects of practising conscious dreaming are far from limited to the time you spend sleeping; in fact, in many ways it is the enhancement of one's daily life that keeps many lucid dreamers attached to the subject for their entire lives. We've already seen how 11% of our daily mental activity is spent dreaming, which is a surprisingly large portion of our conscious experience. However, it is the other 89% that we shall now turn our attention towards.

As you have learnt, many of the skills required for obtaining lucidity are practised during waking hours. These techniques, such as reality testing, are vital when developing a skilful awareness of the world around you, which leads eventually to lucidity within the dreamworld. Of course, such techniques will also enhance your daily awareness, helping improve your observational skills and your general mental clarity.

As you become a proficient lucid dreamer, you should find that your relationship with the waking world also changes. You will become more discerning, less prone to thoughtlessly reacting to external and internal events. You may also find that you become a more reflective individual, one who responds to your waking life in a more thoughtful and adaptive manner. In traditional meditation practices, the term for such a mental state is called 'mindfulness' which, in essence, is a kind of waking-lucidity, an awareness of the current moment and an awareness of awareness itself. Many lucid dreamers find that, not only are they awake in their dreams, but they are also no longer simply sleepwalking through their daily lives; they 'wake up' to the waking world.

Much of this process of increasing awareness is gradual and certainly won't happen overnight. For example, even experienced lucid dreamers miss plenty of cues to reality test, both in the waking and dreaming worlds. Awareness is much like a muscle, in that it takes regular effort and practice to grow; but even the strongest muscle will have moments of weakness when conditions such as diet, health or simply unexpected events put too much strain upon it.

Never be too harsh a judge on yourself if you find your awareness lacking. Simply use every missed chance as an opportunity to learn, as a stepping stone towards increased mental acuity.

Waking awareness, like dream lucidity, is a personal journey, one that is unique to each dreamer. Therefore, there is no guide that will ever account for every possible experience you may encounter. However, in this section we will cover some of the more predictable and likely mistakes and events that you may encounter, offering tips on how to make the most of your growing awareness.

Lucid about Lucidity

If nothing else, the practice of lucid dreaming requires at least a modest level of critical thinking and discrimination. As a result, it is rather surprising how often those new to the subject (and some long-term practitioners) often do not apply these ways of thinking towards the subject of lucid dreaming itself.

As we will cover shortly, the world of lucid dreaming is somewhat of a jungle, and there are many unscrupulous entrepreneurs and those looking to promote other agendas who are peddling various unsavoury products and belief systems, whilst also making extraordinary (and implausible) claims regarding lucid dreaming.

Here, lucid dreamers need to apply the critical and logical thinking required to achieve a lucid dream towards the subject of lucid dreaming itself.

As lucid dreamers, we are in a very unusual position, for here we are studying a subject where there are no obvious qualifications with which to assess the knowledge of those who claim to know what they are talking about. Also, due to the subjective nature of lucid dreaming, it is possible for anyone with a deceptive nature to simply claim they have mastered the skill, without ever having experienced a single lucid dream. There is simply no easy way to prove or deny such claims.

Due to this peculiarity of lucid dreaming, the waking world is awash with those who claim (truthfully or otherwise) to be experts on the subject. There are also many products making exaggerated (or completely unsubstantiated) claims regarding their ability at inducing lucid dreams. It's important to be aware of such potential charlatans and scams before you part with your hard-earned money.

Also, should you spend any time among the online lucid dreaming communities, you will come across certain individuals, often overly enthusiastic youngsters, who are new to the subject and looking to fit in, who will make claims about their experiences that simply do not add up (claims such as having lucid dreams that subjectively lasted a year, or a lifetime, in dreamland but only moments in reality, or other such extreme events that are highly unlikely; whilst time can indeed be distorted in dreams, such an extreme experience is almost certainly nonsense).

Whilst all of these points are somewhat harmless on the surface, at worst wasting your time and money, the real issue here is that it paints the subject of lucidity in a rather poor light. With so much misinformation surrounding the subject, there is a real danger that many people will dismiss lucid dreaming itself based on some of the more obvious nonsense that surrounds the subject.

As lucid dreamers, we need to be vigilant and have very little tolerance for such things. It is easy to simply shrug these things off, assuming they will do no harm, but in doing so we open the doors for further nonsense to encroach upon the subject, burying its real potential.

We must also remind ourselves that a too high tolerance of illogical thinking makes genuine discoveries and experimentation in the field difficult or impossible. We should set high standards of evidence and rational thought for claims made by others, and should attempt to always justify our own assertions equally. In doing so, we will raise the bar of acceptable behaviour in the dreaming community. Also, such critical and logical thinking will increase our own ability to achieve lucidity itself, as we are no longer basing our world view on beliefs and feelings, but on evidence, something that is vital for attaining lucidity and also (and perhaps, more importantly) for establishing the truth behind any matter.

Lucid dreaming and the scientific mind

In many ways, achieving lucidity is a microcosm of the scientific method. A simplistic view of the scientific methods is as follows:

Observation > Hypothesis/Prediction > Experiment > Conclusion

This is essentially the exact same principle that is used when performing a reality test. Let us break it down and see how we can consider inducing lucidity as an example of the scientific method in action.

Observation: Through observation, we notice that there are differences between the waking world and the dreamworld. Over time, we establish our dreamsigns, the unique clues that distinguish dreaming from the waking experience. Once we have established these clues, we continue to observe our experiences looking out for such signs.

Hypothesis/Prediction: In the case of lucid dreaming, should we observe a dreamsign we can make the hypothesis/prediction that we may be indeed be dreaming. The only way to establish our state is through an experiment.

Experiment: To perform a reality test is to perform an experiment. The hypotheses 'I may be dreaming' requires such an experiment in order for us to form our conclusion. Knowing that a reality test will give different results depending on our current state, we are performing a fine-tuned experiment in order to establish the truth of the matter.

Conclusion: Depending on the outcome of our reality test, we are able to make an informed conclusion as to whether we are dreaming or not. Until we perform our experiment, either outcome is possible and it is this gathering of data via experimentation that is the key to successfully inducing lucidity, or knowing for certain that we are currently awake.

When considered in this light, it is clear that (at least, for reality test-induced lucid dreams) the foundations of lucid dreaming are built upon logic, observation and evidence. Therefore, we could say that the scientifically inclined mind is one that is already well-prepared for the experience of lucidity. In today's society, some individuals appear to harbour an odd rejection or suspicion of science. Why this is the case is debateable, but, considering we live in a society that is almost completely dependent upon science, it is a peculiar state of affairs. Here, it is important to remind ourselves what the word 'science' actually means. The word derives from the Latin *scientia*, meaning 'knowledge'. When seen this way, a 'suspicion of knowledge' seems rather strange and more than a little counterproductive. This also brings to mind our old friend Oliver Fox who called his lucid dreams 'dreams of knowledge', a very apt naming for the experience, as it is knowledge (or scientific thinking) that allows for the experience to occur.

The point I am attempting to make is that science is not something that happens only 'in labs' by 'scientists', nor does it need to be something that occurs outside of our everyday experience or comprehension. Any of us who require evidence before we come to a conclusion, and are willing to update our opinions based on evidence (and that means all lucid dreamers), are performing an act of science, or a gathering of knowledge. To be a lucid dreamer is to be a practitioner of the scientific method. Perhaps this way of thinking may help some appreciate the other wonders science has on offer, and also to hopefully apply this way of thinking to other areas in their lives.

It's a jungle out there

We've already touched on the darker side of lucid dreaming, that being the various products and individuals who are attempting to make a quick buck from the subject, generally offering low-quality products that do not live up their claims, or low-quality information (which is generally easily found for free online) and, worse still, a good deal of misinformation also. For those new to lucid dreaming, it really can be a jungle out there. Without wanting to belabour the point too much, your strongest ally to fend off such products and individuals is critical thinking.

Approach any new lucid dreaming product, or individual claiming to be an expert, with a healthy dose of scepticism. Assess the claims that are being made. Do they seem plausible? Or are they more like pipe-dreams and wishful thinking wrapped up in alluring advertising? Educate yourself; check and double-check facts and always look for independent reviews (lucid dreaming forums are a good place for this) before parting with your money. Ebooks are a real danger area; whilst they offer a wonderful platform for independent authors to share their work with a wider audience, it is also a double-edged sword, as it allows those looking to make a quick buck an arena in which they can palm off very poor-quality products with very few overheads.

If you are looking to make purchases on the more famous online ebook stores (which is probably advisable over auction sites, which have even fewer guidelines and less options for customer reviews in place), then be sure to check simple details such as the page count of the book you are looking to purchase, as there are a great deal of 'books' that are under 50 pages long, which can often be a sign of a quick-buck merchant. Obviously, higher page counts do not guarantee quality, so also be sure to use any preview options available also (most books and ebooks will allow for this option; if it's missing, it should make you question why).

When previewing a book, be sure to check for any glaring issues, such as the text being printed in unnecessarily large type, or spelling or grammar issues that would never have made it past a proofreader (having a book proofread is a sign that the author cares about their message!). Also, it can be wise to google a paragraph from the text, to see whether it has simply been lifted from an online encyclopaedia or free information source. This may all seem like hard work, but a little diligence on your part can help you save a good deal of cash (whilst, at the same time, avoiding giving your money to those who behave in such a manner).

There are a great deal of quality independent authors and products available, but often they can get lost in the noise of these other poor-quality products. So, be prepared to do a little searching to find the gems; in doing so, you will also avoid filling your mind with time-wasting misinformation and help support those who are trying hard to educate.

The 'new-age' and esoteric side of lucid dreaming also deserves a mention here. Whilst I believe that everyone has a right to their own beliefs regarding such matters, as a man who prefers evidence for claims I am highly suspicious of a great deal of the products that come from such sources. You will almost certainly come across various 'lucid dream-inducing' crystals, pendants, homeopathy remedies or sound recordings, etc., that claim to aid you in your attempts to attain lucidity. More often than not, such claims are based on flimsy logic with little to no evidence to support them - or, more often, simply belief alone. It is up to you if you wish to experiment with such ideas, but be sure to educate yourself also on such things as the placebo effect before you part with your money. Remind yourself of the logical and critical thinking that is required for lucid dreaming itself, and consider approaching these products with the same level of thoughtful discrimination.

As lucid dreamers, we should be proud of being pioneers of a subject that is still largely unexplored by the population at large. Therefore, it is our responsibility to help keep our 'house in order' for, without such an approach, we risk the subject being consigned in most people's minds as 'wacky' or 'nonsense'.

It's taken a good deal of time for lucid dreaming to be taken seriously by the scientific community and we're still not out of the woods yet. We should all play our part in promoting the subject on its true wonders, namely the power of the human mind. To do so, we must all be sure to help quell the onslaught of pseudoscience and quackery that is constantly attempting to encroach on the subject. This is absolutely not to say that the use of lucid dreaming for spiritual or philosophical purposes is to be avoided; quite the opposite, as these are some of the most personally powerful and interesting uses for the subject. Simply, that we should always make ourselves clear that what we are discussing is fact, speculation or personal belief. We must also all take a stand against those who would do otherwise, simply for the sake of self-aggrandisement or money.

Garbage in Garbage out

The term 'garbage in garbage out' originated in the world of computer programming. The concept is that, regardless of the quality of a system itself, if you input garbage, then your results will also be garbage. It is, in many ways, the software equivalent to the phrase 'you are what you eat'. Both these terms are relevant to the world of lucid dreaming. Our minds are akin to a computer system, in that they can only work with the data they are fed. Should we spend our days filling our minds with a certain kind of information, then it should be of no surprise when our thoughts and dreams reflect this back at us.

A vivid and common example here is the world of horror films. Many people report nightmares or unpleasant thoughts shortly after watching horror films; the more they watch, the higher the intensity of their nightmares - which really should not be all that surprising! This is true of any topic you choose; if you feed your brain garbage, then your thoughts and dreams will spew that garbage back at you. Equally, if you choose a 'healthy diet' for your mind, then the quality of your dreams will also improve accordingly.

There are obvious implications here for lucid dreamers. If we wish to truly make the most of our dreamworlds, then we need to fill our minds with those things we wish to dream about, much like a builder requires quality raw materials with which to work. The knock-on effect of this is that many lucid dreamers will start to be rather discerning about the quality of information with which they are willing to fill their minds. For many, graphic horror films become somewhat less appealing (such grotesque scenes may be bearable on the cinema screen, but less so should you have to deal with them in the realism of the dreamworld!) - unless, of course, the dreamer has an interest in facing their fears. For those who wish to use lucid dreaming for creative problem-solving, then they will be drawn to feeding their minds with as much information and detail as possible on the topics they wish to experience in the dreamworld.

The quality of your daily life and the information with which you feed your brain will, should you continue your journey with lucid dreaming, become something that will become of greater interest to you. You may well learn to realise the value and power of the memories you create; you will also learn that you cannot easily forget that which has been placed within your mind - or, to use the popular phrase, *what has been seen cannot be unseen*. Such a concept comes as both a warning and a boon. So, be sure to feed your mind well.

The ultimate feedback loop

Once we have learnt to appreciate the importance of the quality of the information with which we fill our minds, an interesting feedback loop can occur. As we've discussed, dreams are far from isolated from our waking life, they can impact them in many and varied ways, from improving our creativity to influencing our moods. Likewise, your dreams are reliant on the experiences of your waking life for the raw materials from which they are built. Lucid dreaming can increase your awareness of the subtle interplay between the waking and dreaming worlds; you will become aware that, as a sentient consciousness that moves between worlds, the actions taken in either world will have repercussions in the other. This creates what could be considered an inter-world feedback loop, one which can act as a self-fuelling catalyst for some dramatic changes in your life.

Let's look at this in the simplest terms possible. As you make positive changes in your life, altering the information with which you feed your brain, your lucid dreams will start to become more powerful, interesting, useful and inspiring. This inspiration and positivity from your dreamworld can then feedback into your waking life, fuelling further improvements in your waking world. Of course, this process will then repeat: life improvements = dream improvements = life improvements = dream improvements and so on. This can happen on various levels of the human experience, the most obvious being the psychological level.

Positive psychological experiences in your waking or dreaming life will impact their dreaming or waking equivalent. An example would be for those who suffer with low self-confidence; they may well initially experiment with tackling their confidence issues in the dreamworld, experimenting with new ways to interact with others in this consequence-free environment. Eventually, it is likely that such dream experiments will start to filter into and enhance their waking life confidence. As their confidence improves in the waking world, so it will raise the bar for confidence in the dreamworld. Needless to say, such a feedback loop may continue until such an individual no longer struggles with feelings of low self-confidence.

This feedback loop isn't limited only to the realm of the psychological; skills, hobbies and all manner of human experiences can be improved in such a way. All it takes is the motivation to allow the dreamworld and the waking world to positively influence each other. Of course, with any feedback loop negative patterns could also emerge, so it is important for lucid dreamers to keep a track on their behaviours and the areas upon which they place their focus.

A common area of risk for some dreamers is in letting the consequence-free environment of their dreams filter too strongly into their waking lives. In dreamland, we are all essentially 'gods' of our own private universe; the characters we interact with are temporary and there is zero long-term damage that can be achieved through any negative behaviour we engage in.

There is a small risk here that, for some dreamers, this sense of freedom could negatively influence their behaviour in the waking world, giving them an exaggerated sense of self-importance, or losing empathy for others in the real world. The best way to avoid this is to remind oneself that, even in the dreamworld, we are still accountable to our own sense of right and wrong. It is best to avoid behaviours in dreamland that we would be ashamed of in the waking world. In general, however, such situations are unlikely to occur; more often than not, the freedom of dreamland simply filters into waking life in a positive fashion, helping one see through some of our own self-limiting beliefs about what is or isn't possible.

Also, if we remind ourselves that the characters in dreams are aspects of our own minds, then we are likely to treat them with the respect they deserve. Indeed, such a way of thinking can even improve our empathy and respect for others in waking life, as it helps remind us that, as members of planet Earth, we all have far more in common than we have differences. In many ways, as one species we could almost be considered much as we consider our characters in dreams, as aspects of the same entity (the human race) expressed in different ways. That said, it is important to remind ourselves that a feedback loop can and does occur between the waking and dreaming world and we should still remain vigilant that such a force is moving us in a positive direction.

Developing Mindfulness

If lucid dreaming is being consciously present during a dream, then mindfulness is being consciously present during the current moment, the 'eternal now'. The use of the word 'mindfulness' originates from Buddhist traditions (and is known as *sati* in Pali, or *smṛti* in Sanskrit) and, in its most basic form, is a type of meditative practice. However, one does not need to be a practitioner of Buddhism, or any other spiritual practice, to develop mindfulness; all one needs is the motivation to become fully present in the current moment.

Lucid dreaming is a powerful tool, as well as a useful example for developing and demonstrating such a state - as dream lucidity is in many ways analogous to mindfulness. It may seem odd to most people to consider that we are not fully present in our current waking experience; however, even as you read these words, you may well not be fully engaged in the experience of 'now'.

Take, for example, your breathing - up until reading these words, it is likely that you were not aware of the cold sensation of the air as it enters your nostrils, the feeling as it curves downwards in the back of your throat, or the constant expansion and contraction of your chest. However, these sensations have been constantly there, with or without your attention, as you have gone about your daily business.

Even as your attention becomes focused on this element of the current moment, your mindfulness of others is still lacking. Again, up until this point you may not have considered the sensations in your feet, the feel of your shoes (or lack of them) against the skin, the weight and sensation of gravity as it pulls them down against the surface of the floor. Their temperature, their position, etc.

Each moment in time is a symphony of sensations and experiences, yet our attention is generally rather limited, as our minds have become skilled at creating a sharp focus only on certain elements of interest. This, of course, makes sense as an evolutionary tactic, for animals that are able to remain focused on important tasks, and aware of only significant events, are more likely to survive and pass on their genes than those who are constantly in awe of the kaleidoscope of reality as it unfolds around them.

However, we humans no longer need to be restricted so tightly by the confines of pure survival, for we have built a world around us in which we have (at least to a higher level than most other animals) ensured our basic needs are met, and our physical safety is somewhat more assured. We have also developed complex brains, brains capable of self-reflection and deep and complicated thought. A little more mindfulness, a little more awareness of ourselves and the moment, may now actually be a trait that is beneficial, not only for our appreciation of the universe that we inhabit, but perhaps also to detach us a little from our primal instinctual reactions (which may now no longer be suitable for the complicated world we have created), thus allowing us the ability to see the world more clearly, and respond to our circumstances in more adaptive and far-sighted ways.

Mindfulness is not only about our connection with outside events, but also an awareness of our own inner processes, our thoughts and feelings. Our minds are rather tempestuous; whilst we all like to feel that we are 'in control' of our minds, often our thoughts are in control of us.

Take a moment now to return your focus onto your breathing (and don't be too surprised or distraught if you realised how quickly your attention of this was lost from only moments ago). In a moment (should you be in a safe situation in which this is possible), close your eyes and attempt to focus on the sensation of breathing; count each time you inhale, being sure to be mindful of the experience of breathing. Breathe slowly and naturally and make it your goal to be fully aware of your breathing for an entire 60 inhalations. Should you struggle, or are distracted, do not worry; simply note the experience and then return your focus to your breathing. If possible, do this now before reading further (and, if you're anything like me, resist the urge to skip trying this exercise and simply continue reading - it really is better to experience this rather than simply read about it!).

Welcome back! By this point, unless you are an experienced practitioner of meditation, you are likely to have experienced what is perhaps a little bit of a shock, maybe even a little frustration. As almost all of us will discover, our minds are far from the quiet, tranquil and under-our-control places that we like to imagine. Even the simple act of observing our breath can be incredibly hard to accomplish without distraction, even for such a short duration. It is likely stray thoughts entered your mind, maybe thoughts such as 'This is silly', 'I'm hungry', 'What's the point in this?' etc. Perhaps your body decided to act as a distraction also, maybe a little discomfort here, or an itch. The external world, too, is likely to have interrupted your concentration, maybe the sound of a ticking clock, the roar of traffic, birdsong, or any number of other possibilities.

Such is the nature of the human mind, that Buddhists call this the 'monkey mind', as it is never calm, always jumping and grasping from one thing to another, and here we were, only attempting to focus on the simple act of breathing! How difficult, then, must it be to maintain an awareness of 'the moment', or an awareness of awareness. In our daily lives, we do not notice our 'monkey mind' because, generally, it is in control of us, and we build an illusion of self-control and of our own volition retrospectively to mask this.

For example, you may have felt that you 'decided' to read this book, that it was an independent act of your own free will. But was it? Perhaps you were sitting in your living room, your stomach sent out a pang of hunger, so you reacted and walked to the kitchen to find food. Maybe, whilst in the kitchen preparing a snack, you overheard the radio, a conversation about psychology, perhaps. Feeling a little bored and, with a tired body, maybe you walked to your dining table to sit down and eat. Whilst eating, you were possibly distracted by a noise outside, one that made you walk to look out the window. As you walked to the window, perhaps you noticed this book lying on the table and your mind, already processing thoughts on psychology, led you to pick up the book, it being a related subject.

At the time, it probably felt as if you had 'decided' to read this book. However, in retrospect, all the individual events that led up to this 'decision' were the actions of the monkey mind, mindlessly reacting and jumping from thought to thought, urge to urge. Of course, your own set of 'jumps' will be different; but, if you think about it, was your process all so different? Were you 'in the moment'? Were you responding with awareness of these processes? Or, were you blindly led by them to this current moment? This moment where, once again, you now became aware of the sensation of breathing.

This may all seem a little intimidating. You may be wondering how on earth you can ever truly 'be in the moment'. But the goal here is not to achieve some superhuman rigid awareness of everything, but instead to be present, to be aware of these processes, to see how they guide you, and to allow yourself to either react to them or not. You are not attempting to be something other than what you are, just aware of who and what you are.

Being aware will not stop that itch, but it will allow you to experience it and to respond as you wish. Being aware will not change your emotions, but it may allow you to see them for what they are. You will have the choice to either react or not to react. Such awareness is hard-earned and will not come overnight. It is a potentially lifelong process. But, as you develop a more intimate relationship with the now, which is the place you will always be, you will start to notice the transient nature of both your world, your thoughts, your body, yourself, others and the universe.

Lucid dreaming and its practices with techniques such as reality testing, or looking out for dreamsigns, is a form of mindfulness. It is a way of keeping oneself present in the moment, and to not simply react to events, but to respond accordingly to the individual circumstances. Many lucid dreamers also add other elements of mindfulness practice into their routine, such as meditative walks, where they attempt to be fully present in the simple experience of walking (some even attempt to imagine that the whole experience is a dream, attempting to feel the same sensations and emotions of the dreamworld). Or, some attempt meditative practices such as watching one's breath, as we attempted earlier.

As your journey into lucid dreaming continues, you may find that you experience more moments of clarity, more lucid waking, times when you feel the world around you in all its vibrancy and subtlety. To do so, you must attempt to see each moment with fresh eyes. This (as we have seen) is not as easy as it sounds, but with practice and perseverance your skills will grow, not only in the waking world, but the dreaming world also. Awareness is a true wonder of the universe and a gift that we should all learn to appreciate. Just remind yourself that the journey is just as (if not more) important as the destination. Because the destination is exactly where you currently are - the now.

10
The Future of Lucid Dreaming

Aside from our own personal journeys in the dreamworld, the question of what the future holds for lucid dreaming is one that is wide open to speculation. In recent years, the subject has blossomed with greater numbers than ever enjoying the experience of conscious dreaming. The advent of the Internet has no doubt greatly increased this spread of information on the topic and, as we now live in a world where the web is deeply embedded into the fabric of our society, it is likely that this trend will continue as knowledge of the practice of lucid dreaming filters further into public awareness.

With so many current and future practitioners, it is likely that completely new applications for lucidity will arise and the creative influence of lucid dreaming will no doubt continue to impact upon the arts and other fields. One wonders if Marquis d'Hervey de Saint-Denys would have expected the topic to have spread so widely within the space of less than two hundred years.

What, then, of the next two hundred? Of course, without a crystal ball the answers to such questions remain speculation, but no doubt equally as dramatic shifts will take place in our society. I wonder, then, will lucidity remain a popular subject on the fringe of society, or will it become something commonplace? There are elements to these questions that are simply impossible to guess. Perhaps there will surface a technique, device or medication (or combination of these) that will greatly enhance the accessibility of lucidity to those with only a casual interest. Without such a breakthrough, the effort required to obtain lucidity may continue to limit it to a dedicated minority with an interest in the human mind.

Either way, should the current trend of wealthier, healthier individuals with plenty of leisure time continue (which, in itself, is open to question as, for such a trend to continue, we as a species need to become far more aware of our impact on and limitations of our home the Earth), then it is likely that such individuals will develop a curiosity for the more subtle aspects of the human condition, such as the experience of lucid dreaming. These current trends in technology continue to carry us towards such a future, so it is likely (combined with increasing speeds of information sharing) that the future inhabitants of planet Earth will have both the time and knowledge with which to pursue the subject.

Speculation on possible futures is fun, but almost always far off the mark. Therefore, the following ideas should be treated for what they are, namely pure speculation, and also perhaps as an inspirational nudge for those who may be tempted (and in a position) to help turn them from ideas into a reality.

Lucid dreaming - preparation for a digital life

If we take a look at recent history, there is one area of human experience that is accelerating at breakneck speeds - technology. In a hundred years from now, the world is likely to be a very different place from what it is today. Should humanity have managed to avoid disaster in the meantime, it is likely that our grandchildren will be in possession of technologies that today we can only dream of.

Since the advent of the personal computer, the capabilities of such devices have increased so dramatically, and in such a short period of time, that it is likely that, at some point in our near future, they (along with some new form of interface) will be capable of producing virtual experiences that will rival the realism of both the waking and dreaming worlds. Our descendants may well spend a good deal of their time living in realistic virtual worlds, living a digital life.

Today's technology, whilst impressive, still has a long way to go until we are likely to mistake virtual realities for actual reality. Even the most advanced computer systems of today at best produce realistic visual and audio reproductions of reality, but lack the ability to reproduce the full spectrum of human sensory experience, at least in a way that isn't clumsy and obviously fake. Our only truly convincing virtual reality of today is the experience of dreaming. We are then, it seems, given a chance to understand and experience through lucid dreaming what may well one day be a commonplace event for future humans: convincing virtual worlds.

Of course, lucid dreaming has certain benefits over the possible virtual worlds of the future; they are uniquely personal (being built from our own minds), utterly private, require the creativity of our own (and not someone else's) imaginations, and are free from product placement and advertising. However, perhaps we can learn something in advance from lucidity that may benefit our descendants. How we interact with and control our dreams, the way in which our minds accept an experience as 'real', the psychological impact of experiencing a virtual reality, are all elements that we can study today, without waiting for technology to catch up.

We can, through the study of lucid dreaming, prepare ourselves for our future digital lives. Perhaps future virtual worlds will (and I think should) have dreamsigns or their equivalent built into them, aspects to the world that can be used as a reality test, signs that can inform the experiencer which world they are currently inhabiting. Without such signposts, it is likely that future virtual worlds could cause significant psychological issues for their users.

Even on the simplest level, a study of how current day lucid dreamers interact with the dreamworld, the way in which we control the experience, may help future virtual reality designers build a user interface that is intuitive, something that feels right. Consider, for example, the experience of flight in a dream. It is something we can do effortlessly, without a great deal of thought. However, think of the difficulties one would face in attempting to design the same experience in a computerised virtual world - how would the user inform the system that they wish to fly?

Today, we simply use a combination of button presses, etc., to initiate actions in our rather primitive computer games, but future systems will be attempting to mimic reality with minimal distraction. By studying the common practices of lucid dreamers, such an interface could be designed to feel completely natural.

Artificial intelligence is another area that humans are currently wrestling with, yet we all experience convincing and seemingly sentient artificial intelligence whenever we interact with a dream character. These and many more elements of the virtual worlds of our future can all be explored, understood and studied today, long before the technologies exist. Lucid dreaming may well be a glimpse of humanity's future. Understanding what we have now could very well be the preparation we require to enter such a future in an informed and knowledgeable way; it may help us avoid problems we cannot even envisage today.

Communication between dreamers

I have long thought that a very plausible area for exploration in the field of lucid dreaming is the ability for dreamers to communicate with each other. We have already seen that experiments conducted in the late 1970s and early 1980s allowed lucid dreamers to communicate with the outside world. We also know that signals can be sent to dreamers from the waking world that will become embedded in the dream itself, such as the flashing lights of the various lucid dream induction devices that exist, or the more common experience of when our alarm clocks infiltrate our dreams and become sirens or other similar sounds within the dreamworld.

The logical next step, it would seem, would be for two dreamers to communicate from one dreamworld to another. This should be completely achievable with current technology, although such signals would be rather limited. Limited or not, such a signal would be the first time in history that two apparently sleeping individuals have communicated with one another.

But how would it be achieved? Well, as we have seen, predetermined eye movement signals during REM can be recorded via an external device. A small addition to this principle is all that is required. I would envision the simplest form of this experiment, as follows.

Two dreamers would attempt to synchronise their sleep cycles, aiming to fall asleep and awaken at the same times. The reason for this behaviour is to increase the chances of them both experiencing REM concurrently. Both dreamers would (whilst sleeping) be wearing electronic sleep masks, masks that will monitor their REM patterns. These masks would be connected via a computer system, and both masks would be capable of both monitoring REM and signalling the dreamer (either through light, sound or another means).

The dreamer who is to act as the messenger will have arranged for the system to be on the lookout for one of several eye movement patterns. Each pattern would be associated with and cue a particular signal in the mask of the other dreamer - let's say a single flash of light for one eye movement pattern, two flashes for the second, and three for the third. Once the system has been set up, the dreamer who is to be the receiver of the message will be informed that they are to look out for any flashing lights within their dreams and to count the number of flashes. They could also be told to perform a recognition eye movement signal on receipt of the message (one that the system will also be programmed to await).

With these preparations completed, the dreamers will simply need to retire to bed, wearing their sleep masks. The dreamer who is to act as a messenger will attempt to attain lucidity during their night's sleep and, on doing so, decide if they wish to send the message one, two or three. Upon attaining lucidity, they would perform the relevant eye movement signal for that particular message. At this point, the system will (if both dreamers are seen to be in the REM state) transmit the correct amount of flashing lights to the receiving dreamer via their eye mask. If the receiving dreamer becomes aware of such a signal, they will perform their own 'recognition' eye movement signal that will, in turn, cue both masks to sound an alarm to wake both dreamers.

At this point, neither dreamer should be allowed to communicate with each other; instead, they would be requested to share their sent and received messages to an independent judge. This judge will then assess if the message sent and the message received are the same; if this is the case, then the first (albeit simple) message between two dreaming minds will have occurred.

Whilst the practical uses for such an experiment are very limited, it will at the very least demonstrate that communication between two dreaming minds is possible. Over time, more complicated messages could be sent, perhaps with each dreamer learning a simple code system (such as morse code) which could be sent and received in a similar manner. This would allow for more spontaneous and complicated messaging.

As technology grows and human computer interfaces advance, it may well be possible for dreamers to communicate in far more complicated ways. If, at some point in the future, it is possible to establish the content of thought verbal communication purely from the activity within the brain, such information could easily be transmitted directly to another dreamer. I would imagine that, if such technology were available, then it is likely also that similar technology for influencing brain activity may also be available, allowing for the receiver to 'hear' the message within the dream. This would create what would be a form of electronic telepathy between dreamworlds.

For the time being, even the simplest form of this experiment has yet to be achieved. So, for those of you looking to mark your place in the history of the science of lucid dreaming, perhaps such an experiment would secure you a place. I would welcome those who are inspired by such an idea and have the means with which to attempt to make it a reality to do so.

The Final Frontier

Humanity has exploration in its blood. Since our earliest times we have explored, visiting new lands and making them our home. Even the act of lucid dreaming is a form of exploration, that of the frontier of the mind. We have reached a point in history where the surface of the Earth no longer offers us the excitement of adventure we crave, as it is all but known. However, we face other, more pressing, issues. As the population of our planet continues to rise and the resources of Earth become too few to sustain us all, we are now looking outwards, to the planets and stars, looking for new frontiers to explore, new homes. At this current point in time, humanity has all of its proverbial eggs in one basket; our species is confined to one fragile rock in the vastness of space. It would take only one disaster to erase the human race from the universe forever. It is, therefore, imperative that we explore the stars, that we spread ourselves out into the cosmos - our very survival demands it.

Such exploration is already underway, if moving rather slowly and somewhat underfunded. Even at the time of writing, the recent successful landing of the Mars Curiosity rover is making headlines, as well as significant advancements in human knowledge. However, a robot cannot sustain the species, and soon we will need to send humans to other worlds; we will need to colonise space.

It is estimated that the minimum amount of time before the first humans set foot on our nearest semi-hospitable neighbouring planet, Mars, is 30 years away, and preparations and planning for such an expedition are already well underway. However, such a journey is not without peril and risk, and there is one element to these issues where lucid dreaming may well be the solution.

A journey to Mars can take between 150-300 days, depending on launch speed and the alignment between Earth and Mars. Of course, the same amount of time is required to return. Some even speculate that the first visitors to Mars will be making a one-way journey, as they will have no immediate means of returning home to Earth. Even if this were not the case, such adventurers would be far from home for a very long time; far from friends, family and all the comforts and familiarity of our planet.

The psychological strain of such isolation and distance would be immense. The journey there alone, cooped up in such a small living space, with only a handful of other explorers to keep you company, would be a very different experience to living on a planet with an estimated population of seven billion. The ability to 'phone home' will also be very limited. Radio contact between Earth and Mars can take as long as 30 minutes between a message being sent and received - which, as you can imagine, could lead to some very long awkward pauses in conversation!

So, how does lucid dreaming fit into such grand adventures? The answer is something that has already been discussed (albeit in a different form) in many works of science fiction. One example (as we discussed in earlier chapters) is shown in the famous television series *Star Trek: The Next Generation* in which was featured a form of fictional virtual reality on board the *Enterprise*. This virtual reality was called the 'holodeck' which, in essence, was a computerised version of a shared lucid dream.

What is interesting here is that the writers of the show must have realised that the experience of long durations in space would put a psychological pressure on the crew, and that they may well need a place in which they could feel more at home. They would need somewhere to experience what it felt like to be on a familiar planet, or with loved ones; basically, somewhere to unwind.

The same would be true for our future pioneers of space - they will be isolated, far from home and in an alien environment. However, unlike the worlds of fiction, it is unlikely that virtual reality will be sufficiently advanced in time to help ward off such feelings of isolation. The simulation will just not be convincing enough to be effective. Furthermore, such systems will be expensive, requiring both additional energy and space. Most probably, they will be considered an unnecessary luxury by those who foot the bill for such missions.

However, these astronauts will still need a way to connect with Earth.

They will need their very own form of virtual reality in which they can escape the confines of their ship, or the hostile planet upon which they are trapped. Luckily, such a virtual reality already exists in each and every human mind (it is, as you almost certainly have guessed, lucid dreaming). Not only that, but it is free, requires no additional power or storage, and is perfectly suited to those with high motivation and an eye for detail (which, I imagine, are just some of the prerequisites for becoming an astronaut).

It may seem far-fetched, but lucid dreaming could very well be the perfect tool for maintaining a healthy psychological state for the crews of such missions. Space travel is almost certainly going to become more prevalent as humanity advances, and the duration of such journeys will increase. It is therefore likely that, until our technology develops to a stage where either a form of suspended animation or more convincing low-cost virtual realities are possible, lucid dreaming could well be the solution to these future problems.

Celebrating Lucidity

So far, we've only discussed aspects of the future of lucid dreaming that are beyond the reach of the majority of practitioners. However, we can all do our bit to help guide the future of lucid dreaming. One simple area that we can all partake in is the promotion and celebration of the topic. Keeping online blogs, creating video tutorials or journals of our personal experiences, connecting with other dreamers either through workshops or dream groups, sharing our creative pursuits that are inspired by our dreams, etc., are all very good places to start.

I believe if all lucid dreamers do their part in promoting the subject, especially in a logical, creative and accessible way, then we will certainly see the subject continue to grow in popularity. I would imagine that, in the near future, as we reach a 'critical mass' of lucid dream practitioners, we will see various social developments in the field that have currently yet to surface. One that I would particularly like to see is an increase in real-world communication and social elements surrounding the topic. For example, festivals or other such celebrations of the subject would be a wonderful way for lucid dreamers to connect and share their experiences and creativity.

Perhaps a good way to start this ball rolling is to put aside one day a year when those of us interested in the subject make a concerted effort to share, reflect and enjoy the subject. Therefore, I would like to suggest the idea of a 'lucid dreaming day', a day when we as lucid dreamers can come together and enjoy what it means to be conscious in the dreamworld. There are many dates we could choose for such a day, but I believe the best choice is the 12th April, in celebration and remembrance of the day when the first scientifically recorded signals from a lucid dream were recorded, signals that demonstrated the existence of lucid dreaming as a verifiable state.

It would be nice for such an idea to catch on, as gestures such as this can do a lot to create cohesion within a community, something the lucid dream community currently struggles with a little. As for suggestions on what to do to celebrate 'lucidity day', well part of the fun will be coming up with your own ideas. I, personally, am rather fond of the idea of arranging get-togethers, putting on parties and talks on the subject, anything that you feel is suitable and fun.

Of course, we can celebrate such a day in the world of dreams, also. Perhaps we could use our skills at lucid dreaming to induce a lucid dream in which we meet those characters who have been historically important in the field, such as Oliver Fox, Saint-Denys, Frederik van Eeden, etc., as it seems rather fitting that they, too, should get to take part in the celebrations. I'll leave this idea for the community of dreamers to either take on board or not.

One thing is certain: as a lucid dreamer, you will be shaping the future of the field. The subject is still very much in its infancy, and in reality all lucid dreamers are pioneers. It is perfectly plausible that you yourself may make completely new and unique discoveries. If nothing else, be sure that your dreams do not remain locked in your own mind - connect with other dreamers, share your stories and experiences. Your journey is part of a bigger story, a story we are all collectively writing. Share your dreams and who knows where the future will take us!

Afterword:
On the Edge of Reality

As we come to the end of our wander together through the world of lucid dreaming, your personal journey is only just beginning. Conscious dreaming is one of the true wonders of the human experience, and as a species we are only just beginning to probe and understand the depths of the human mind. It could easily take a lifetime to explore the universe that exists inside each and every one of us, and each inner cosmos is as unique as the dreamer who experiences it.

Every night we stand on the edge of reality, the shoreline where the waking world gives way to the ocean of sleep and dreams. So far, we have only just played in the surf, examined our options and learnt the basic skills required to navigate this new world. But this journey is a uniquely personal one, an exploration that we can only ever undertake alone. Over the coming days and years, you will discover hidden treasures, strange new lands and all manner of peculiar and exotic beings. You will become a pioneer at the frontier of your own mind, an explorer of worlds that no other human will ever experience.

This is no simple undertaking, nor is it trivial. You will be traversing the byways of your own 'soul', unearthing aspects of yourself that may have lain hidden, deep in the shadows of your mind your entire life, silently awaiting discovery. It will take a certain kind of strength to confront our own inner world this way, so be prepared for a journey like no other. There are no health and safety inspectors in dreamland, so it will be your responsibility to approach this adventure with appropriate caution and wisdom.

It is easy for us all to lose sight of the fact that our minds are not our property, not somehow separate from us as individuals. We *are* our minds, we *are* the products of them. Therefore, tread lightly, as such adventures are an exploration of an untamed force of nature: you. There is much more to all of us than meets the eye. This is not to say that our enterprise should be avoided; far from it, as we are all in a unique position simply from the very act of being alive, one that demands we wake up and savour all the beauty and wonder our universe has to offer.

Lucid dreaming is just one element of a life fully lived, a single piece of the vast kaleidoscopic puzzle of existence. We are creatures with an innate curiosity, and it is this trait that has continued to drive our species forward through the ages and into new and previously uncharted realms of understanding. Each of us now has the opportunity to turn the focus of curiosity inwards towards our dreams and ourselves, and to become wiser, more knowledgeable beings for doing so.

I would like to offer one last word of advice before we part ways. As a lucid dreamer, you are likely, as I and many others have, to encounter many strange attitudes towards your exploits. Many will question what you do, perhaps seeing it as rather strange or unusual. It is up to you how you deal with such reactions, although do not be disheartened by these opinions. I have found the best way to deal with this way of thinking is to put our lives into perspective. We are, each of us, born into this world facing the insurmountable mystery of our own existence. Whilst some may claim otherwise, there is not one of us who enters this world with any more of an idea of who or what we are than any other.

We are essentially a world of seven billion (and rising) individuals all looking for answers in the vast and swirling mystery of the universe. In practical terms, every one of us is the result of an unbroken thread of reproduction, the endless march of evolution that has spanned the eons, with our distant ancestors being little more than the most primitive forms of life. We are currently relatively intelligent, hairless primates that have learnt to ask questions beyond those of the mere mechanics of survival. We are clinging to a speck of dust, a ball of rock that circles a single star in a universe of at least

100 sextillion stars (that's 100,000,000,000,000,000,000,000, while some even believe the actual number is at least three times larger).

In the cosmic perspective, each of us is very small indeed. Yet, as individuals we are incredibly complex creatures, made up (depending on the estimate) of 10 trillion cells, 120 billion (or thereabouts) of which make up the neural architecture of our brains. In a way, our bodies are like miniature universes.

Yet, here we are, hairless and almost clueless primates journeying around a gigantic ball of plasma - our sun - at 66,000 miles an hour (and spinning at 900 miles an hour). We are lost in the vastness of time and space, both of which we are still desperately struggling to understand. We go about our 'normal' daily lives, taking all this and much more for granted. But if this is 'normal', then who are we or anybody else to define what is strange? Our existence itself is so utterly and unfathomably peculiar it boggles the mind. To explore your own inner worlds, to attempt to understand something as intimate as our own mind, is far from strange. In fact, I would go as far as to say, it is strange to lack the curiosity to do so.

So from one dreamer lost in the vastness of time and space to another, I wish you a pleasant journey, not only in your dreams but throughout your life also. Remember to stay alert, aware and constantly curious. Oh, and one last thing... Are you dreaming?

For further resources and to continue your journey, visit:

www.areyoudreaming.co.uk
or
www.exploringluciddreams.com

Acknowledgements

My deepest gratitude to all these wonderful people for their help, inspiration, patience and support, and without whom this book would not have been possible; My Parents & family, Andrew Brown (an especially huge thank you!), Al Wadlan, Benjamin Tallamy, Chin Jung Huang, Jess Gowing, Dr Keith Hearne, Madeline Hopkins, Meng Meng Li, Paul Morris, Simon Best, and the many scientists, researchers and dream enthusiasts whom I have either referenced or been inspired by, and whose dedication and work continues to drive the subject of lucid dreaming ever forward.

References and Bibliography

References are listed in approximately the order in which they are cited in the text. As a bibliography this list is by no means exhaustive.

Chapter 1

Maslow, A.H. *Religions, Values, and Peak Experiences* (London, Penguin, 1978)

Myers, D. *Psychology.* 7th edition. (NY, Worth Publishers, 2004)

Chapter 2

Fossil Reanalysis Pushes Back Origin of Homo sapiens. (Scientific American. February 17, 2005)

Aristotle. "On Dreams", from Gallop, D., ed., *On Sleep and Dreams*. 2nd Edition. (Oxford, Aris & Phillips Ltd, 1996)

Kelsey, M.T. *Gods, Dreams and Revelation* (NY, Augsburg, 1974)

Shah, I. *The Sufis* (London, Octagon Press, 1964)

Aquinas, St. Thomas. *Summa Theologica.*, vol. 1 (NY, Benziger Brothers, 1947)

Schatzman, M. *Dreams and How to Guide them* by Hervey de Saint-Denys, translated by Nicholas Fry. (London, Duckworth, 1982)

de Saint-Denys, H. *Les Revés et les Moyens de les Diriger* (Paris, Amyot, 1867)

Freud, S. *The Interpretation of Dreams* (NY, Avon, 1980)

van Eeden, F. "A study of dreams". *Proceedings of the Society of Psychical Research.*, 26, 431-61 (1913)

REFERENCES

Arnold-Forster, M. *Studies in Dreams* (London, Allen & Unwin, 1921)

Fox, O. *Astral Projection* (New Hyde Park, NY, University Books, 1962)

Ouspensky, P. *A New Model of the Universe* (London, Routledge & Kegan Paul, 1931)

Moers-Messmer, H. von. "Träume mit der gleichzeitigen Erkenntnis des Traumzustandes". *Archiv für Psychologie.,* 102, 291-318 (1938)

Green, C. *Lucid Dreams* (Oxford, Institute for Psychophysical Research, 1968)

Green, C. & McCreery, C. *Lucid Dreaming* (London, Routledge, 1994)

LaBerge, S. *Lucid Dreaming* (NY, Ballantine, 1986)

Faraday, A. *The Dream Game* (NY, Perennial Library, 1976)

Faraday, A. *Dream Power* (NY, Berkley, 1972)

Garfield, P. *Creative Dreaming* (NY, Simon and Schuster, 1974)

Castaneda, C. *Journey to Ixtlan* (NY, Simon and Schuster, 1972)

Castaneda, C. *The Art of Dreaming* (NY, HarperCollins, 1993)

Gackenbach, J. & Bosveld, J. *Control your Dreams* (NY, HarperCollins, 1989)

Gackenbach, J. & LaBerge, S. *Conscious Mind, Sleeping Brain* (NY, Plenum Press, 1988)

Hearne, K. *The Dream Machine* (Wellingborough, Aquarian Press, 1990)

LaBerge, S. *Lucid Dreaming* (NY, Ballantine, 1986)

LaBerge, S. & Rheingold, H. *Exploring the World of Lucid Dreaming* (NY, Ballantine, 1990)

Yuschak, T. *Advanced Lucid Dreaming* (Raleigh, Lulu, 2006)

Chapter 3

Payne, J.D. & Nadel, L. *Sleep, dreams, and memory consolidation: The role of the stress hormone cortisol* (Online). Available: http://learnmem.cshlp.org/content/11/6/671.full (July 2012)

Fahey, J. "How Your Brain Tells Time". *Out Of The Labs*. (NY, Forbes, 2009)

Hall, R.H. *Circadian Rhythms* (1998) (Online). Available: http://web.mst.edu/~rhall/neuroscience/03_sleep/circadian.pdf (July 2012)

Hall, R.H. *Sleep Stages* (1998) (Online). Available: http://web.mst.edu/~rhall/neuroscience/03_sleep/sleepstages.pdf (July 2012)

Rechtschaffen, A. & Kales, A. *A Manual of Standardized Terminology, Techniques and Scoring System for Sleep Stages of Human Subjects* (Washington, Public Health Service, US Government Printing Office, 1968)

Silber, M.H.; Ancoli-Israel, S.; Bonnet, M.H.; Chokroverty, S.; Grigg-Damberger, M.M.; Hirshkowitz, M.; Kapen, S.; Keenan, S.A. et al. "The visual scoring of sleep in adults". *Journal of Clinical Sleep Medicine.,* 3 (2), 121–31 (2007)

Iber, C., Ancoli-Israel, S., Chesson, A., & Quan, S.F. for the American Academy of Sleep Medicine. *The AASM Manual for the Scoring of Sleep and Associated Events: Rules, Terminology and Technical Specifications* (Westchester, American Academy of Sleep Medicine, 2007)

Dang-Vu, T.T., McKinney, S.M., Buxton, O.M., Solet, J.M., & Ellenbogen, J.M. "Spontaneous brain rhythms predict sleep stability in the face of noise". *Current Biology.,* Vol. 20 (15), R626-R627 (2010)

Saletin, J.M., Goldstein, A.N., & Walker, M.P. "The Role of Sleep in Directed Forgetting and Remembering of Human memories". *Cerebral Cortex.,* 21, 2534–2541 (2011)

Cash, S.S.; Halgren, E.; Dehghani, N.; et al. "Human K-Complex Represents an Isolated Cortical Down-State". *Science.,* 324, 1084–87 (2009)

Hobson, J.A. "REM sleep and dreaming: towards a theory of protoconsciousness". *Nature Reviews.,* 10 (11), 803–813 (2009)

REFERENCES

Aston-Jones, G., Gonzalez, M., & Doran, S. "Role of the locus coeruleus-norepinephrine system in arousal and circadian regulation of the sleep-wake cycle". *Brain Norepinephrine: Neurobiology and Therapeutics*. (Cambridge, University Press, 2007)

Siegel, J.M. "REM Sleep". *Principles and Practice of Sleep Medicine*. 5th ed. (Philadelphia, Elsevier, 2010)

Mavromatis, A. *Hypnagogia* (London, Thyrsos Press, 2010)

Stickgold, R., Malia, A., Maguire, D., Roddenberry, D., & O'Connor, M. "Replaying the game: Hypnagogic images in normals and amnesics". *Science.,* 290(5490), 350–3 (2000)

Sleep Paralysis (Online). Available: http://www.webmd.com/sleep-disorders/guide/sleep-paralysis (July 2012)

Hersen, M. & Beidel, D. *Adult Psychopathology and Diagnosis*. 6th Edition. (Hoboken, John Wiley & Sons, 2012)

Hearne, K. *The Dream Machine* (Wellingborough, Aquarian Press, 1990)

McNally, R.J. & Clancy, S.A. "Sleep Paralysis, Sexual Abuse, and Space Alien Abduction". *Transcultural Psychiatry.,* 42 (1), 113–122 (2005)

Terrillon, J. & Marques-Bonham, S. "Does Recurrent Isolated Sleep Paralysis Involve More Than Cognitive Neurosciences?". *Journal of Scientific Exploration.,* 15, 97-123 (2001)

Liberman, A. *Word Origins And How We Know Them* (Oxford, Oxford University Press, 2005)

"The Science Behind Dreams and Nightmares". *Talk of the Nation*, national Public Radio. (30 October 2007)

Highland, J. *Foods high in Choline & Methionine* (Online). Available: http://www.livestrong.com/article/249591-foods-high-in-choline-methionine/ (July 2012)

Davis, J.L. & Wright, D.C. "Case Series Utilizing Exposure, Relaxation, and Rescripting Therapy: Impact on Nightmares, Sleep Quality, and Psychological Distress". *Behavioral Sleep Medicine.,* 3 (3), 151–157 (2005)

Krakow, B.; Hollifield, M.; Johnston, L.; Koss, M.; Schrader, R.; Warner, T.D.; Tandberg, D.; Lauriello, J. et al. "Imagery Rehearsal Therapy for Chronic Nightmares in Sexual Assault Survivors with Posttraumatic Stress Disorder: A Randomized Controlled Trial". *JAMA: the Journal of the American Medical Association.,* 286 (5), 537 (2001)

Green, C. *Lucid Dreams* (Oxford, Institute for Psychophysical Research, 1968)

Russell, B. *Human Knowledge: Its Scope and Limits* (London, Allen and Unwin, 1948)

Chapter 4

Hall, R.H. *Neurotransmitters and Sleep* (1998) (Online). Available: http://web.mst.edu/~rhall/neuroscience/03_sleep/sleepneuro.pdf (July 2012)

Yuschak, T. *Advanced Lucid Dreaming* (Raleigh, Lulu, 2006)

LaBerge, S. & Rheingold, H. *Exploring the World of Lucid Dreaming* (NY, Ballantine, 1990)

Martin, P. *Counting Sheep* (London, Flamingo, 2002)

Hearne, K. *The Dream Machine* (Wellingborough, Aquarian Press, 1990)

Risse, G.B. *Mending bodies, saving souls: a history of hospitals* (Oxford, Oxford University Press, 1990)

Chapter 5

Kahan, T.L., LaBerge, S., Levitan, L., & Zimbardo, P. "Similarities and differences between dreaming and waking cognition: An exploratory study". *Consciousness and cognition.,* 6, 132-147 (1997)

LaBerge, S. & Rheingold, H. *Exploring the World of Lucid Dreaming* (NY, Ballantine, 1990)

Hall, R.H. *Neurotransmitters and Sleep* (1998) (Online). Available: http://web.mst.edu/~rhall/neuroscience/03_sleep/sleepneuro.pdf (July 2012)

REFERENCES

Yuschak, T. *Advanced Lucid Dreaming* (Raleigh, Lulu, 2006)

LaBerge, S., Phillips, L., & Levitan, L. "An hour of wakefulness before morning naps makes lucidity more likely". *NightLight.,* 6(3) (1994)

Fuller, P.M., Lu, J., & Saper, C.B. "Differential rescue of light- and food-entrainable circadian rhythms". *Science.,* 320(5879), 1074-7 (2008)

Machlin, L.J. *Handbook of Vitamins: Nutritional, Biochemical, and clinical Aspects* (NY, Marcel Dekker, 1984)

Institute of Medicine. *Dietary Reference Intakes: Vitamins* (Online). Available: http://www.iom.edu/~/media/Files/Activity%20Files/Nutrition/DRIs/DRI_Vitamins.ashx (August 2012)

USDA. *National Nutrient Database for Standard Reference* (Online). Available: http://ndb.nal.usda.gov/ndb/foods/list (August 2012)

Yuschak, T. *Advanced Lucid Dreaming* (Raleigh, Lulu, 2006)

University of Massachusetts Lowell. *Research Shows Benefits of Apple Juice on Neuro-transmitter Affecting Memory* (2006) (Online). Available: http://www.uml.edu/News/press-releases/2006/research_shows_benefit_of_appl.aspx (August 2012)

Tchantchou, F., Chan, A., Kifle, L., Ortiz, D., & Shea T.B. "Apple juice concentrate prevents oxidative damage and impaired maze performance in aged mice". *Journal of Alzheimer's Disease.,* 8(3), 283-287 (2005)

Ebben, M., Lequerica, A., & Spielman, A. "Effects of pyridoxine on dreaming: a preliminary study". *Percept Mot Skills.,* 94(1), 135-40 (2002)

LaBerge, S., Phillips, L., & Levitan, L. "An hour of wakefulness before morning naps makes lucidity more likely". *NightLight.,* 6(3) (1994)

LaBerge, S. *Lucid Dreaming* (NY, Ballantine, 1986)

LaBerge, S. & Rheingold, H. *Exploring the World of Lucid Dreaming* (NY, Ballantine, 1990)

Hearne, K. *The Dream Machine* (Wellingborough, Aquarian Press, 1990)

Hall, R.H. *Neurotransmitters and Sleep* (1998) (Online). Available: http://web.mst.edu/~rhall/neuroscience/03_sleep/sleepneuro.pdf (July 2012)

Yuschak, T. *Advanced Lucid Dreaming* (Raleigh, Lulu, 2006)

Chapter 6

Gregory, R.L. *The Oxford Companion to the Mind.* 2nd Edition. (Oxford, Oxford University Press, 2004)

Martin, P. *Counting Sheep* (London, Flamingo, 2002)

Roddenberry, G. (Executive Producer). *Star Trek: The Next Generation* (Television Series). (United States, Paramount Television, 1987)

Myers, D. *Psychology.* 7th edition. (NY, Worth Publishers, 2004)

Roehrs, T. & Roth, T. *Sleep, Sleepiness, and Alcohol Use* (Online). Available: http://pubs.niaaa.nih.gov/publications/arh25-2/101-109.htm (August 2012)

Yuschak, T. *Advanced Lucid Dreaming* (Raleigh, Lulu, 2006)

Abu-Jayyab, A. *Nutritional Pharmacology Of Sleep & Depression* (Online). Available: http://www.selfgrowth.com/articles/Nutritional_Pharmacology_of_Sleep_Depression.html (August 2012)

LaBerge, S. & Rheingold, H. *Exploring the World of Lucid Dreaming* (NY, Ballantine, 1990)

Chapter 7

Gackenbach, J. & LaBerge, S. *Conscious Mind, Sleeping Brain* (NY, Plenum Press, 1988)

Bancroft, J. *The endocrinology of sexual arousal* (2005) (Online). Available: http://joe.endocrinology-journals.org/content/186/3/411.full (August 2012)

REFERENCES

Parmeggiana, P.L. & Morrison, A.R. "Alterations in autonomic functions during sleep". *Central Regulation of Autonomic Functions.* (NY, Oxford University Press, 1990)

van Campen, C. *The Hidden Sense: Synesthesia in Art and Science* (Cambridge, Massachusetts, MIT Press, 2007)

"The Science Behind Dreams and Nightmares". *Talk of the Nation*, national Public Radio. (30 October 2007)

Hartmann, E. *The Nightmare* (NY, Basic Books, 1984)

Bishay, N. "Therapeutic Manipulation of Nightmares and the Management of Neuroses". *British Journal of Psychiatry.,* 147, 67-70 (1985)

Garfield, P. *Creative Dreaming* (NY, Simon and Schuster, 1974)

Marks, I. "Rehearsal Relief of a Nightmare". *British Journal of Psychiatry.,* 135, 461-465 (1978)

Stevenson, R.L. *Across the Plains* (NY, Charles Scribner's Sons, 1892)

Turner, S. *A Hard Day's Write: The Stories Behind Every Beatles Song*. 3rd Edition. (NY, Harper, 2005)

Cross, C. *The Beatles: Day-by-Day, Song-by-Song, Record-by-Record* (Lincoln NE, iUniverse, 2005)

Benfey, O.T. "August Kekulé and the Birth of the Structural Theory of Organic Chemistry in 1858". *Journal of Chemical Education.,* 35, 21-23 (1958)

Hartman, E. *Biology of Dreaming* (Springfield, Charles C. Thomas Publications Ltd, 1997)

Bricker, D. *The life of an Idea* (Online). Available: http://homepages.indiana.edu/web/page/normal/10042.html (August 2012)

Chapter 8

Godwin, M. *The Lucid Dreamer* (Shaftesbury, Element Books, 1994)

Herbert, N. *Quantum Reality: Beyond the New Physics* (NY, Anchor Books, 1985)

Kaempffert, W. *A Popular History of American Invention Vol II* (NY, Scribner, 1924)

Ellis, H. quoted in Dement, W.C. *Some Must Watch While Some Must Sleep* (San Francisco, Freeman & Co., 1972)

Hanh, T.N. *Breathe! You Are Alive: sutra on the Full Awareness of Breathing* (Berkeley, Parallax Press, 1990)

Blake, W. *Auguries of innocence* (NY, Grossman Publishers, 1968)

Chapter 9

Gackenbach, J. & LaBerge, S. *Conscious Mind, Sleeping Brain* (NY, Plenum Press, 1988)

Tholey, P. "Techniques for Inducing and Maintaining Lucid Dreams". *Perceptual and Motor Skills.,* 57 (1983)

Okasha, S. *Philosophy of Science: A Very Short Introduction* (Oxford, Oxford Paperbacks, 2002)

Godwin, M. *The Lucid Dreamer* (Shaftesbury, Element Books, 1994)

Hagen, S. *Buddhism Plain and Simple* (London, Penguin Books, 1997)

Rimpoche, T.W. *The Tibetan Yogas Of Dream And Sleep* (NY, Snow Lion Publications, 1998)

Chapter 10

Kurzweil, R. *The Singularity is Near* (London, Duckworth Overlook, 2005)

REFERENCES

Kaku, M. *Physics of the Future: How Science Will Shape Human Destiny and Our Daily Lives by the Year 2100* (NY, Allen Lane, 2011)

LaBerge, S., Levitan, L., Rich, R., & Dement, W. "Induction of lucid dreaming by light stimulation during REM sleep". *Sleep Research.,* 17, 104 (1988)

Gackenbach, J. & LaBerge, S. *Conscious Mind, Sleeping Brain* (NY, Plenum Press, 1988)

LaBerge, S. & Dement, W. "Voluntary control of respiration during REM sleep". *Sleep Research.,* 11, 107 (1982)

Hearne, K. *The Dream Machine* (Wellingborough, Aquarian Press, 1990)

Roach, M. *Packing for Mars: The curious Science of Life in the Void* (NY, Norton & Company, 2010)

Zubrin, R. *The Case for Mars: The Plan to Settle the Red Planet and Why We Must* (NY, Free Press, 2011)

Roddenberry, G. (Executive Producer). *Star Trek: The Next Generation* (Television Series). (United States, Paramount Television, 1987)

Sagan, C. *Pale Blue Dot: A Vision of the Human Future in Space* (NY, Ballantine, 1994)

Hearne, K. *The Dream Machine* (Wellingborough, Aquarian Press, 1990)

Afterword

Buescher, C. *100 sextillion stars wasn't enough* (Online). Available: http://www.examiner.com/article/100-sextillion-stars-wasn-t-enough (August 2012)

Campbell, N.A., Williamson, B., & Heyden, R.J. *Biology: Exploring Life* (Boston, Pearson Prentice Hall, 2006)

Sagan, C. *Shadows of Forgotten Ancestors* (London, Century, 1992)

Scientific American. *The Scientific American Book of the Brain.* (NY, Scientific American, 1999)

Sagan, C. *Pale Blue Dot: A Vision of the Human Future in Space* (NY, Ballantine, 1994)

Index

N

O

P

Q

R

V

W

Y

Z

Printed in Great Britain
by Amazon.co.uk, Ltd.,
Marston Gate.